An Economic Justice Classic

A PLEA *for* Peasant Proprietors

With the Outlines of a Plan for Their Establishment in Ireland

By William Thomas Thornton, C.B.

(1848, 1874)

Author of
"Over-Population and Its Remedy"; "On Labor";
"Old-Fashioned Ethics and Commonsense Metaphysics";
"Indian Public Works and Cognate Indian Topics"

Foreword by Michael D. Greaney, CPA, MBA
Director of Research
Center for Economic and Social Justice

First Edition
London
John Murray, Albemarle Street
1848

Revised Edition
London
Macmillan and Company
1874

CESJ Economic Justice Classic Edition
Arlington, Virginia
Economic Justice Media
2011

Foreword, additional notes, Appendices III through XIII
and Index © 2011 Center for Economic and Social Justice

Published by Economic Justice Media, an imprint of the
Center for Economic and Social Justice
P. O. Box 40711, Washington, D.C. 20016, U.S.A.
(Tel) 703-243-5155 • (Fax) 703-243-5935
(Eml) thirdway@cesj.org • (Web) www.cesj.org

International Standard Book Number: 978-0-944997-10-9

Library of Congress Control Number: 2011942382

Cover design by Rowland L. Brohawn

TO MESSIEURS

LÉONCE DE LAVERGNE & ÉMILE DE LEVELEYE

PRE-EMINENT *among* LIVING WRITERS *on* RURAL ECONOMY

THIS EDITION

OF

"A PLEA FOR PEASANT PROPRIETORS"

THE RESULT OF RESEARCHES IN A CORNER OF THE SAME FIELD

IS

WITH AN ADMIRING FELLOW RESEARCHER'S CORDIAL REGARD

INSCRIBED BY THE AUTHOR

A PLEA

FOR

PEASANT PROPRIETORS;

WITH

THE OUTLINES OF A PLAN FOR THEIR ESTABLISHMENT IN IRELAND.

BY

WILLIAM THOMAS THORNTON,

AUTHOR OF "OVER-POPULATION AND ITS REMEDY."

Modum agri imprimis servandum.
PLINII NAT. HIST., Lib. xviii.—7.

The lands of a country cannot be properly distributed, nor its agricultural economy be of the most improved description, unless it contain a due admixture of small, and of moderate-sized, as well as of large farms.
MACCULLOCH ON SUCCESSION TO PROPERTY.

LONDON:

JOHN MURRAY, ALBEMARLE STREET.

1848.

Foreword
William Thomas Thornton and the Just Third Way

Ireland is in crisis. Its economy is on the verge of collapse. Short-term "solutions" are only buying time until the next disaster. Politicians, academics, and business leaders are floundering helplessly in the face of the failure of a global financial system that they never understood in the first place. Proposals to correct the problem are only making matters worse and increasing the magnitude of the inevitable breakdown. In this, Ireland is a bellwether of where the global economy is headed.

Growing agitation about the crisis is spreading throughout the world. People from across the political spectrum are complaining about the economy. From the "Tea Party" movement in the United States, to the recent "Occupy Wall Street" phenomenon, complaints are becoming louder, in some cases violent — but nobody is doing or suggesting anything more than proposals that have already failed miserably.

There is a solution — and one that applies not only to Ireland, but to the United States and the rest of the global economy. The solution is one developed more than a century and a half ago to address a catastrophe in comparison with which today's problems pale in significance. While it was ignored then, Thornton's solution and vision of a more just and humane future for all was relevant 150 years ago. Updated to the needs of a technologically advanced civilization, it is even more relevant today.

Following "Black '47," the worst year of the Great Famine in Ireland (1846-1852), William Thomas Thornton, a clerk in the London office of the East India Company, proposed a solution to the disaster that had struck Ireland. Thornton's remedy was revolutionary, though hardly new or unique: vest the common people of Ireland with direct ownership of the landed capital of Ireland. Thornton believed his solution would end the famine, eliminate widespread poverty, diminish the threat of violence and rebellion, and establish a native "middle class." He published his proposal in 1848 as *A Plea for Peasant Proprietors*.

Thornton's proposal was a logical development of an analysis he had published two years before. In his first major work in 1846, *Over-Population and Its Remedy*,[1] Thornton refuted Thomas Malthus's scarcity-based theories. Thornton's analysis in *A Plea for Peasant Proprietors* countered an idea implicit in Malthus's *Essay*: that ownership of capital *must* be concentrated if the rich are to accumulate sufficient savings to finance new capital and provide jobs for workers who own nothing except consumer goods and their own labor. Like other philosophers and political scientists through the ages,[2] Thornton made clear that a program of widespread capital ownership has the potential to make people politically as well as economically free.

Nor did Thornton ignore the rights or concerns of propertyless non-agricultural workers. In fact, Thornton's proposal bears a striking resemblance to that of Louis Kelso and Mortimer Adler published in the late 1950s and early 1960s.[3] In 1869, Thornton published *A Treatise On Labour: Its Wrongful Claims and Rightful Dues, Its Actual Present and Possible Future*,[4] revising it in 1870. This work strengthened his point that the only solution to the conflict between "labor" and "capital" is for workers and owners to form an alliance, with workers becoming own-

---

[1] William Thomas Thornton, *Over-Population and Its Remedy*. London: Longman, Brown, Green, and Longmans, 1846.

[2] A brief list includes Aristotle, the Gracchi (noted by Thornton), Plutarch, the 6th century Byzantine "Farmers' Law," John Locke, George Mason, William Cobbett, Benjamin Watkins Leigh, and Daniel Webster.

[3] See Louis O. Kelso and Mortimer Adler, *The Capitalist Manifesto*. New York: Random House, 1958; *The New Capitalists*. New York: Random House, 1961.

[4] William Thomas Thornton, *A Treatise On Labour: Its Wrongful Claims and Rightful Dues, Its Actual Present and Possible Future*. London: Macmillan and Company, 1869.

ers with defined rights to profits and control. As he summarized the benefits of such an alliance,

> For mistrust and dislike or indifference on the one side, and for envy and jealousy on the other, would be substituted something of that fellow-feeling which can scarcely help growing up between those who, in serving themselves, are helping each other. With those laborers who had taken shares, some sympathy with capital would tincture the old headlong passion in favor of labor. With those who had not yet become shareholders the possibility of their becoming so subsequently would have a like effect.[5]

Not surprisingly, this had also been the contention of Charles Morrison in his pivotal *An Essay on the Relations Between Labour and Capital*[6] published in 1854 — and would be repeated by Pope Leo XIII in the epochal *Rerum Novarum* in 1891, usually regarded as the first social encyclical, "On Capital and Labor"[7]:

> We have seen that this great labor question cannot be solved save by assuming as a principle that private ownership must be held sacred and inviolable. The law, therefore, should favor ownership, and its policy should

---

[5] William Thomas Thornton, *On Labour: Its Wrongful Claims and Rightful Dues, Its Actual Present and Possible Future, Second Edition*. London: Macmillan and Company, 1870, 394.

[6] Charles Morrison, *Essay on the Relations Between Labour and Capital*. London: Longman, Brown, Green, and Longmans, 1854. Morrison's book was influential in the reform of the Law of Partnerships and adoption of the Limited Liability Act of 1855 (18 & 19 Vict c 133), his goal being to lift one of the chief barriers preventing or inhibiting worker ownership.

[7] Pope Leo XIII, *Rerum Novarum* ("On Capital and Labor"), 1891. N.B.: "On Capital and Labor" is the current official title in English, http://www.vatican.va/holy_father/leo_xiii/encyclicals/documents/hf_l-xiii_enc_15051891_rerum-novarum_en.html. Many other titles have been used.

be to induce as many as possible of the people to become owners.[8]

Still, the Great Famine seemed to confirm Malthusian theory. Population had, evidently, outstripped existing food supplies. The Four Horseman of the Apocalypse — Famine, Disease, War, and Death — had consequently put in their expected appearance.

The irony is that Ireland was one of the few food exporting countries in Europe. The land provided more than enough to feed the Irish and the propertyless workers of England. Even in 1847, the worst year of the Great Famine, there were massive exports of food from Ireland.[9]

To Thornton, the Great Famine represented not a confirmation of Malthusian theory, but its refutation. As he had argued in 1846, "over-population" is caused *by* systemic poverty and lack of widespread ownership of capital, not the other way around. In Europe, the potato blight caused hardship, as small landowners who depended on the potato for their basic subsistence had to shift to more expensive foodstuffs.

In Ireland, with virtually no small landowning class and afflicted with "tenancy-at-will" (which meant that landlords could evict a tenant for any reason or none at all), the blight was a disaster of unprecedented magnitude. More than enough food was grown in Ireland to stave off the Great Famine, but it did not belong to the common people. They died by the hundreds of thousands as food was shipped out of the country.

Unfortunately, the British government paid no attention to Thornton's proposal for Ireland. As he complained in 1874 in his revision of the *Plea*, "The time for creating a numerous peasant proprietary in the summary mode suggested has, however, long gone by, and is not now to

---

[8] *Rerum Novarum*, § 46.
[9] Christine Kinealy, *This Great Calamity: The Irish Famine, 1845-1852*. Dublin: Gill and Macmillan, 1995, 354.

be recovered. How seldom, alas, does England, in respect of Irish reforms, take time by the forelock!"[10]

The two and a half decades between the first and second editions of *A Plea for Peasant Proprietors* saw the rise and fall of the "Young Ireland" movement,[11] the "Fenian" uprising of 1867,[12] the "dynamite campaign" of terror, growing discontent over the continued failure of land reform[13] and renewed agitation for the repeal of the Act of Union of 1800 and restoration of "Home Rule" to Ireland.[14] Thornton's aim in his revision was to put before the public a "what might have been" scenario had his proposal been adopted in 1848[15] — thereby avoiding all the violence and discontent that shook Ireland in the latter half of the 19th century.

In his 1874 revision, Thornton did modify his stand somewhat. He expressed the hope that the new land legislation of the 1870s would remove legal disabilities from the Irish so that the broadening of ownership to all citizens could proceed naturally. As we note in Appendix VI on the "Irish National Land League," however, this hope proved ephemeral.

While things are not yet as bad in the world today as they were in Ireland in the 1840s, most people are as dependent on wage system jobs as the Irish were on the potato. The vast majority of today's citizens have no access to other sources of income (from, in particular, capital ownership), except government welfare. The fact is, as we explain in Appendix III, there are other barriers that inhibit or prevent universal access to the means of acquiring ownership of capital and the establishment and main-

---

[10] William T. Thornton, *A Plea for Peasant Proprietors*. London: Macmillan and Company, 1874, 261.
[11] See Appendix V.
[12] *Ibid.*
[13] See Appendix VI.
[14] See Appendix IV.
[15] 1848 also saw the publication of Karl Marx's *The Communist Manifesto*, that advocated the *abolition* of private property and (unlike Thornton and Kelso and Adler) has *not* been ignored.

tenance of a just, third way beyond both capitalism and socialism. A major barrier remains lack of democratic access to capital credit for financially feasible projects.

The root cause of lack of democratic access to capital credit is a fixed belief, found primarily in Keynesian economics, but also in the Monetarist/Chicago and Austrian schools. Keynes held that for new capital to be financed, consumption must be reduced and money savings accumulated. This has resulted in a situation in modern Ireland with disturbing parallels to the 1840s. A similar problem afflicts virtually every nation on earth. The world's "social safety nets," while they have staved off the worst effects so far, are nearly bankrupt in most countries.

Fortunately, today's economic problems in Ireland and elsewhere are amenable to the same solution Thornton proposed: establish and maintain universal *direct* ownership of capital as fast as possible. Equally fortunate, the problem of how to finance a program of rapid capital expansion — in agricultural, industrial, and commercial capital — can easily be solved by applying advanced techniques of corporate finance, and maintained by applying sound principles of justice and market economies in our management systems.

Perhaps not surprisingly, however, while Thornton's observations and remedies can readily be applied to the current crisis, there remains a great deal of built-in resistance in politics and academia — the same barriers that Thornton faced in his day. Nevertheless, if we understand that both land and technology are simply different forms of capital, and that we don't have to confiscate, condemn, or redistribute existing capital that belongs to some people so that other people can become owners, then we quickly realize that it is possible for everyone on earth to become an owner of a capital stake that could generate an income sufficient to meet common household needs. The financing of new capital would not come from existing savings, but from the present value, the "future savings," of the capital that has yet to be formed.

We can sit idly or helplessly by while discontent, anger and despair continue to grow throughout the world. We can blame government indifference, corporate greed, or the selfishness of the developed countries or the wealthy. Or, we can look to a new way to avert the crisis and repair the economic system — empowering every citizen to become an owner of productive capital. As Thornton presaged in the concluding chapter of his 1874 revision:

In every quarter of the United Kingdom a storm against landlordism is audibly brewing, which, if allowed to break, will shake the edifice to its foundations, not, assuredly, leaving undislocated the superstructure. Yet landlordism, even if a hundred times more unpopular than it has, so far, become amongst ourselves, might be rendered one of the most popular of institutions, by simply having its privileges, now so invidiously concentrated, made freely accessible to all — the meanest farm laborer included; and to this change in its character the only remaining impediments are legal ones, of which landlords and their legal advisers are the chief upholders.[16]

Michael D. Greaney, CPA, MBA, editor
Director of Research
Center for Economic and Social Justice

---

[16] Thornton, *A Plea for Peasant Proprietors, op. cit.*, 265.

Preface to 1874 Edition

This work appeared originally in 1848, and has been long out of print. Some years ago, while the discussions which terminated in the passing of the Irish Landlord and Tenant Act were at their height, it came greatly into request, and I was strongly urged by the late Mr. Mill[1] and other friends to republish it; but to do so required an amount of preliminary labor for which I neither then had, nor have since, until recently, been able to find, leisure. For the last few months, however, my spare half-hours have been occupied with little else. Every portion of the book has been searchingly revised; the first Chapter has been almost rewritten, two new Chapters (the fourth and seventh) have been introduced, and to or in all the rest material additions, corrections, and other alterations have been made. No pains, in short, have been spared to render this edition an adequate exposition of its subject, and also an effective aid to study of the still greater subject with which it is inextricably bound up.

Of neither subject of neither Peasant Proprietorship nor Landed Property in general is the daily increasing interest likely to begin to diminish for some generations to come.

Cadogan Place; January, 1874.

---

[1] [John Stuart Mill (1806-1873), British utilitarian philosopher and political economist who enjoyed a friendly rivalry with Thornton.]

Preface to 1848 Edition

Such a work as this, if published a few years ago, might have been expected to attract but little notice. The question of which it treats was then somewhat prematurely regarded as finally settled, and an attempt to revive it, if not resented as an impertinent intrusion on public attention, would probably have been received with that scornful indifference with which antiquarian dissertations are common received by the busier portion of mankind. Small farmers and small proprietors had been summarily condemned, and having been condemned unheard, the sentence passed upon them was on that very account the less likely to be reversed, inasmuch as no opportunity had been afforded for the statement of anything in their favor. To have appealed against a decision which had obtained such general acquiescence, would have been almost hopeless.

There is, however, in Truth an inherent force, which is sure to prevail in the end against every obstacle. Its light may long burn dimly, but it is never totally extinguished; and, when least heeded, is slowly gaining strength to disperse the mists of error and prejudice in which it is enveloped. Even when public opinion was most decidedly in favor of large farms, and when their progress in this country was hailed as matter for national exultation, there were still a few who doubted whether the change that was taking place was productive of unmixed good, and whether the good which had obviously resulted from it, might not have been secured by other means, without so much social disturbance. The doubts of these skeptics were confirmed by further experience and more extended observation, and only timidly hinted at first, began by degrees to be expressed more distinctly and with more and more confidence. At length the avowed dissenters from the established creed became numerous enough to constitute a sect. No person, perhaps, is better entitled to be styled its founder than that shrewd annotator on men and things, Mr. Laing,[1] the well-known traveler. Mr. Blacker[2] and Mr. Poulett Scrope[3] also did good service in propagating the doctrines; but its greatest accession of strength was received more recently, when it was joined by a powerful section of the "fourth estate," the conductors of the *Morning Chronicle*, and by one whose name must ensure respect for any cause which has the advantage of his support — Mr. John Stuart Mill — assuredly, whether as a dialectician, or as a political economist, without any living superior.

The example of such distinguished adherents has had its due effect, and the opinion maintained by them is visibly gaining ground. Its success, however, though sufficient to warrant sanguine hopes of its ultimate triumph, has hitherto been impeded by the prevailing ignorance with respect to the principles of which it rests. Each of the writers mentioned has done his part for the vindication of peasant proprietors; but the task has been undertaken systematically by none except the last, and even he, having been able to allot to it only a portion of a work embracing a variety of other topics, has not treated this one at the length which its importance deserves. It has, therefore, been thought that a distinct treatise on the subject, in which the arguments on both sides should be fairly confronted, and in which no mere speculations, however ingenious, should be permitted to pass without being submitted to the test of experience, might now prove neither useless nor unacceptable to a large and increasing class of readers. It might help to guide them to a decision on a question which, wherever human subsistence is derived from the soil, and in every community of which husband-

---

[1] [Samuel Laing (1780-1868), Scottish travel writer.]

[2] [Lieutenant-Colonel William Blacker (1776-1850), Irish British Army officer and member of the Royal Irish Academy. He is sometimes confused with his brother, Valentine Blacker (1778-1826), a Lieutenant-Colonel in the private army of the Honourable East India Company.]

[3] [George Julius Poulett Scrope (1797-1876), English geologist, political economist and magistrate.]

men form a considerable part, must be of immense importance; but which possesses a ten-fold interest at this moment, and in this country, and which must be satisfactorily solved before any well-founded hope can be entertained of extrication from our present embarrassment.[4]

With this view the following pages have been written. They are called a "Plea," and the title confesses them to be the work of an advocate, — of one whose mind is made up, and who is anxious to bring others to his own way of thinking. Advocacy, however, when the result of honest conviction, is perfectly compatible with impartiality. The author has, of course, done his best to answer every argument opposed to his own views, but contending for truth alone, he has not been satisfied with the semblance of victory, nor condescended to disguise his weakness by misrepresenting what he could not refute. On the contrary, he has been careful to state both sides of the question with equal fairness, so that the reader whom he failed to convince might at least be furnished with ample materials for forming his own unbiased judgment.

He thinks it due to himself to add, that the scheme proposed in the last chapter for the reclamation of the Irish waste lands is his own. Suggestions of a somewhat similar character have been made by Mr. Blacker and Mr. Scrope, but the outlines of the present author's plan were traced in a work published by him more than two years ago,[5] when, so far as he is aware, Mr. Scrope had not alluded to the subject either in or out of parliament, and before Mr. Blacker's *Essays*,[6] although published much earlier, had been seen or heard of by him.

---

[4] [The Great Famine, *An Gorta Mór*, of 1846-1852.]

[5] [William Thomas Thornton, *Over-Population and Its Remedy, Or, an Inquiry Into the Extent and Causes of the Distress Prevailing Among the Labouring Classes of the British Islands, and Into the Means of Remedying It*. London: Longman, Brown, Green, and Longmans, 1846.]

[6] [William Blacker, *An Essay on the Improvement to be Made in the Cultivation of Small Farms* (1837).]

He mentions this with no desire of claiming originality which belongs more justly to another, but solely with the view of protecting himself against a charge of plagiarism of which he is wholly guiltless.[7]

---

[7] [This seems like an odd statement for an author to make, but in his *History of Economic Analysis* (New York: Oxford University Press, 1954), Joseph A. Schumpeter hints that Thornton may have been the victim of allegations of plagiarism at some point in his career. Discussing John Stuart Mill's "recantation" of a portion of his formulation of the "wage fund doctrine" — of which, not surprisingly, [John Ramsay] Macculloch managed to establish himself as the premier exponent (*ibid.*, 669) — Schumpeter explained, "[Mill] paid no attention to the attacks, if he knew of them, by [Richard] Jones and [Francis Davy] Longe. But in response to the elaborate restatement of the latter's arguments by William Thornton, he wrote a review article that did not indeed spell complete surrender and, in particularly, did not induce him to change any of those passages — for example, the Fourth Proposition on Capital — that ought to go out if the wage fund does. But it surrendered a phrase, which was all the public took in. The Longe-Thornton argument, as accepted by J. S. Mill, did not amount to more than denying that there exists any definite quantity of wage goods that 'must' under any circumstances go to labor." In a note to the passage quoted here, Schumpeter carefully stated that, "The word Restatement is to denote a fact but is not to insinuate a charge of plagiarism, though Longe did complain that neither Thornton nor Mill mentioned him — inferring (the optimist!) from having sent his pamphlet to Mill that the latter had read it. Moreover, though Longe anticipated the substance of Thornton's criticism of the wage-fund theory, the latter's book contained several points that were new. Outstanding among them is his emphasis on *expected* consumers' demand as the true guide of the producers. In view of the importance the element of expectations has gained of late, Thornton's book must be allocated a place in this history of analysis that is quite independent of the particular wage-fund issue. J. S. Mill's review article appeared in the *Fortnightly Review*, May 1869, and was, besides being a remarkable display of good feeling in the face of what other men would have taken as a provocation, a gentle correction of superficial misunderstandings rather than a retraction." *Ibid.*, 669-670.]

Note on the Text

The text of this edition of William T. Thornton's classic *A Plea for Peasant Proprietors* is taken primarily from the revised 1874 edition, correlated with the first edition of 1848. Some notes from the 1848 edition omitted by the author in the revision have been restored, while the spelling of "Macculloch" has been retained from the first edition instead of the "M'Culloch" used in the revised edition. New notes added by the editor as well as insertions into the text are indicated by brackets, [insertion], while spelling has, in most cases, been updated to modern American usage. The French spelling "Département" has been used in the case of a specific political division, but the English "department" has been used for the general term. Chapter summaries have been moved from the Table of Contents to the head of each chapter. The author's prefaces from both the 1848 and 1874 editions have been retained, as well as the original Appendix from 1848 ("Appendix I" in this edition), and the new Appendix from 1874 ("Appendix II" in this edition). Appendices III through XIV are additions by the editor, and do not necessarily reflect the thought of the original author. Appendix XV consists of material removed from the 1848 edition for the 1874 revision.

The preparation of this edition of William Thornton's classic work on expanded capital ownership was made possible through the generous assistance of Dr. Norman Kurland, president of the Center for Economic and Social Justice (CESJ) in Arlington, Virginia; Dawn Brohawn, Director of Communications; Rowland Brohawn, Art Director; and a grant from CESJ. The editors also acknowledge the invaluable contributions of Dr. Robert H. A. Ashford of the Syracuse University School of Law and, of course, Patricia Hetter-Kelso of the Kelso Institute in San Francisco, California, in preserving and advancing the work of Louis Kelso and Mortimer Adler.

Table of Contents

1. Comparative Productiveness of Large and Small Farms

Prejudices entertained by English Economists against Small Farms — Examination of the Objections to them — Comparison of Small with Large Farmers in respect to Command of Capital Copiousness, of Crops — Livestock — Use of Manure — Arrangements for Drainage and Irrigation — Use of proper Implements and Machinery — Facilities for Division of Labor and Rotation of Crops — Singular Industry of Small Farmers — Obligations of most advanced British Agriculturists to lessons taught by Flemish Peasantry — Bigoted attachment to old customs one defect of Peasant Farmers — Comparative amounts of Net Produce sent to market by Large and Small Farmers — Large non-agricultural population of certain countries of Small Farms — Comparison in that respect between England and the Channel Islands[1]

Large landed estates by no means necessarily imply large farming, but small farming is an almost invariable concomitant of small proprietorship; for numerous petty properties welded together into a single farm would generally have long to wait before finding favor in the eyes of an eligible tenant. Whatever evils, therefore, are inherent in peasant farms must be scarcely less inseparable from peasant properties, and no plea for the latter can be perfectly satisfactory which does not entirely exculpate the former also.[2]

---

[1] [From the 1848 edition: "Prejudices entertained in this country against Small Farms — Examination of the Objections to them — Their Productiveness — Liberal use of Manure by Small Farmers — Their arrangements for Drainage and Irrigation — Abundance of their Live Stock — Their ability to procure proper Implements — to effect a proper Division of Labor and Rotation of Crops — Their extraordinary Industry — Their bigoted attachment to old Customs — Produce sent to Market by Large and Small Farms — Great amount of Non-Agricultural Population in some Counties of Small Farms — Comparison between Great Britain and the Channel Islands — General Result of the Comparison between Large and Small Farms.]

[2] [The 1848 edition started with the subsequent paragraph.]

Now, ever since political economy was raised by Adam Smith[3] to the dignity of a science, its British professors have been almost unanimously of opinion that small farms are incompatible with the prosperity either of agriculture or of agricultural laborers. Land, they assert, cannot be properly cultivated unless it be held in large quantities by men of capital, nor can its cultivators be in a satisfactory condition unless they be hired servants, and chiefly dependent for subsistence on the wages they receive. The eminent men by whom this notion has been promulgated have supported it by many ingenious and plausible arguments; nor has their advocacy been confined to theoretical reasoning. They have ventured to appeal to experience and observation, and have been able to point to several facts which at first sight, and until carefully examined, seem to justify their views. So long, indeed, as their attention was confined to their own country, the conclusion at which they arrived was just such as might have been expected. Eighty or ninety years ago, when their doctrine was coming into fashion, farms of 1,000 or 1,500 acres, though much less numerous than at present, were already not unknown in England; and, though a more usual size was a hundred acres or thereabouts, farms of less than that extent were gradually becoming less common, and the cottage tenements of a dozen acres or less had almost entirely disappeared.[4] Simultaneously with this change in the arrangement of land, agriculture had made undeniable progress, and its improvement was most remarkable on the larger farms. Farm laborers, indeed, having lost the land anciently at-

---

[3] [Adam Smith (1723-1790), Scottish social philosopher and pioneer political economist. Smith's *The Theory of Moral Sentiments* (1759) detailed a political philosophy that was applied in *An Enquiry into the Nature and Causes of the Wealth of Nations* (1776), considered the first modern work of economics.]

[4] Can my sons share from this paternal hand
The profits with the labors of the land?
No! though indulgent Heaven its blessing deigns,
Where's the small farm to suit my scanty means?
— Bloomfield's *Farmer's Boy*, 1799.

tached to their habitations, were not so well fed or so expensively clad as some centuries earlier, when sumptuary laws had been thought necessary to restrain their excesses in diet and dress; but the memory of those golden days was retained by few except professed antiquarians, and the result of a comparison with more recent times might have appeared favorable to the actual state of things. During the reign of George II[5] and the first thirty years of George III[6] the English peasant was in a better position in many respects than in the preceding century. His wages were higher, though provisions and most other articles of consumption were cheaper. His supply of necessaries, if not plentiful, was at least not scanty, and the progress of the arts had placed many conveniences and luxuries within his reach which were utterly unknown to his wealthier ancestors. With glass panes in his casement, a glass tumbler or two and some plates and dishes on his shelves, and some potatoes, and possibly a little tea and sugar in his closet, it would have seemed ridiculous to question his advantage over his rude forefathers, whose horn casements excluded the light and admitted the wind, who ate and drank out of wooden bowls and bickers,[7] and ate and drank little but what their own ground furnished. His superiority over the serfs of Germany and Russia, who, like his own ancestors, were paid for labor, not in money, but in land, was, of course, taken for granted. To have questioned it would have been a reflection on British freedom. It was therefore assumed that the actual social position of the English agricultural laborer was the highest which he had ever attained; and it was further assumed, that the occupation of land by the lower class of peasants was a mark or relic of serfdom and barbarism, and that their deprivation of land and conversion into laborers for money-wages, was an indispensable step in their progress to freedom and civilization. Adam Smith himself, who appears to have subsequently taken a juster view of the subject, speaks in one of the early chapters of

---

[5] [1727-1760.]
[6] [1760-1820.]
[7] [Drinking vessel.]

his great work of "the diminution of the number of cottagers and other small occupiers of land, as an event which has, in every part of Europe, been the immediate forerunner of improvement and better cultivation."

These inferences from experience of large farms in England, were shortly afterwards confirmed by the observed results of the formation of small farms in Ireland. The partition of the immense pastures by which so large a portion of that island had been overspread, was followed by the creation of a body of small farmers, poor, ignorant, and unenterprising at first, and poorer and more spiritless in every succeeding generation, and by the excessive multiplication of a cottier[8] peasantry, whose debasement and misery were at once the wonder and the scandal of the age. Some explanation will hereafter be offered of the peculiar circumstances which caused the subdivision of land to be followed in this instance by such deplorable consequences. Suffice it in this place to admit the fact, and to acknowledge that it affords some justification for the opinion which has been founded upon it. With small farms, sloth and misery on one side of St. George's Channel,[9] and on the other, large farms, tolerably cultivated and moderately productive, together with a peasantry in a condition which, by comparison, might almost be styled comfortable, even careful inquirers might be excused for inferring that the several phenomena in juxtaposition bore to each other the relation of cause and effect. Whether the inference was correct as well as pardonable, and whether such hasty generalization was quite consistent with the rules of induction, are questions which may be better answered when we come to extend our field of observation, and having collected additional facts, shall have ascertained how far they can be reconciled with the theory at present in vogue.

---

[8] [A cottier is a peasant farming a small piece of land under "cottier tenure" — not more than half an acre at a rent of not more than £5 per annum.]

[9] [The stretch of water between Ireland and Wales connecting the Irish and the Celtic seas.]

But how narrow soever may be the basis on which the theory rests, the superstructure itself must be confessed to be very cleverly put together, and to present a very imposing aspect. Nothing, indeed, could be more satisfactory than the way in which the superiority of large to small farms has been accounted for, provided only that the superiority were real, and that the advantages claimed for the former, and the evils imputed to the latter, actually existed. The arguments used have not only obtained very general acceptance among persons without adequate means of testing them; they have prejudiced the minds of many against the admission of opposite evidence, and have stood their ground in situations where everything around bore testimony against them. Their fallacy can scarcely therefore be exposed without a patient and minute investigation; and it is hoped that the space here allotted to that purpose will not be thought excessive, when the difficulty as well as the importance of the subject is considered.

It is asserted, in the first place, that small farms must needs be badly cultivated. "The produce of a farm of five, ten, or twenty acres, may perhaps enable its occupier to preserve his family from downright starvation; but it will never," we are told, "enable him to accumulate stock to any extent." He must consequently be too poor to bear the expense of properly manuring, draining, or irrigating his fields; he cannot afford to "use any but the simplest machines," nor to avail himself, except very insufficiently, "of the powers of the lower animals," nor of those improvements which in rich and enlightened countries are continually being made in his art. Neither can he properly vary his crops, but, for want of space for judicious alternation, must injure his land by making it bear similar sorts of produce too frequently. Moreover, not only is he mainly dependent on manual labor, with little aid from mechanism or from the inferior animals, he cannot even make the best use of that labor. The same man must by turns apply to every sort of work, and consequently will do every job worse than it would be done on a large farm, where separate persons, it is said, would be "plowmen, thrashers, hedgers, shepherds, cowherds, oxherds, lime-burners, drainers, *etc.*" Finally, the small farmer is seduced into idle habits by temptations too strong for his virtue, or forced into them by influences beyond his control. Not being subject to the same compulsion as the hired laborer, he "naturally" allows himself more frequent intervals of relaxation. "A cottager, however small his possession, has some species of produce to dispose of. This," it seems, "leads to a habit of going to market, where much precious time is lost in the adjustment of trifling bargains." "Nothing," as Arthur Young[10] has very justly, but somewhat superfluously, remarked, "can be more absurd than a strong, hearty man walking some miles, and losing a day's work in order to sell a dozen of eggs, or a chicken, the value of which would not be equal to the labor of conveying it if he were properly employed." Then it is assumed that farms cannot be small without being too small to afford constant employment to their occupiers. But the latter, when they have nothing to do at home, cannot find work elsewhere, at least if all the neighboring farms be of much the same size. In consequence, they contract habits of indolence which are too frequently converted ere long into habits of dissipation. Of course, an idle drunkard, who keeps neither a horse nor a cow, whose only tools are the spade and hoe, who seldom manures, and never drains, but nevertheless overcrops his land, is a wretched farmer, and it would be perfectly marvelous if his farm were not the counterpart of himself.[11]

Here is a tolerably long list of charges, yet they form but one clause in the bill of indictment. Let us examine them separately, beginning with the culprit's alleged inevitable indigence.[12]

Of such indigence, if it were real, two explanations might be suggested. Either there might be circumstances

---

[10] [Arthur Young (1741-1820) was an English writer on agriculture, economics, and social statistics.]

[11] *Encyclopaedia Britannica*, Art. Cottage System.

[12] [The subsequent passage was substantially rewritten for the 1874 edition. The original is included in Appendix XV.]

inseparable from small farming rendering it less efficient and less productive than large, or, whatever the productiveness of small farms, the conditions of occupation might be such as to prevent their tenants from retaining as much of the produce for their own use as larger holders would be permitted to appropriate from the same extent of land. Now, that this latter cause very frequently operates is not to be denied. Personal habit, reinforced by family tradition, the potent and manifold charms of a country life, ignorance of, or sense of unfitness for, any other career, all unite to dispose the sons of farmers to follow the calling of their fathers, and to compete with each other for the possession of any farm there may be to let. The smaller the farm, the less the capital required for its cultivation, and the larger the number of qualified competitors, whose competition, where farms are very small indeed, is often so fierce that, in order to obtain what seems to them their sole means of livelihood, they enter into engagements that leave them barely wherewithal to support life, and would not leave even that if enforced to the letter. So it used to be in Ireland in the dismal decades immediately previous to the famine of 1846, when all the potatoes grown on the four- or five-acre, or still smaller plots, which then took up nearly a twentieth of the cultivated area, would in many instances not have sufficed for the rent which the cottier had, in his desperation, undertaken to pay, and when, therefore, all that remained for his subsistence was just so many potatoes as the compassion of the landlord or of the landlord's agent suffered him to keep. Things, however, can scarcely reach to quite so deplorable a pitch except where land, besides being excessively subdivided, is also held at-will.[13] In that case a spade or mattock[14] and a barrowful of tubers[15] for seed may constitute the entire farming stock looked upon as indispensable; whereas, wherever farms are not so diminutive as to render leases ridiculous, and leases are

---

[13] [That is, as a tenancy-at-will, which can be terminated "at will" by the landlord without warning or compensation.]

[14] [A digging or grubbing tool similar to an adze, ax or pick.]

[15] [Potatoes or other root crops.]

actually adopted, every incoming tenant is expected to be the possessor of some capital, which he, on his side, will be disinclined to invest except upon conditions that leave him a reasonable prospect of obtaining such moderate return as sufferance, the badge of all his tribe, has taught him to deem adequate. Still, even in Flanders, where nine-year leases generally prevail, the small tenant-farmers fare as to diet little better than their own laborers, who, while the hardest worked, are also about the worst fed of their class that Europe can show.[16] In short, it may as well at once be frankly acknowledged that, wherever the terms on which land is held are the result of a bargain with a landlord exercising full proprietary rights, the small tenant's share of the produce will be considerably less than a large farmer would have insisted on. It does not, however, follow that the small farmer must have relatively less money than the large to lay out on the land. There is no reason why his capital on entering should not be at least as great in proportion as the other's, since, whatever be the proper amount per acre, from £5[17]

---

[16] So says M. de Laveleye, writing in 1863 (*Économie Rurale de la Belgique*, p. 69). The Flemish farm-laborer's actual bill of fare, however, as transcribed by him in 1870, is one which most Englishmen of the same class may well envy. "For breakfast; bread-and-butter with chicory, coffee, and milk; for dinner; potatoes, vegetables, and bread; at 4 P.M., bread-and-butter again; and for supper, the same fare as for dinner; very seldom, a little bacon, and as for butchers' meat, four or five times a. year." *Cobden Club Essays*, 1st series, pp. 264, 265.

[17] [Prior to the monetary reform of 1970, the pound was divided into 240 pence. A shilling in England was 12 pence, while a crown or dollar was 5 shillings. The symbol for shilling was "*s*" or /, from *solidus*, an ancient Roman denomination, while the symbol for penny was "*d*" from *denarius*, another Roman denomination. The symbol for pound remains £, from *librum*, a Roman pound of silver. In the early 19th century, shillings in Ireland, Guernsey, and Jersey had different values. The Irish and British currencies were amalgamated in 1821. In 1877 in Jersey the shilling was revalued from 13 Jersey pence to 12. Until 1921, there were twenty-one Guernsey shillings to the pound.]

to £20, there will always be more bidders with £25 or £100 to spend upon five acres than with £2,500 or £10,000 to spend upon five hundred acres. Neither — although the five-acre tenant would probably be much the more highly rented of the two, so that, unless he somehow managed to get more gross produce out of the land than the other, his own net rate of profit would be less, and it would therefore be harder for him to add to his original capital — does it follow that, because less able to afford expenditure on his land, he must therefore spend less. He might perhaps choose to stint himself in order not to stint the land, which, as he would well know, could not, unless generously treated, be induced to yield him wherewithal to meet the onerous obligations he had incurred. And this, in fact, is what he commonly does.

In East and West Flanders, where the average size is about five acres and seven acres and a-half respectively, the capital with which a tenant enters averages at least £8 an acre, and this is gradually increased, and often doubled, during the currency of the lease; whereas in two other Belgian regions, the Hesbayan, whereof one-tenth is occupied by farms of 100 acres and upwards, and the Condrusian, where farms as large as 250 acres abound, the capital invested in the soil is estimated at between £5, 12s, and £6, 8s, and between £3 and £4 respectively, while in England its average is probably not above £6.[18] True, whereas the English farmer expects ten percent on his capital, the Fleming is fain to be satisfied with two percent, and to content himself with rye bread, potatoes, a few beans or other vegetables, and buttermilk, scarcely ever tasting meat, or even bacon, or any beverage

---

[18] *Économie Rurale de la Belgique*, par Emile de Laveleye, pp. 49-51, and 161, and 186-8. La Hesbaieis, strictly speaking, merely the portion of the province of Liege westward of the Meuse; but in the agricultural and more extended sense in which, after M. de Laveleye's example, the term is here used, it includes also the whole of Brabant and Hainault. Le Condroz, the territory of the ancient Condrusii, occupies the portions of Namur and Liege bounded by the rivers Meurthe, Ourthe, and Lesse.

stronger than chicory,[19] and reserving beer for high days and holidays; while many an English farmer breakfasts on game, or veal-and-ham pie, according to the season, can produce a bottle of '34 port for a favored guest, sends a son to Cambridge, and is lulled into his after-dinner nap by the performance of his daughters on a semi-grand piano. But the Fleming's obligation to the practice of such severe economy is an incident of tenure, not a necessity of small culture. Small farms are not always rack-rented. In some territories the landlord's exactions are restrained by custom having the force of law; in others, the occupant is altogether rent-free. Were it not so, the present volume would lack an adequate pretext, for there would then be no Peasant Proprietors to plead for. Some such people, however, being certainly existent, a further certainty regarding them is that, since small tenants, with only a small portion of the produce of their fields at their disposal, can, nevertheless, lay out upon their land more in proportion than large tenants do actually lay out, small proprietors, to whom the entire produce belongs, cannot but be able to do the same. This certainty is independent of the comparative productiveness of small and large farming, and does not, therefore, require for its corroboration that the second of the possible causes of the penury of small farmers, *viz.*, the comparative unproductiveness of small farms, should be disproved. On other accounts, however, it may be of use to show how absolutely overwhelming against the reality of such unproductiveness is the preponderance of evidence.

In contrasting small with large culture, the most legitimate course might seem to be to observe the respective aspects presented by them in one and the same country, and to note, for example, that, on the ten-acre farms of Flanders, the crops are heavier by a fourth[20] than on the hundred-acre farms of La Hesbaie, and as heavy again as on the farms of two hundred and fifty acres in Le Condroz. This seemingly fair mode of comparison, however,

---

[19] [As a coffee substitute.]
[20] [That is, 25% greater.]

might, in the hands of a skillful manipulator of statistics, become exceedingly misleading, bringing out almost any results desired, according to the country to which it was applied, and testifying almost as strongly in England to the superiority of large farms, as in Belgium to that of small. If our object be, not to fortify any foregone conclusion, but simply to get at the truth, we had better go for our materials of comparison to distinct regions in which, on the one hand large, and on the other small, culture appears to most advantage. Now, in England — the country in which large farms are both more numerous and in general far better tilled than in any other — the average yield of wheat per acre was, in 1837, only twenty-one bushels; the highest average for any single county being no more than twenty-six bushels.[21] The highest average since claimed for the whole of England is thirty-two bushels; but this is pronounced to be much too high, by that best perhaps of all authorities, Mr. Caird,[22] who gives twenty-six and a-half bushels as the "average of figures furnished to him by competent judges in all parts of the country;" adding, as the result of his own observation, that "thirty-two bushels, as an average produce, is to be met with only on farms where both soil and management are superior to the present average of England."[23] In Jersey, however, where the average size of farms is only sixteen acres, the average produce of wheat for the five years ending with 1833 was, by official investigation, ascertained to be forty bushels.[24] In Guernsey, where farms are still smaller,[25] thirty-two bushels per acre were, according to Inglis,[26] considered about the same time, "a good but still a very common crop;" and the light soil of the Chan-

---

[21] See Table in Macculloch's *Statistics of British Empire*, vol. i. p. 482.

[22] [Sir James Caird (1816-1892), British politician and agricultural writer.]

[23] English Agriculture, pp. 480-522 and 3.

[24] *Guernsey and Jersey Magazine*, vol. iii. p. 186.

[25] Owing, says Inglis, to there being "no law, as in Jersey, forbidding the subdivision of land below a certain extent."

[26] [Henry David Inglis (1795-1835) British travel writer.]

nel Islands is naturally by no means particularly suitable for the growth of wheat. That of Flanders, originally a coarse siliceous sand, is particularly unsuitable, and accordingly very little wheat is sown there, but of that little, the average yield, at least in the Waes district, is, according to a very minute and careful observer, from thirty-two to thirty-six bushels.[27] Of barley, a more congenial cereal, the average is in Flanders forty-one bushels, and on good ground sixty bushels;[28] while in England it is probably under thirty-three, and would certainly be overstated at thirty-six bushels. Of course, the English averages are considerably exceeded in particular localities, on such farms for instance as those of Mr. Paget,[29] near Nottingham, and of Mr. Stansfeld[30] in the West Riding of Yorkshire, wheat crops of forty-six bushels per acre being not extraordinary, and of fifty-six bushels not unknown.[31] But these exceptional cases may be more than matched in Guernsey, where the largest yield of wheat per acre in each of the three years ending with 1847, was proved, to the satisfaction of the local Agricultural Society, to have been not less than seventy-six, eighty, and seventy-two bushels respectively. Of potatoes, ten tons per acre would, anywhere in England, and even on the rich "warp lands" bordering the tidal affluents of the Humber, be considered a high average crop;[32] but in Jersey, the average is reckoned at fifteen tons,[33] and near Tamise, in Eastern Flanders, Mr. Rham[34] found a cultivator of eight acres of poor

---

[27] *Outlines of Flemish Husbandry*, by the Rev. W. Rham, in Library of Useful Knowledge, p. 92.

[28] Laveleye, *ut supra*, p. 84.

[29] [Charles Paget (1799-1873), Labour Member of Parliament for Nottingham, 1856-1865. He sponsored many reforms on his own estate, considered a "model landlord."]

[30] [Sir James Stansfeld (1820-1898), British politician and Radical member of parliament.]

[31] Caird's *English Agriculture*, pp. 211 and 289.

[32] *Ibid.*, p. 301.

[33] *Guernsey and Jersey Magazine*, vol. iii. p. 106. Inglis gives 29,077 lbs., or nearly 13 tons, as the average Jersey crop.

[34] [William Lewis Rham (1778-1843), Dutch-born English clergyman and member of the Royal Agricultural Society.]

land raising nearly twelve tons from one of them.[35] Clover, again, "the glory of Flemish farming," is nowhere else found in "such perfect luxuriance" as in Flanders, where it exhibits "a vigor and weight of produce truly surprising" especially when it is discovered "that such prodigious crops are raised from six pounds of seed per acre."[36] The superiority in productiveness of the best small over the best large farming, of which these are illustrations, is no more than might be expected by any one who considered that, the smaller the farming, the nearer, if good of its kind, it approaches to gardening, and who recollected, too, how hopelessly, with reference to copiousness of crops, the greatest of our agricultural giants — our Pagets, Puseys,[37] Huxtables,[38] and Mechis[39] — are distanced by their dwarf competitors, the market gardeners of our metropolitan suburbs. The same superiority alone can explain the eagerness with which agricultural laborers will accept from the farmer who employs them, allotment plots at as high a rent per rood[40] as their employer grumblingly pays for the same land per acre. Still, whatever the productiveness of small farming, it is of course possible for a farm to be so small that its total produce will not be more than enough for the subsistence of its cultivator; who, in that case, unless he possesses supplementary resources of some sort, cannot prevent the land from becoming rapidly impoverished. Not so, however, if the holding be of as much as ten or twelve acres, or reach to even half that size. Many a leaseholder of five or six acres spends, acre for acre, on

---

[35] *Flemish Husbandry*, p. 92.

[36] Rham, p. 35-7, and Macculloch's *Geographical Dictionary*, vol. i. p. 331.

[37] [Philip Pusey (1799-1855), reforming agriculturalist, member of parliament, and friend and follower of Sir Robert Peel, who was instrumental in the passage of the Bank Charter Act of 1844.]

[38] [Anthony Huxtable (1808-1883), English clergyman and agriculturalist.]

[39] [John Joseph Mechi (1802-1880), English agriculturalist of Italian extraction.]

[40] [Unit of land measure equal to ¼ acre, or 40 square rods, *cir.* 0.10 hectare.]

improvements, not simply as much, but a great deal more than the largest agricultural practitioners. His entire profits might not, indeed, even though he sat rent free, enable him to do some few things that are occasionally done by managers of large properties. Assuredly he could not, "to improve the breed of his sheep, give a thousand guineas[41] for the hire of a single ram for a single season;" nor "send across the kingdom to distant provinces for new implements, and for men to use them;" nor "employ and pay men for residing in provinces where practices were found which he might wish to introduce." But with all deference to Arthur Young, who says that such efforts are common in England, they are never made except by the very largest farmers, and very rarely even by them; while, as to all the more ordinary expenses of cultivation, if the small farmer be not equally able to bear them, it can only be because he is usually more heavily rented.[42] Otherwise, with as much ease as the tenant of two or three square miles, he ought to be able, if need were, to "cover his whole farm with marl at the rate of 100 or 150 tons an acre;" to "drain all his land at the expense of £2 or £3 an acre;" to "pay a heavy price for the manure of towns, and convey it thirty miles by land carriage[43];" or to "float his land at the expense of £5 an acre."

But why do I say "ought to be able"? He is able. Disproportionately rented as he almost always is, the small farmer often contrives to spend upon his land more in proportion than more than one in a thousand of the largest farmers ever does. So far from being "unable to accumulate stock to any extent," his accumulations of livestock are often such as might well fill his rival with humiliating surprise. "It would startle," says Mr. Rham, "the English farmer of 400 acres of arable land, if he were told that he should constantly feed 100 head of cattle; yet this would not be too large a proportion if the Flemish system

---

[41] [At the time Thornton wrote, the guinea was a unit of account in the amount of 21 shillings.]
[42] [That is, pays a high rent.]
[43] [Land transport.]

were strictly followed . . . a beast for every three acres being a common Flemish proportion, and *on very small occupations*, where spade husbandry is used, the proportion being still greater. "That the occupier of only 10 or 12 acres of light arable soil should be able to maintain four or five cows may appear astonishing, but the fact is notorious in the Waes country."[44] To possess plenty of livestock is to possess in equal abundance the first requisite of fertility. "No cattle, no dung; No dung, no crop" is a Flemish adage; and the wealthiest of English farmers are less prodigal of manure than those poor Flemish peasants, who, by the continual intermixture of animal and vegetable refuse, have converted mere powdered flint, through which, in its natural state, water runs as through a filtering stone, into a dark rich mould, of a fertility unsurpassed on this side the Alps. Mr. Caird cites as something remarkable that, for a farm six miles from Manchester, manure should have been bought at the rate of twelve or thirteen tons an acre;[45] but this, which in England passes for lavishness, might seem more like niggardliness in Flanders. For there, from ten to fifteen tons of good rotten dung, and ten hogsheads of liquid from the urine tank, per acre, are quite common sacrifices and li-

---

[44] *Flemish Husbandry*, pp. 59, 60, and 94. The statements in the text are of somewhat ancient date, but are still as applicable as ever. During a tour last summer (that of 1873) through Belgium, I visited two farms near St. Nicolas in the Pays de Waes, the two first that came in my way. On one of ten acres I found four cows, two calves, one horse, and two pigs, besides rabbits and poultry. On the other, of thirty-eight acres, one bull, six cows, two heifers, one horse, and seventy-five sheep; these last, however, being allowed, in addition to what they got on their owner's land, the run of all the stubbles of the commune, the whole commune on the other hand being allowed the use of the bull gratis. A few days afterwards I went over a farm of thirty-two acres a few miles from Ypres. On this I counted eight cows, six bullocks, a calf six weeks old, and four pigs; and was told by the farmer, in the presence of his landlord, that, over and above what his own cattle yield, he purchases no less than 200 shillings worth of manure annually.

[45] *English Agriculture*, p. 270.

bations to the Sterculine Saturn; and some thirty shillings' worth of purchased fertilizers — bones, wood-ashes, linseed-cake, and guano — are not unfrequently superadded. Nay, when potatoes are the crop for whose increase the deity is invoked, sixty tons of manure per acre are no unusual quantity to lay on.[46] In the Channel Islands also, manure is employed with great liberality, ten cart loads of seaweed, worth fifty shillings, besides stable dung, being the ordinary allowance per acre.[47] Drainage is an operation which, in many situations, cannot be effectually executed unless it be undertaken on an extensive scale; but that the necessity of combining for the purpose does not prevent small occupiers from properly performing this important part of their business, is shown by the example of the Netherlands, the country above all others in which drainage is most indispensable, and in which also it is most amply provided for. Combination equally enables small farmers to construct expensive works for irrigation. Perhaps the most ingenious contrivances of the kind which anywhere exist are to be found, not among the scientific and wealthy agriculturists of Europe, but among the Bedouins of some Arabian oases, which owe their fertility to the labor and skill exerted by the inhabitants in order to obtain supplies of water. The greater part of the country being destitute of running streams on the surface, springs are sought in high places beneath it, and in order to reach them the ground must often be opened to a depth of forty feet. "A channel from the fountainhead is then, with a very slight descent, bored in the direction to which it is to be conveyed, with apertures at regular distances, to afford light and air to those who are occasionally sent to keep it clean. In this manner water is frequently conducted from a distance of six or eight miles, and an unlimited supply is obtained. The channels are usually about four feet broad and two feet deep, and contain a clear rapid stream."[48] If the small farmer use only the "simplest machines," it is probably because experience has taught

---

[46] Rham's *Flemish Husbandry*, pp. 31 and 92.

[47] Duncan's *History of Guernsey*, p. 294.

[48] Wellsted's *Travels*, vol. i. p. 93. c 2.

him, as we shall hereafter see, that the simplest tools are by far the most efficient. Those who keep no horses are chiefly they whose holdings are so small that they seldom have occasion for them, and for whom it is cheaper to hire them when required. It happens, however, that Flemish tenants of twenty-five acres and upwards do keep a good many horses. In 1846 it was reckoned that in Western Flanders there were between three and four, and in Eastern nearly six, horses for every hundred acres. In disproof of the small farmer's alleged inability to avail himself of the services of others of the "lower animals," it may suffice to cite Mr. Rham, whose statement, that it is quite common for Flemish tenants of nine acres to keep as many as three cows, has already been quoted, and who also speaks of a tenant of barely five acres, the only drawback from whose happiness was that he could not immediately afford the money to buy a second cow, although he knew he could have maintained two very well. Such a farmer in Belgium would use the spade only for trenching the ground; but among equally small occupiers in the Channel Islands, whether from attachment to old custom, or from some other cause, not only is the plow in general use, but a plow called "la grande querrue," so large and lumbering that not less than eight or ten horses or oxen are often employed to draw it. Very few of the peasants are rich enough to possess one of these ponderous engines, or the number of cattle required for it; but the poorest has no difficulty in borrowing both the one and other from his neighbors; who, moreover, cheerfully assist each other in busy seasons. The good feeling subsisting between the people of the Channel Islands allows this exchange of services to be effected by barter; but, even if money were employed in the transaction, it is obvious that every one, with the hire of his own services, would be able to purchase an equal quantity of work from others, and that thus the division of labor could be practiced even on small farms, although not nearly to the extent to which it is carried on in large ones.[49] So much must be admitted in favor

---

[49] "Jersey laborers are not to be obtained for hire, but willingly exchange labor. Hired laborers are English, Irish, or French."

of the latter; but of all the claims hitherto enumerated, set up on their behalf, this is the only one which can be even partially conceded. The assertion that a suitable rotation of crops is impracticable in small farms, must sound strangely to anyone who from the top of a church tower in the Pays de Waes, has looked admiringly down on the country round, glowing like a Turkey[50] carpet, with intermingled patches of red, blue, yellow, white, violet, and green, of every tint. The Flemish peasant is for nothing more remarkable than for the great variety of plants among which he distributes his attention; finding room, as he does, within the scope of ten or twelve acres, for wheat, rye, barley, or oats, rape and clover, flax or hemp, hops, chicory, poppies or tobacco, peas, beans, French beans, vetches, or cabbages, potatoes, turnips, carrots, and beet-root. Is it the number of these that is supposed to prevent their rotating, instead of multiplying the facilities for interchange of situations?[51]

But of all the charges brought against small farmers the most amazing is that which represents them as slothful, so diametrically is it opposed to truth, which literally leaps into the eyes of all who are willing to look in the right direction. Small farmers (such of them, that is, as are either owners or leaseholders of their farms, and it must be distinctly understood that this vindication is intended to apply to no others) are not only not generally indolent, but their most distinguishing characteristic is ardent, constant, nay, almost excessive, industry. Circumstances may, no doubt, be imagined in which it would be impossible for them to be uninterruptedly employed. If in any district all the farms were of the same size, and if that size were insufficient to occupy the entire labor of one man, the occupiers would sometimes be without work at home, and would be unable to procure it elsewhere.

Inglis's *Channel Islands*, vol. i. p. 82. See also Le Quesne's *Ireland and the Channel Islands*, p. 113.

[50] [Turkish.]

[51] [The rewritten passage ends here. The subsequent passage is substantially unchanged from the 1848 edition.]

But, when small farms are defended, it is of course understood, either that the smallest is sufficiently large to keep its tenant in full work, or that, if any are below that size, a proportionate number are above it. Unless, therefore, it be supposed that small farms have a tendency to decrease in size (a point to which we shall come hereafter), the apprehension that small farmers must necessarily be occasionally idle from absolute deficiency of work, may be at once dismissed. It is further asserted, however, that the small farmer, even when he has work to do, will be apt to shirk it. He is subject to no immediate compulsion. No one can forbid his sitting down as soon as he is tired, or taking a holiday whenever he feels inclined; and it is presumed that he will not fail to abuse this liberty. But, although he is exempt from the same compulsion, he is stimulated to exertion by influences much stronger than any that affect the hired laborer. The latter must not, indeed, openly dawdle about his business, or he may be dismissed; but, provided he work hard enough to content his master, he is himself content, and aims at nothing more. He has little or no inducement to exert himself further; he has no certainty of gaining an increase of wages by so doing; it is far more probable that virtue in his case would be suffered to be her own sole reward; and industry is a virtue too nearly related to fatigue to allow of such a reward being very eagerly coveted. On the contrary, lease-holding cottage-farmers work for themselves; their remuneration is regulated by their exertions; the fruits of their industry, after a certain fixed deduction has been made, belong to themselves, and the produce of any extra labor is wholly their own. Day-laborers never work so hard as when paid by the piece; but a cottage-farmer does nothing else but piece-work. Human nature would be even more inconsistent than is commonly supposed, if a man would waste time, of so much value to himself, either in rest, recreation, or marketing, and yet would exert himself diligently as a day-laborer, in order to avoid dismissal from a situation not nearly so remunerative. In truth, the only instances of idleness on the part of cottage-farmers are taken from countries where they are only yearly tenants.[52] But the reputation of rack-rented yearly cottiers has already been acknowledged to be too rotten to be patched up, and must be abandoned to the mercy of their censors. The small farmers with whom we are at present dealing, are such only as, being either leaseholders or proprietors, have a secure hold upon the land, and the industry of these is admitted even by their most determined opponents. Mr. Macculloch[53] represents them as contracting "indolent habits," as being "incapable of continuous and vigorous exertion," and as not accumulating capital "in one case out of a hundred." Yet the same Mr. Macculloch confesses that "the very large produce obtained by the Flemish farmer is solely attributable to indefatigable industry; for that the soil is naturally poor and the climate by no means especially favorable;"[54] and M. de Laveleye[55] shows in eloquent detail how indefatigable that industry is. There is not a day on which the husbandman may not be seen plowing, digging, harrowing, hoeing, manuring, sowing, or finally garnering the heterogeneous fruits of his unremitting toil; while his children, who have been since dawn on the roads or commons, are carefully picking up, and depositing in their little cart, everything which, as a German traveler delicately says, "attests the passage of horses or sheep." Arthur Young, as zealous a champion as anyone of large farms, although in the course of his tour through France he could see nothing else "respectable" in small properties, yet admits that he found "a most unremitting industry." "Though," says he, "the husbandry I met with, in a great variety of instances,

---

[52] [That is, short-term tenants with no long-term interest in the land.]

[53] ["M'Culloch" in the 1874 edition, also spelled "McCulloch." John Ramsay Muculloch (1789-1864), a Scottish economist, author and editor.]

[54] Compare *Statist. Acct. of Brit. Emp.*, vol. i. pp. 150 and 151; and *Geog. Diet.*, vol. i. p. 330.

[55] [Émile Louis Victor de Laveleye (1822-1892), Belgian economist in favor of "primitive property."]

on little properties, was as bad as can well be conceived, yet the industry of the possessors was so conspicuous and meritorious, that no commendations would be too great for it."[56]

In order to accumulate evidence to the same effect, it is only necessary to turn to any country in which the peasantry cultivate their own lands. Such is the case in Zürich, as well as in several other Swiss Cantons; and, accordingly, says Inglis, "Anywhere in the neighborhood of Zürich, in looking to the right or the left, one is struck with the extraordinary industry of the inhabitants. In the industry they show in the cultivation of the land, I may safely say they are unrivalled. When I used to open my casement between four and five in the morning to look out upon the lake and the distant Alps, I saw the laborer in the fields; and when I returned from an evening walk, long after sunset, as late perhaps as half-past eight, there was the laborer, mowing his grass or tying up his vines. But there are other and better evidences of the industry of the Zürichers than merely seeing them late and early at work. It is impossible to look at a field, a garden, a hedge, scarcely even a tree, a flower or a vegetable, without perceiving proofs of the extreme care and industry that are bestowed upon the cultivation of the soil. If, for example, a path leads through or by the side of a field of grain, the corn is not, as in England, permitted to hang over the path, exposed to be pulled or trodden down by every passer-by; it is everywhere bounded by a fence; stakes are placed at intervals of about a yard, and about two and four feet from the ground boughs of trees are passed longitudinally along. If you look into a field towards evening where there are large beds of cauliflower or cabbage, you will find that every single plant has been watered. In the gardens, which around Zürich are extremely large, the most punctilious care is evinced in every production that grows. The vegetables are planted with seemingly mathematical accuracy; not a single weed is to be seen, nor a single stone. Plants are not earthed up as with us,

---

[56] *Travels in France*, vol. i. p. 412.

but are placed in small hollows, into each of which a little manure is put, and each plant is watered daily. Where seeds are sown, the earth directly above is broken into the finest powder, every shrub, every flower, is tied to a stake; and where there is wall-fruit, a trellis is erected against the wall to which the boughs are fastened, and there is not a single twig that has not its appropriate resting-place."[57] In another place he says, "When speaking of the Engadine" (with respect to which he had previously stated that the whole of the land belongs to the peasantry), "I did not sufficiently enlarge upon the industry of the inhabitants, but it deserves a panegyric. There is not a foot of waste land in the Engadine, the lowest part of which is not much lower than the top of Snowdon.[58] Wherever grass will grow, there it is; wherever a rock will bear a blade, verdure is seen upon it; wherever rye will succeed, there it is cultivated. Barley and oats have also their appropriate spots; and wherever it is possible to ripen a little patch of wheat, the cultivation of it is attempted."[59] Mr. Laing confirms these statements, and applies the description to Switzerland generally. "The little spots of land," he says, "show the same daily care in the fencing, digging, weeding, and watering." The owners "have a kind of Robinson Crusoe industry about their houses and little properties; they are perpetually building, repairing, altering, or improving something about their tenements."[60] In Germany, Mr. Howitt,[61] after mentioning that the land "is for the most part in the hands of the people," and "parceled out amongst the multitude," describes the peasantry as laboring "early and late, because they feel that they are laboring for themselves. There is not an hour of the year," he adds, "in which they do not find unceasing occupation. In the depth of winter, when the weather permits them by any means to get out of doors, they are always finding

---

[57] Inglis's *Switzerland and South of France*, vol. i. pp. 32 and 33.
[58] [At 3,560 feet, the highest mountain in Wales, possibly (outside Scotland) the highest in the British Isles.]
[59] *Ibid.* pp. 145 and 146.
[60] *Notes of a Traveler*, pp. 354 and 355.
[61] [William Howitt (1792-1879), English miscellaneous writer.]

something to do. They carry out their manure to their lands while the frost is in them. If there is not frost, they are busy clearing ditches and felling old fruit-trees, or such as do not bear well. Such of them as are too poor to lay in a sufficient stock of wood, find plenty of work in ascending into the mountainous woods and bringing thence fuel. It would astonish the English common people to see the intense labor with which the Germans earn their firewood. In the depth of frost and snow, go into any of their hills and woods, and there you find them hacking up stumps, cutting off branches, and gathering, by all means which the official wood-police will allow,[62] boughs, stakes, and pieces of wood, which they convey home with the most incredible toil and patience."[63] In another place he says; "In England, with its great quantity of grass lands and its large farms, so soon as the grain is in and the fields are shut up for hay grass, the country seems in a comparative state of rest and quiet. But here they are everywhere and forever hoeing and mowing, planting and cutting, weeding and gathering. They have a succession of crops like a market-gardener. They have their carrots, poppies, hemp, flax, sainfoin,[64] lucerne,[65] rape,[66] colewort,[67] cabbage, rutabaga,[68] black turnips,[69] Swedish[70]

---

[62] [The expression, "By hook or by crook" comes from the Medieval English practice of permitting peasants to collect whatever wood they could cut with a billhook or shepherd's crook, as well as deadfalls from a lord's forest or common land.]

[63] Howitt's *Rural and Domestic Life of Germany*, pp. 50, 51.

[64] [A forage crop of the legume family, also valuable as a source of nectar for honey.]

[65] [Alfalfa]

[66] [Also known as "field mustard," the source of canola oil.]

[67] [A generic term for brassica, "the cabbage family."]

[68] [Yellow turnip, also Swedish turnip or swede; a cross between cabbage and the turnip.]

[69] [Black radish.]

[70] [In Ireland, rutabagas are called "Swedish turnips," or "swedes." This may be an inadvertent redundancy on Thornton's part.]

and white turnips, teazles,[71] Jerusalem artichokes, mangel-wurzel,[72] parsnips, kidney-beans, field beans and peas, vetches,[73] Indian corn,[74] buckwheat, madder[75] for the manufacturer, potatoes, their great crop of tobacco, millet — all, or the greater part, under the family management, in their own family allotments. They have had these things first to sow, many of them to transplant; to hoe, to weed, to clear of insects, to top, many of them to mow and gather in successive crops. They have their water meadows of which kind almost all their meadows are to flood, to mow, and to re-flood; watercourses to re-open and to make anew; their early fruits to gather, to bring to market with their green crops of vegetables; their cattle, sheep, calves, fowls, and poultry, to look after; their vines, as they shoot rampantly in the summer heat, to prune and thin out the leaves where they are too thick; and anyone may imagine what a scene of incessant labor it is."[76] As Mr. Inglis had declared the industry of the small proprietors of Zürich to be "unrivalled," so Mr. Howitt calls the small proprietors of Germany "the most industrious peasantry in the world;" the truth being, as Mr. Mill aptly observes, in commenting on this remark of Mr. Howitt's, that "whoever is acquainted with only one region in which there are peasant proprietors, invariably thinks the peasantry of that particular region the most industrious in the world." Enough surely has now been said to prove that there is no vice with which small fanners are less justly chargeable than with idleness, and it cannot be necessary to produce other witnesses in their favor from the Channel Islands, the Tyrol, or from the Saxon colonies of Transylvania.

---

[71] [A plant formerly used in textile processing, as its head made a natural comb for smoothing cloth.]

[72] [A beet developed in the 18th century as animal fodder; also known as mangold, mangel beet, field beet, and fodder beet.]

[73] [A legume, one of the earliest known cultivated crops.]

[74] [Maize.]

[75] [A vegetable dye plant.]

[76] *Ibid.*, p. 44.

It seems,[77] then, that they are not necessarily poor, but, on the contrary, as their rate of profit is higher, are likely to be relatively richer than large farmers; they can lay out more money on their land in proportion to its extent; they can use more manure; they can buy for themselves all ordinary agricultural implements; and, by combination among themselves, can obtain the use of the most costly machines, or effect the most expensive improvements; the idea of their being prevented by want of space from varying their crops, is merely fanciful; and, although they may be unable to carry the division of labor as far as might be desirable, their disadvantage in that and all other respects is much more than counterbalanced by the superiority of their industry.[78]

The reader, indeed, if tolerably versed in agricultural history, may not improbably have been tempted to groan under the foregoing accumulation of proof that the disabilities represented as inseparable from the condition of small farmers have no existence, and that there is really nothing in that condition incompatible with the practice of the most approved methods. Why, it is precisely the practice of good small farmers that the best large farmers have taken as their model. It is mainly by copying the former, that the latter have become what they are. It is from Flanders that our mediaeval kings brought over colonists to settle down in the Welsh peninsula of Gower, and in the Irish Baronies of Forth and Bargey; and to teach husbandry to such of the wild natives as their devastating wars had spared. To Flanders our ancestors owed the hop, and several culinary vegetables, and in especial that "good root" for whose English vocative Mrs. Quickly's[79] spelling would, a little before that worthy lady's time, have been in a double sense appropriate.[80] It

---

[77] ["It appears," 1848.]

[78] [The subsequent passage was substantially rewritten for the 1874 edition. The original is included in Appendix XV.]

[79] ["Mistress Quickly" is a character in four of Shakespeare's plays, *Henry IV, Part I, Henry IV, Part II, Henry V,* and *The Merry Wives of Windsor.*]

[80] *Sir Hugh Evans.* What is the focative case, William?

was of "the Husbandry used in Brabant and Flanders" that Sir Richard Weston[81] wrote, and Thomas Hartlib in 1650 published a "Discourse, showing wonderful improvement of land there, and serving as a pattern for our practice in this Commonwealth." From Flanders it was that soon afterwards our countrymen learned to make artificial fields of clover, which, as Weston tells us, was previously unknown in England as a cultivated crop, and found only amongst natural grasses in rich meadows; and, from what he observed in Flanders when passing through in George the Second's train, that Lord Townshend[82] conceived the enthusiasm for turnip cultivation which gained for him the nickname of "Turnip-tops"[83] as his reward. Now, from the earliest period to which farming can be traced back in Flanders, it seems always to have been on a small scale. To anyone who endeavors to picture to himself the maritime districts of Belgium as they must have shown themselves in the sixth and seventh centuries — a mere intermixture of sandy waste and salt marsh, over which the sea continually broke, and a few Menapian[84] stragglers plodded or paddled — it cannot but seem singular that a region so utterly unattractive should have been selected by agricultural adventurers as a field for experiment. The following may perhaps be a partial solution of the enigma. The primitive civilizers of the Netherlands may have been refugees from neighboring Romanized cities of Gaul or Rhenish Germany, who, when those countries were overwhelmed by barbarian invaders, took shipping, and sailed away in search of an asylum elsewhere.

William. O, vocative, O.

Evans. Remember, William, focative is *caret.*

Quickly. And that's a good root.

— Merry Wives of Windsor.

[81] [Sir Richard III Weston (1591-1652), English canal builder and agricultural improver.]

[82] [Charles Townshend, Second Viscount Townshend (1674-1738), British statesman and leader in the "Agricultural Revolution" as the period from the 17th to the end of the 19th centuries is called.]

[83] [The Wikipedia says, "Turnip Townshend."]

[84] [A glacial period in Northern Europe.]

The very dreariness of the Dutch and Belgian coasts, which in other circumstances would have been so repulsive, might now be welcome, as promising the wanderers security against molestation from either dispossessed natives or fresh immigrants. We know that it was by considerations of this kind that the fugitive citizens of Aquileia were led to select the muddy islets at the mouth of the Brenta, whereon to lay the foundations of Venice. Like the Venetians, too, these settlers in the Low Countries may well have begun by devoting themselves almost exclusively to foreign commerce, from sheer want of any other suitable occupation; for, except by becoming the carriers of northern Europe, they could not immediately have earned a livelihood. The example of Venice, again, shows what great wealth they might acquire in that capacity; commercial wealth would supply the means of creating manufacturing wealth, and the two combined, while causing corn, wine, and oil to be imported, would create a demand for provisions of other sorts which could not be brought from a distance, and which, to be had at all, would have to be grown near at hand. Wherever numerous human habitations are collected together, the prime requisite for the fertilization of land cannot be absent; whoever would undertake to reclaim a piece of the apparently irreclaimable wastes that surrounded the early Flemish settlements would freely be allowed to do so rent-free. But, with so intractable a soil, his only chance was to attack it spade in hand; and it would be but a very small piece that a single individual could succeed in subduing with the spade. Whence it would naturally result that the belts of cultivation that gradually encircled the Flemish towns, and, gradually widening till they met, at length enveloped the whole open country, would consist almost entirely of garden-plots, tended for the most part by their own freeholders. To the still existing race of gardening farmers who descended from these in lineal succession, the greatest of English agriculturists are indebted for most of the improvements on which they pride themselves; having by them been, first introduced to an acquaintance with green crops, next taught to substitute an unceasing alternation of green and white crops for the previous ruinous rotation of one or more cereal crops and a fallow; and being even now in process of being by them initiated into the sterculine mysteries of "the maturation of manure under cover, the special value of naturally liquid manure, and the importance of liquidizing solid manure."[85]

Still it is not pretended that small farmers, even the best of them, are all that they might be, or that the generality are not a very long way indeed behind ideal perfection. Living usually on the same spot, with little leisure for reading, and few opportunities of comparing their own doings with those of other people, they are exceedingly averse to change, bigoted to old habits, and proportionately disdainful of foreign practices. Those most skillful and successful of all small farmers, the Flemings, used to be as obnoxious as any to this reproach. Most likely they have altered a good deal for the better within the last thirty years; but, previously, there were none who adhered more pertinaciously to hereditary usages, or were more unwilling to adopt modern inventions, or to listen to the counsels of modern science. "There are few books on husbandry," said Mr. Rham, in 1838, "published in Flanders, and if there were, the Flemish farmers would not read them. New productions or new methods are not read-

---

[85] Likewise into another cognate mystery, of which M. de Lavergne thus writes; "Les cultivateurs flamands ne s'en contentent pas" (i.e. des masses énormes d'engrais fournies par leurs animaux); "ils y ajoutent les boues de ville, les tourteaux, les os, les sables de mer, et surtout un genre particulier de fumure, dont personne ne connaît aussi bien qu'eux la préparation et l'emploi, l'engrais humain. Rejeté avec répugnance par beaucoup de peuples, *notamment par les Anglais*, qui commencent à se raviser, cet engrais est des plus énergiques; *en le perdant, on laisse échapper une immense richesse.* C'est par lui que les Flamands ont pu étendre leurs cultures épuisantes, sans nuire à la fécondité de leur sol, et se montrer supérieurs même aux Anglais, comme production. Tandis que l'Angleterre consacre les trois quarts de son territoire à la nourriture du bétail, la Flandre n'emploie qu'un quart, bien quelle nourrisse proportionellement plus d'animaux; elle y supplée par l'engrais humain." *Économie Rurale de la France*, pp. 71, 72.

ily adopted by any farmers, and least of all by the Flemings." No ground can be more carefully tilled than theirs, more thoroughly drained or kept freer from weeds; but their implements of husbandry, though handy, are rude and simple in comparison with the ingenious agricultural machines so common in this island; the horses are oppressed by massy wooden collars, and broadcast sowing has only to a very moderate extent given way to drilling. But this prejudice in favor of antiquated customs, instead of furnishing a warrant for the unqualified condemnation of small farming, really proves conclusively that there must be some more than counterbalancing excellence in a system which, in spite of such drawbacks, is in its results more than a match for the most imposing combinations of capital and science. However ignorant of theory the small cultivator may be, however inefficient his tools, however much of his time may be lost in turning repeatedly from one job to another, he does nevertheless somehow persuade his land to yield larger returns than the large occupier, with all his advantages, manages to extort from an equal area. That this is the case has now, it is hoped, been sufficiently demonstrated to leave no doubt as to the side in whose favor the verdict should be given, if the question at issue between large and small culture were to be determined by their respectively proportionate amounts of gross produce.[86]

Gross produce is not, however, the only thing to be considered; for, as Arthur Young remarks, so many hands might be employed to raise the larger amount, as to afford nothing for the market. In such a case there could be no towns, no exchange of raw produce for manufactures, no division of labor into rural and urban; all the members of the community would be husbandmen, and would raise or manufacture every article at home. Everything, although very badly made, would have cost a great deal of labor. Little progress could be made in the arts of life; society would remain in its rudest stage, and, instead of the

---

[86] [The rewritten passage ends here. The subsequent passage is substantially unchanged from the 1848 edition.]

blessings of civilization, there would be at best only a sort of coarse abundance. For these reasons, Young pronounces that to be the best system of cultivation which allows of the largest produce being carried to market; but neither is this test altogether unexceptionable. The largest surplus produce might be supplied by those cultivators who retained least for themselves, but it would surely be preferable that their necessities should first be adequately supplied, even though somewhat less should remain for the consumption of others. That is the best system of agriculture, not which provides for one class at the expense of another, but which insures the greatest plenty to all; and small farms, therefore, might possibly be preferable to large ones, even though it should appear that a smaller surplus produce were sent from them to market.[87]

Waiving, however, this consideration,[88] and accepting unconditionally the test proposed by Young, we shall still find that small farms are not only the most productive in proportion to their extent, but that the supplies sent from them to market are also relatively the largest. In proof of this it will not suffice to discover that land, when divided among numerous occupants, pays commonly a much higher rent than when united into a few extensive holdings; that whereas, for example, in England, £30 an acre would be thought a fair, and indeed rather a high, rent for middling land, it is only inferior land that, in Guernsey and Jersey — where the average sizes of farms are respectively eleven, and sixteen acres — will not let for at least £4,[89] while in Switzerland the average rent is £6 an acre. For, as already intimated, these higher rents might be results of an incident not of culture but of tenure, which, although unhappily a very frequent, is not a necessary, concomitant of small farming. Neither will it suffice to show that, although the agricultural population in a

---

[87] [The subsequent passage was substantially rewritten for the 1874 edition. The original is included in Appendix XV.]

[88] ["these considerations," 1848.]

[89] According to Mr. le Quesne, the average rent of good land in the Channel Islands may be estimated at 6 shillings and its value at £150 an acre. *Ireland and the Channel Islands*, p. 123.

minutely divided territory is always far denser than in one of large farms, certain territories of the former description are also among those which maintain in addition the largest manufacturing and commercial population — Belgium, for instance, being second to England alone in that respect, and Switzerland and Rhenish Prussia being further illustrations of the same fact. For it may readily be objected that the non-agricultural sections of a community need not be dependent for their subsistence on home produce, but may derive part of their supplies from abroad, and it may generally be impossible to ascertain what is the proportion imported. This objection does not, however, apply to the Channel Islands. We are there able to determine pretty accurately the quantities of food imported and exported, and after making the needful allowance on that account, we shall find that two small territories occupied exclusively by small farmers, and affording employment to four times the number of cultivators that would be thought requisite on large farms, do nevertheless furnish a sufficiency of food, not only for those cultivators and their families, but for a non-agricultural population, in addition, twice or four times larger than is maintained by an equal extent of land in Great Britain.

The extent of cultivated land in England is, according to the estimate of Mr. Caird,[90] 27,000,000 acres, of which about one-fourth, or 6,833,500, is under wheat, barley, oats, or rye, another fourth under green crops, and the remainder under grass. At the rate of 34 bushels per acre, the annual produce of the corn-land would be about 29,000,000 of quarters, and, at a similarly liberal rate, that of the remaining acreage, a quantity of food equivalent to 46,000,000 of quarters, making a total of indigenous provisions equal to 75,000,000 of quarters of corn. But, in addition, in the three years ending with 1870, about 14,000,000 of imported corn, together with the equivalents in rice, cattle, butchers' and salted meat, fish, cheese, butter, lard, and eggs, of 11,000,000 or 12,000,000 more, or 25,000,000 of quarters altogether, were on an

---

[90] *English Agriculture*, pp. 521 and 522.

average annually retained for home consumption; so that of the population of England proper — according to the Census of 1871, about 24,500,000 — one-fourth would seem to be fed from abroad. The Tables of the last Census, so far as yet published, do not show the classification of the people according to occupation, but in 1861 the number of persons in England connected with agriculture was 1,600,000. It is possible that, owing to the growing use in husbandry of mechanical and other labor-saving contrivances, this number may not have much increased, and if it alone be deducted from the present total population, the non-agricultural residue will appear as somewhat under 23,000,000, of whom nearly 6,000,000 have been shown to subsist on foreign imports, so that only 17,000,000, exclusive of cultivators, remain to be fed by our 27,000,000 of acres of cultivated land. This is at the rate of less than one person for every acre and a half. The total population of Guernsey was in 1861, 24,243; in 1871, 30,593; the corresponding figures for Jersey 55,613 and 56,657; the agricultural population of Guernsey in 1861, about 2,850; that of Jersey, 5,063; but the other statistics in my possession available, for the desired comparison of those islands with England, are only those collected by me for the purpose a full quarter of a century back. In 1841, Guernsey contained 10,240 acres of cultivated land; her total population was 21,440; of whom, on the presumption that the proportions were much about the same in that year as they were subsequently in 1861, the agricultural portion was 2,530, the non-agricultural 18,910. In the year 1834, foreign provisions were imported to the value of £81,400. But, whereas corresponding imports into Great Britain are paid for almost entirely with manufactured goods, in the Channel Islands they are to a great extent bartered for other agricultural produce. The exports of provisions from Guernsey in 1835 were worth £27,500,[91] so that the

---

[91] The authorities for these statements and for those in the next paragraph are partly tables in Montgomery Martin's *History of the British Colonies*, vol. v. pp. 481 and 482, and in the *Guernsey and Jersey Magazine*, vol. iii. pp. 106-9, and partly oral commu-

value of the surplus imports was £53,900 only; which, at the rate of £10 a head — a very moderate rate for a community so generally well off as that of Guernsey — would suffice for the maintenance of 5,930 persons. Deduct that number from the nonagricultural population referred to above, and there will remain 12,980 persons, exclusive of cultivators, to be fed with the produce of 10,240 acres. This is at the rate of very nearly two persons for every acre and a half.

The results exhibited by Jersey are still more striking. In 1841, the cultivated portion of that island contained about 18,000 acres; the total population was 47,500, the number of cultivators, on the same presumption as before, 4,320, and the non-agricultural residue, 43,200. In the year 1834, foreign provisions were imported to the value of £80,000, but provisions were exported to the value of nearly £60,000, so that the value of the net imports was £20,000.[92] This sum might suffice for the maintenance of 2,000 persons, leaving nearly 41,200, besides cultivators, to be fed with the produce of 18,000 acres. This is at the rate of very nearly four persons for every acre and a half.[93]

Thus it appears, that in each of the two principal Channel Islands, the agricultural population is more than four times as dense as in England, there being in the latter country only one cultivator to seventeen acres of cultivated land, while in Guernsey and Jersey there is one to about four. Yet the agriculture of these islands maintains, besides cultivators, non-agricultural populations, respectively twice and four times as dense as that of England.

---

nications made to myself during a six-weeks' sojourn in the Channel Islands in 1847.

[92] Compare with these the corresponding particulars for the Isle of Wight, which, says Mr. Cliffe Leslie, "has not one peasant proprietor, and, with 86,810 acres of land, has a population of 55,362, and scarcely any commerce or shipping." *Land Systems and Industrial Economy of Ireland, England, and Continental Countries*, p. 74.

[93] [The rewritten passage ends here. The subsequent passage is substantially unchanged from the 1848 edition.]

This difference does not arise from any superiority of soil or climate possessed by the Channel Islands, for the former is naturally rather poor, and the latter is not better than in the southern counties of England. It is owing entirely to the assiduous care of the farmers and to the abundant use of manure. The results of the comparison just made may be surprising to most English readers, but the Channel Islanders themselves are not insensible of the advantages they derive from their method of farming, and very reasonably congratulate themselves upon it. "There are larger estates in England," says a late Bailiff of Guernsey, Mr. Brock,[94] "than the whole of this island; but where will one be found that produces the quantity of provisions sent to market by our small farms? Let the production of the island be compared to that of any ten thousand acres kept in one, two, or three hands in Great Britain, and the advantage of small farms will be obvious. Independently of the two thousand families living in the country, compare the surplus produce sent to market with the surplus produce of any ten thousand acres in one, two, or three hands elsewhere, and see on which side the balance will be found."[95] Surely the particulars mentioned above must be sufficient to establish the truth of the opinion in support of which they have been cited. If they had been known to Arthur Young, they must have induced that candid writer to lay aside his prejudices, and to acknowledge that, tried by his own test, small farms had come off victorious, as best answering what he had himself pronounced to be the main purpose of agriculture, so that if they were nevertheless still to be condemned, it must be on some other ground than that of ingratitude for the pains bestowed on them.[96]

---

[94] [Daniel de Lisle Brock (1762-1842), Bailiff (Chief Justice of Guernsey or Jersey) from 1821-1842.]

[95] *Guernsey and Jersey Magazine*, Oct. 1837, p. 258.

[96] [A passage was deleted here from the 1848 edition. See Appendix XV.]

2. Social Effects of Peasant Proprietorship

Special advantages of Small Proprietors — Their peculiar
Resources and Incentives to Diligence — Alleged tendency of
Small Properties to Excessive Subdivision, and to promote
Pauperism — Examination of arguments in favor of that opinion
— Evidences against it from History of the Jews — of Ancient
Rome — and Greece — and of England — From the Past and
Present condition of Norway — Switzerland — the Tyrol — and
the Channel Islands — Objection of Mr. G. W. Norman and Judge
Longfield to Peasant Proprietorship[1]

The preceding chapter was principally intended as a
vindication from the reproach of infecundity of small
leasehold farms, although some of the illustrations contained in it were drawn from peasant properties. It is obvious, however, that the arguments urged in favor of the
former apply with greatly increased force to the latter. A
small landowner, whose whole produce belongs to himself,
is of course richer than he would be if he had to pay rent;
he can more easily bear the expenses of cultivation, of
procuring proper implements and manure, of drainage
and irrigation, and he can keep more livestock. Small
leaseholders, as a class, can lay out more money on their
land in proportion to its extent than larger occupiers; but
a small freeholder has more to lay out than a leaseholder
of the same degree, and has, besides, very much stronger
motives for liberal expenditure. "A small proprietor," says
Adam Smith, "who knows every part of his little territory,
who views it with all the affection which property, especially small property, naturally inspires, and who, upon
that account, takes pleasure not only in cultivating, but in
adorning it, is generally of all improvers the most industrious, the most intelligent, and the most successful." It
may be added that he is also the most enterprising. He
need not carefully calculate whether an outlay will be
fully repaid to him within a certain number of years; he
has only to consider whether the addition to the annual

---

[1] ["Objection of Mr. G. W. Norman and Judge Longfield to Peasant Proprietorship" was added to the 1874 edition.]

value of his land will be equal to the interest of the sum which the improvements will cost; he does not consider it essential that the principal should ever be returned; he is satisfied to sink it for ever in his own land, provided that, in that safest of all investments, it yield a perpetual annuity equal to what would be its annual increase in another employment. Nay, if he be tolerably frugal, devoting to domestic and miscellaneous expenses no more than the leaseholder of a similar property would so appropriate, he may even grow rich. Inglis tells us that "many Swiss peasants have amassed large fortunes;" in the village of Bergun, in the Grisons, he heard that there were two persons holding money in the British funds, one, £1,000, and the other somewhat less; and in another village of the same sequestered canton he found two peasants said[2] to be worth each £20,000 sterling; and in the Channel Islands, men working in the fields in smock frocks are frequently pointed out to a stranger as possessors of considerable property. Compare this state of things with England, where Burke's remark, that "a farmer's trade is a very poor trade," still holds good, and where it is still as rare as ever to find an instance of one occupying from 150 to 400 acres, who, "after a course of the most unremitting parsimony and labor, dies worth more than pays his debts, leaving his posterity to continue in nearly the same equal conflict between industry and want, in which the last predecessor, and a long line of predecessors before him, lived and died."[3]

Again, the peasant proprietor has the strongest possible incentives to diligence. A man never works so well as when paid by the piece, but even then the more he is paid the better he works. The small leaseholder, not less than the small proprietor, is paid in proportion to his labor; but the latter is paid at a higher rate, for he takes to himself the whole fruit of his exertions, while the former must content himself with part. The proprietor, too, knows that, if his labor increase the productiveness of his land,

---

[2] Inglis's *Switzerland*, vol. i. pp. 91, 109.
[3] *Thoughts on Scarcity.*

his remuneration will increase likewise; whereas that of the tenant, if augmented for a while by his own exertions, is pretty certain to be reduced to its former level at the expiration of his lease. Besides, many rural operations yield no profit until after a long lapse of time, and yield so little even then that the enjoyment of it in perpetuity seems requisite to recompense the labor expended. Such operations are seldom undertaken except by proprietors. No others would think of planting an orchard such as Arthur Young saw near Sauve, on a tract consisting "seemingly of nothing but huge rocks;" or, as in the mountains of Languedoc, would "carry earth in baskets on their backs to form a soil where nature had denied it;" or would enclose and till fields and gardens on a "wretched blowing sand, naturally as white as snow." But, as Young exclaims, in spite of himself, "give a man the secure possession of a bleak rock, and he will turn it into a garden;" there is "no way so sure of carrying tillage to a mountaintop as by permitting the neighboring villagers to acquire it in property. The magic of property turns sand to gold."[4] It may be objected that the gold realized does not repay the expense of transmutation, and that therefore the labor employed upon it has been misapplied; and no doubt any moneyed speculator who should engage in such alchemy with hired labor might never recover the amount of his outlay. But — and here comes a conclusive answer to those who, instead of admiring such agricultural achievements, condemn them as waste of power — the peasant who performs them on his own account, performs them without other outlay than that of labor which would otherwise have lain useless at that particular time. When the hired laborer has earned his daily wage, and gives himself up to rest or amusement, the small freeholder is content to recreate himself by turning to some lighter work. For him it is sufficient diversion to weed and water his cabbages, or train his fruit trees; and in wet or wintry weather, when outdoor work is scarcely worth paying for, and when the day-laborer must often remain idle because

---

4 *Travels in France*, vol. i. pp. 50, 51, 88, 412.

no one will give him work, then it is that the cottager builds up terraces on the steep hillside, or lays the site of a garden amongst rocks. It is, in short, a prime excellence of peasant proprietorship that it stirs into activity labor which would otherwise not have been exerted, in other words, would not have existed, and the fruits of which, consequently, however insignificant, are, at any rate, all pure gain.

In short, whatever may be the absolute merits of small properties, they must be acknowledged to be preferable to equally small leasehold farms in all those respects which we have hitherto considered. They have, however, been subjected to one accusation, to which leasehold farms are less obnoxious, and which, if well-founded, would completely neutralize all their advantages, and would indeed justify their unqualified condemnation as one of the greatest curses with which a country can be afflicted. It is asserted that small properties have a strange tendency to become smaller by subdivision, and that, as an increase in the number of properties implies a corresponding multiplication of proprietors, an excessive agricultural population must soon come into existence. An estate may be just sufficient to afford full occupation to its owner, and to enable him to maintain his family in comfort; but, on his death, his children may divide the land amongst themselves, and may convert their separate shares into so many distinct farms. But if the original property were but just large enough for the employment and maintenance of one family, the separate portions must each be too small for those purposes; yet the partition need not stop here. In another generation or two, the number of owners may be so much increased, and the size of their respective shares so much diminished, that the whole produce of the land belonging to each family may just suffice to keep it from starvation. A similar partition may take place on every small estate, so that a country entirely occupied by small proprietors may, in the course of two or three generations, be filled with a peasantry as numerous as the whole produce of the soil can preserve in existence. Not only would such a peasantry be reduced to the lowest depth of misery, they would also be the sole inhabitants of their country; for as, in order to live, they would be obliged to consume whatever provisions they were able to raise, they would have none left to exchange for manufactured goods, no surplus to send to market for the subsistence of a town population. The whole country might be justly described as a vast "pauper-warren," and such, we are told, is the fate impending over every country in which the actual cultivators are at the same time owners of the soil.

In inquiring into the grounds for these frightful predictions, our first consolation is derived from the reflection, that they take for granted the right of all the children of a deceased landowner to share his estate amongst them. But peasant proprietorship and custom of gavelkind,[5] or the like, although often found together, are two distinct things, and the first may exist quite independently of the second. Peasant proprietors may be conceived to exist, who should be at liberty to bequeath their lands to whomsoever they chose, or who should be forbidden to divide them into portions of less than a certain size. Besides, it is not obvious why the baneful influence of gavelkind should be confined to small properties, and should not operate on estates of all sizes. If the children of the owner of twenty acres might divide their patrimony into portions of five acres, the inheritors of an estate of twenty times the size might split it into farms of a hundred acres. One of these, on the occurrence of another death, might undergo a second partition, and the grandchildren of the original gentleman-farmer would then sink to the degree of peasants. Thus, the only difference between dividing a country into estates of twenty and into estates of four hundred acres, would appear to be, that the evils apprehended in the former case would in the latter be retarded by some two generations.

It may, however, be urged, that a peasant's sons have more than ordinary motives for effecting a partition of their patrimony. It has even been asserted that they have

---

[5] [A system of land tenure that requires an estate to be equally divided among all qualified heirs.]

no alternative. The younger sons of an agricultural capitalist may seek their fortunes in trade; but in a country of small farms, a farmer's sons, it has been said, have no means of gaining a livelihood without becoming farmers themselves. Such a country, according to the late Mr. Macculloch, "can never furnish surplus produce sufficient, after satisfying the wants of the cultivators, to feed a numerous body of merchants, handicraftsmen, *etc.*, nor would small occupiers have any demand for the products or services of such persons. There could, therefore, be no demand for that surplus population which an agricultural society is always producing, and the division of the paternal properties would be the only way in which families could be provided for."[6] Of this it need only be said, that it is a false inference from false premises. It has been shown that well-managed small farms send to market not only as large, but a much larger surplus produce than corresponding portions of the best-managed large farms, and may afford subsistence for more numerous bodies of artisans, manufacturers, traders, and other inhabitants of towns. Consequently, where they abound, the greatest abundance and variety of nonagricultural employments may likewise be found; so that the necessity for adopting the business of husbandry because no other is open to him, should apparently be felt by no man so little as by the son of a peasant proprietor. Mr. Macculloch, however, uses some additional arguments, which are much more to the purpose, and cannot be so summarily disposed of. He insists much on the preference which the young peasant, even if enjoying liberty of choice, is likely to show for the business in which he has been brought up. "The strong predilection," he observes, "entertained by the great bulk of the children engaged in agriculture for the pursuits of their fathers, has been remarked by every one in any degree familiar with rural affairs." Children at liberty to divide their father's estate, possess "the greatest facilities for gratifying their natural inclination." They have "the power of continuing in the line of life in which they have

---

[6] *Encyclopaedia Britannica*, Art. Cottage System.

been educated, and which must in consequence be endeared to them by all those early associations which exert so strong an influence over future conduct." Moreover, "the possession of a piece of ground gives a feeling of independence to a small capitalist or a poor man that he cannot otherwise experience." A possession of this sort may fail to render him comfortable, "but it gives him a security against want. It furnishes him with a cottage, and unless it be unusually small, it will enable him to raise such a supply of potatoes, as will go far to support himself and his family. In no way, therefore, can a poor man be so independent. The possession of a piece of ground renders him in some measure his own master. It exempts him from the necessity of severe labor and unremitting application." From these considerations Mr. Macculloch concludes, that the children of small landowners will choose "to reside on the little properties they have obtained from their ancestors, and that the process of division and subdivision will continue until the whole land has been parceled out into patches, and filled with an agricultural population equally destitute of the means and the desire of rising in the world."[7]

This reasoning, no doubt, possesses much force, and might perhaps not inexcusably be looked upon as decisive if the question at issue were merely hypothetical, and related only to what might be expected to take place in circumstances hitherto untried. Arguments on the other side are not indeed wanting, and some shall be forthwith produced; but they may not perhaps do more than make the balance of probabilities equal; facts may need to be thrown in to turn the scale.

Nothing can be said in opposition to the alleged fondness of young country people for a country life —

'Tis born with all; the love of Nature's works
Is an ingredient in the compound man,
Infused at the creation of the kind.

---

[7] Macculloch's Edition of the *Wealth of Nations*, vol. iv. pp. 462-4.

Man, though immured in cities, still retains
His inborn, inextinguishable thirst
Of rural scenes.[8]

In those born and bred amongst them, then, the attachment to such scenes may well be a sort of passion. But the love of country pursuits is common to all country-folk; agriculture is the favorite occupation of agriculturists of every degree, of the gentleman-farmer not less than of the peasant proprietor. The sons of either are equally attached to the business in which they have been brought up, and would make equal sacrifices rather than relinquish it. If the son of an owner of twenty acres would be satisfied with the possession of five acres, so also might the son of a proprietor of an estate of four hundred acres apply himself as contentedly to the cultivation of one hundred, and the son's son to that of twenty. By so doing, the last-mentioned would, it is true, sink below the condition in which he was born, and would degrade himself from the rank of a petty gentleman to one little above that of a peasant; but the peasant's son also has a station in society to maintain, he also is ambitious of remaining on an equality with the companions of his youth, and would fear to be looked down upon by the twenty-acre men of his father's acquaintance. Rather than submit to such debasement, he probably, like the young gentleman with whom we have been comparing him, would sell his inheritance, and with the help of the proceeds endeavor to make his way in some new walk of life. His little capital might not perhaps enable him to establish himself immediately as his own master, and he, like his betters, might be compelled to begin with a subordinate situation; but perhaps also he would have sense enough not to estimate at more than its real value the independence he had forfeited. Certainly he would not value it at all on that particular account on which Mr. Macculloch lays most stress, *viz.*, for the exemption which it would afford from the necessity of severe labor. No one works harder than the peasant

---

[8] [William Cowper (1731-1800), "The Task," *The Task and Other Poems*, 1785.]

proprietor; nowhere could he find a stricter taskmaster than himself; he is not likely then to refuse to take the service of another from the mere fear of being overworked.

Two advantages land certainly possesses over most other kinds of property; there is less risk of its being lost, and it is tolerably certain to yield some annual produce. The amount may be small — too small, perhaps, for the comfortable subsistence of the owner, or even for his preservation from want; but it will help, more or less, to save him from starvation; whereas, if the land were sold, and the proceeds invested in trade, the speculation might prove unprofitable, or the money might be totally lost. Suppose that this and other considerations should determine several sons of a small proprietor not to sell the paternal acres, but to trust entirely to them for subsistence, does it follow that they must divide the land? Would it not be more natural, as well as wiser, to cultivate it in common as in their father's lifetime, and to continue to live together in the family dwelling? They could scarcely be dissuaded from doing so by the fear of not agreeing about the mode of cultivation, or insist upon a partition, "in order that each might pursue his own plan of farming, and avail himself of what he might suppose his own superior sagacity."[9] Such causes of dissension might well exist among great agricultural capitalists, men whose enterprise and ardor for improvement were proportioned to their means; but they could scarcely have place among peasant proprietors, whose "inveterate retention of local and hereditary usages" furnishes such abundant matter for reproach. Whatever might be their points of difference, they would at least agree in reverencing old-established customs, and would probably be only too unanimous in abiding by the rules of their forefathers. Discord might possibly gain admittance amongst them, but would certainly not be introduced by the spirit of innovation.

But it may be argued, that, without dividing the land, the co-proprietors could not build separate cottages for the reception of their respective families. We have now

---

[9] Macculloch, *ut supra*.

reached the foundation-stone of the whole theory of the tendency of small properties to endless subdivision. It is based upon the assumption that members of the lower classes are apt to marry as soon as they have a prospect of a bare subsistence. This, which is true of the lowest class, where that lowest class is sunk in the depths of destitution, is false of every class enjoying a moderate share of the conveniences of life, and is, in substance, admitted to be false, even by those who maintain it in words. Men do not, in general, marry, when, as a necessary consequence, they must permanently sacrifice their position in society, and adopt a mode of life greatly inferior to that to which they have been accustomed. An Irish beggar, who being already at the bottom of the social scale, cannot sink lower, and whose means of livelihood cannot well become more defective or precarious, runs no risk of this kind, and need not hesitate to take a wife from among the companions of his wretchedness, as soon as he is rich enough to pay the wedding fees, and to buy potatoes and whisky for the wedding feast. But those to whom fortune has been more bountiful are, in general, proportionably careful not to forfeit her favors by matrimonial imprudence. There are exceptions to all rules, but the son of a man of five thousand a year is seldom content to marry upon a thousand a year, nor the son of a man of a thousand a year on two hundred a year; neither does the son of a proprietor of twenty acres undertake to bring up a family on the produce of five acres, or the son of an owner of five acres on the produce of one acre. Even the very slight acquaintance with the conveniencies of life which the person last mentioned might be supposed to possess, would probably endow him with the requisite modicum of prudence. If he had been brought up sufficiently well to have discovered that there is such a thing as domestic comfort, he would not recklessly throw away his chance of attaining it. If he had passed his youth in a substantial cottage, and had been fed at a tolerably well-covered table, he would not be satisfied with Mr. Macculloch's magnificent dowry of a hovel and a sufficiency of potatoes. He would have a standard of comfort; not a very high one indeed, but still one below which he would, nevertheless, be anxious not to fall; for peasants, as well as peers, are little disposed to forfeit, by their rashness, advantages to which they have been accustomed. Indeed, the owner of a small piece of ground, yielding little more than enough for his own maintenance, is the less likely to marry without adequate means, as he, of all men, is in least danger of over-rating his resources. If his farm were larger, or if he were a day-laborer, his gains would depend, in a great measure, on changes in the market, or in the rate of wages, and his income being uncertain, might be reckoned at more than its real amount. But as it is, he is liable to no such mistake. He knows pretty accurately what is the annual average produce of his land, and how much, if at all, it exceeds the quantity required for his own use. He has no accidental sources of increase to look to, and no excuse for trusting anything to luck. He cannot expect that two stalks of corn will, by mere chance, grow where but one grew before. He can calculate, without risk of serious error, the amount of his income, and whether or not it will enable him to maintain a family; and if it is insufficient for that purpose, it would be pure insanity in him to marry. It is more charitable to suppose that he would remain single until some favorable change should take place in his circumstances, until he could captivate some village heiress, or obtain an accession to his little territory by the death of a relation. Until then, he would have no adequate motive for requiring a partition of the property held by him in common with his brothers; and when he did demand his separate share, he would do so in order to annex it to the other lands which he had acquired by marriage or inheritance. In this manner, properties when divided might immediately be recomposed, and their average size might remain undiminished.

This question does not, however, depend entirely upon argument, and need not be determined merely according to the balance of probabilities. It has been submitted, over and over again, to actual experiment. Ever since the Flood it has been almost constantly under trial, and abundant evidence whereon to found a confident judgment may be procured, either from the records of the past, or from observation of the present.

The pastoral tribes, by which most civilized countries were at one time occupied, have almost invariably been followed, either immediately, or after a certain interval, by a race of peasant proprietors. The revolution has taken place at different stages of national progress, but scarcely an instance can be mentioned in which it has not occurred sooner or later. In territories of very small extent, very barren, or much divided by mountains, rivers, or other natural barriers, it has commonly been effected as early as the first appropriation of land by individuals. In such situations, the tribes or clans constituting the as-yet nomad community, must necessarily be small for want of pasture; and the same cause must prevent any individual from acquiring very great numbers of cattle, and from very greatly surpassing his companions in wealth or power. There can be no great inequality of rank, nor any authority save that of the assembled heads of families, which a freeman, after emancipation from parental control, need acknowledge. The chief of the tribe himself holds merely honorary office, is simply *primus inter pares*, and unable to take any public action in peace or war without consent of the other heads of families, since these, by combination, could effectually resist his commands. Whenever, therefore, the members of this tribe, after having partially exchanged pasturage for tillage, find it convenient to divide part of their land amongst themselves, instead of holding it all in common, every family has a voice in the partition, and makes good its claim to a share to be held in fee simple. If, on the other hand, there be abundance of good pasture, a tribe may expand indefinitely, and the cattle of a single herdsman may be counted by thousands and tens of thousands. Such an one may be raised by a concurrence of fortunate circumstances far above his companions in wealth and power, and may become their chief in reality as well as in name. Successful wars, first with other tribes, and then with other nations, may extend his dominion, and increase the disparity between himself and his subjects, until his authority becomes as absolute as that of the

authority becomes as absolute as that of the Genghis Khans and Tamerlanes, who have from time to time succeeded in reducing all the wandering tribes of Tartary under their sway. Even if no individual be able to exalt himself in this manner, and though there be instead a considerable body of rich herdsmen pretty nearly on a level, the existence of such an aristocracy is fraught with equal danger to the liberty of their inferiors. Each of its members must maintain a number of dependents, captives taken in war, or poor clansmen of his own, to look after his cattle, and as these have no means of subsistence but what their master furnishes, so neither have they any law but their master's will; nor dare they refuse to assist him in any act of oppression, or among others, in that of bringing smaller herdsmen into subservience to him. Suppose now the tribe to pass from a migratory and pastoral to a stationary and agricultural condition — every wealthier herdsman acquires complete suzerainty over all the land allotted to himself and his followers. Part of the land is appropriated by such of these latter as possess a few cattle of their own; but these continue to acknowledge their allegiance to him as leader, and, from clients of a patron, are insensibly converted into vassals of a lord. As for his more immediate retainers, the slaves or servants fed and clothed by his bounty, they are settled on the demesnes reserved by him for himself; and besides tending his flocks and herds as before, are required to till portions of his land, accepting in payment of these services certain other portions assigned to them, to be cultivated for their own behalf. Their previous subjection to their master is exchanged for a bondage still more stringent; from servants they become serfs, bound to the soil by ties of personal attachment, and also by consciousness of having lost the facilities for escape which they possessed when dwelling in a camp. It was in this manner that the bulk of the wandering Goths and Scythians of antiquity degenerated into German and Russian serfs, as completely at their master's disposal as any other part of his livestock. So too, in all probability, had the nomad races of Gaul and Spain been long before degraded, and, if the serfdom in which the peasantry of these countries were found at the date of Roman annexation was subsequently alleviated during the period of Roman domination, it was certainly restored in all its rigor by the barbarians who overran the Roman provinces.[10]

Although, however, the earlier generations of serfs may hold neither property nor life by any better tenure than their lord's permission, their successors imperceptibly acquire in the course of ages important rights and privileges. Their lord may, if he please, deprive them entirely of the fruits of their labor; but in a thinly peopled country, in which manufactures have made little progress, and foreign commerce is unknown, a great landowner would be simply encumbered by larger contributions of raw produce than his household can consume. His own proper demesnes, together with the prescribed dues of his tenantry of various grades, supply him with fully as much as he requires, and leave him without motive for extortionate demands on the lower orders of serfs. These latter, if the country remain long in a nearly stationary condition, may equally long continue without having their rents sensibly raised, and be left undisturbed in possession of their respective holdings from sheer want of any reason for ejecting them. In process of time customs become confounded with rights, so that at length it would be looked upon as a piece of injustice to assess a serf at an advanced rate, or to oust him from his tenement, as long as the old rate was punctually paid. If, while this was the state of feeling, an influential middle class were to grow up, or if the Crown became desirous of curbing the power of the nobles, the rights of the peasantry would be more boldly asserted and more generally recognized, until at length they became formally established. Their proprietary title, at first merely prescriptive, would be eventually legalized, either by judicial decisions or statutory enactments; and thus

---

[10] [This appears to be a somewhat sarcastic reference to the "Germanic superiority" thesis of Edward Gibbon and Edward Creasy, in *The Decline and Fall of the Roman Empire* (1776-1789) and *Fifteen Decisive Battles of the World* (1851), respectively.]

villains and serfs would be metamorphosed into independent and high-spirited yeomen.

In one or other of these ways, almost every country on the face of the globe which has passed regularly through the various stages that separate barbarism from civilization, has been at some period, as many are still, occupied partially by peasant proprietors. Ample opportunity must consequently have been afforded for the development of those evils by which every community so constituted must, it has been said, be inevitably overwhelmed. Let us inquire, then, whether the apprehensions of certain writers have ever been realized; whether one single country can be named in which landed property has been so minutely divided that the produce barely sufficed for the consumption of the cultivators; in which there were no towns, no manufacturers, no artisans, none but a rural and agricultural population, and that plunged, as it assuredly would be, in the circumstances supposed, in destitution and barbarism.

Our first example shall be taken from Jewish history. It is evident from the Scriptural account of the occupation of Canaan by the Israelites, that the land was divided among the whole people, and that, although the partition was made without perfect regard to equality, still every head of a family obtained a share. Moreover, extraordinary precautions were taken to prevent an allotment from ever passing away from the descendants of the first grantee. If poverty compelled any one to sell part of his domain, he might at any time redeem it by returning what would remain of the purchase money, after deduction of the annual profit which the purchaser had made while the land had been in his possession. Even if the land were not redeemed, it could only be retained by the purchaser until the jubilee, which took place once in fifty years, and was then to be restored unconditionally to the seller. Thus the consolidation of estates was very anxiously guarded against, since it could not legally occur except when a family became extinct; but no precautions were adopted against the opposite evil of excessive subdivision, to which indeed the law afforded every facility. The only inequality which was sanctioned in the partition of an inheritance, was that the eldest son should obtain a double portion; the remainder of the property was to be divided equally among the other sons, or among the daughters, if there were no sons. Thus were united the conditions required by the theory we are examining — peasant proprietorship, and a custom of inheritance differing very slightly from gavelkind, — yet the consequences were the very opposite of those which, it is said, should have ensued. Landed property among the Israelites never became too much subdivided; on the contrary, the prophets inveigh loudly against its unjust consolidation; and as long as the Mosaic law on the subject was strictly administered, poverty was almost literally unknown. Five hundred years after the death of the lawgiver, when ample time had been allowed for the development of whatever germs of evil his system contained, few or no instances could be found of destitute persons whose indigence was not the result of their own misconduct. David did not hesitate to say, that in the whole of his life he had never "seen the righteous forsaken, nor his seed begging bread;" and this assertion, which might otherwise be regarded as an Oriental hyperbole, may very likely have been strictly correct in a country of peasant proprietors. At this day, the Bailiff of Guernsey, confining his observations to the natives of his own island, might with perfect truth use the same and even stronger language than that of the King of Israel. Certainly there is not a beggar within the limits of his jurisdiction, and an able-bodied person very rarely, if ever, seeks admittance into either of the two hospitals or asylums for the poor. The security against want possessed by the ancient Israelites is expressly stated to have been of the same nature as that of the present inhabitants of the Channel Islands. To every family belonged a portion of land which only needed to be diligently cultivated to maintain its owners in plenty. He who tilled his land, Solomon tells us, had plenty of bread. Those only who kept idle company, and neglected their business suffered from poverty.[11] Such was the state of things while the law of Moses continued in full force; but under the later kings its authority became insufficient for the protection of the peasantry, whose rights were then frequently set at naught. We may be sure that the tyranny of Ahab found many imitators among his licentious nobles, if, even in the days of good Hezekiah, the Lord "looked for judgment, but behold oppression; for righteousness, but behold a cry."[12] The cry was the same that was heard, and the oppression the same that was practiced long afterwards in England, in the time of the Tudors, when "husbandmen were thrust out of their own" by their rich neighbors, who, with the assistance of their "man of law," would "pretend some title," and sometimes "by covin[13] and fraud," sometimes "by violent oppression put them beside it, or by wrongs and injuries so weary them, that they were compelled to sell all."[14] Even so, ages before, in Palestine, did Scribes and Pharisees, whose legal knowledge gave them peculiar facilities for interfering in questions of disputed inheritance, defraud the fatherless, and "devour widows' houses." So did rich landholders "covet fields, and take them by violence; and houses and take them away; so did they oppress a man and his house, even a man and his heritage."[15] So did they "join house to house," and "lay field to field, till there was no place, that they might be placed alone in the midst of the earth."[16] This is something very different from the minute division we were bidden to expect; and it is highly deserving of notice that

---

[11] Prov. xxviii. 19.

[12] Isaiah, v. 7.

[13] [Covin is a type of fraud, a secret agreement between two or more persons to defraud another of his or her rights.]

[14] Sir T. More's *Utopia*, St. John's Edition, pp. 32-4, and Massinger's "New Way to Pay Old Debts." [Thornton appeared to understand that *Utopia* is a satire, and the abolition of private property in Utopia was intended to mirror and ridicule the effective abolition of private property in capital under the Tudors.]

[15] Micah, ii.

[16] Isaiah, v. 8.

pauperism, which is said to be inseparable from small properties, scarcely made its appearance in Palestine until separate properties were forcibly united. From that time, indeed, the Jews seem to have had "the poor always with them," although, as the main body of the peasantry, notwithstanding the grievous injustice inflicted on individuals, were never probably very generally dispossessed of their proprietary rights, the poor may never have formed a very numerous class. Those of whom the Scriptures afford us glimpses were chiefly infirm of body or mind, sick, halt, maim or blind.

The primitive Romans were likewise peasant proprietors. The *ager Romanus*, the original territory of Rome, extended in no direction more than five miles from the walls; and as, for some time after the foundation of the city, it constituted the entire property of the three patrician tribes, who were at first the only inhabitants, the portion belonging to each proprietor must have been exceedingly moderate. So late as the third century of Rome, the haughty Cincinnatus is said to have received the news of his nomination to the dictatorship in his shirt sleeves, while digging or plowing in his little farm of less than three acres;[17] and the story, whether true or false, proves equally, that, when Livy wrote, tradition still preserved the memory of a time when the noblest citizens could dispense with the aid of hired laborers, and worked with their own hands for their own subsistence. Nor was this mode of life peculiar to the Romans; it was common at the same period throughout Latium, as well as in many other parts of Italy. Most of the little precipitous cliffs, in which terminate so abruptly the low hilly ridges of the now desolate Campagna, were once surmounted each by its citadel, rising out of a collection of houses inhabited by the petty freeholders of the adjoining canton. When these townlets were subdued, after a succession of bloody contests, the remaining inhabitants of some were compelled to take up their residence in Rome, and Roman colonies were placed

---

[17] *Quatuor jugerum agrum*. A juger contained 28,800 square feet.

in others, but in no case were the conquered people allowed to retain the whole of their former territory. Part was invariably confiscated, nominally for the benefit of the Roman government, but often in reality for the exclusive benefit of the patricians, who frequently divided the so called public domains amongst themselves, and became, in consequence, immensely rich. But although the aristocracy were thus exalted, the bulk of the nation, the Roman commons, consisting of the descendants of the several conquered nations, retained for some time longer their ancient social position, the subsistence of a family being commonly derived from the portion of land which it possessed in full property. That, in the early ages of the Republic, some freehold property was considered essential to personal independence, may be inferred from the fact, that when, soon after the sack of Rome by the Gauls, four new tribes were created, a grant of seven jugers (between four and five acres) was made to every family; and it also seems probable that the size of these grants was determined by the average size of the plebeian freeholds previously existing. The great mass of the Roman commons may be presumed to have been proprietors, possessing on an average nearly five acres each. In many other parts of Italy, landed property was not less divided than in Latium. In Samnium, Sabinum, and generally in the highlands of the Apennines and Alps, the peasantry were undoubtedly freeholders; and even in Etruria, where the native Pelasgi had been reduced to vassalage by foreign conquerors, they retained at least the same proprietary rights as the serfs of modern Europe. Held either by a free or by a servile tenure, the lands cultivated by the native peasantry throughout the peninsula, seem to have belonged to themselves. It must be added, that the Roman law of inheritance resembled that of Moses, so far as to require the property of a man dying intestate to be equally divided among all his children, Such having been the distribution of land in ancient Italy, and such the facilities for its further partition, what consequences ensued? Did the land become continually more and more subdivided, and did the proprietors, daily growing more numerous, sink daily deeper and deeper into indigence and misery? On the contrary, the lordly usurpers of the public domain rapidly displaced their humble neighbors, and annexed fields and gardens to their own overgrown estates. This is, indeed, the danger really to be apprehended in all similar circumstances. Comparatively little care is required to prevent the division of peasant properties; of that there need be no fear, provided they be in the first instance of a suitable size, and provided, also, that their owners enjoy the protection of equitable law. The true difficulty is to save them from the grasp of the rich and powerful, who have everywhere too many expedients for seizing upon the possessions of small landowners. Open violence and legal fraud, or, where neither of these can be resorted to, the temptation of a high price, are influences which peasants are frequently unable to resist; and thus it is that so many tracts, once divided among several, have been brought under the sway of a single master. One hundred and forty years before the birth of Christ, as Tiberius Gracchus returned from a campaign in Spain, he found remaining in Italy neither peasant properties nor even a native peasantry; both had utterly disappeared. The scene which presented itself to him was that of a country whose only cultivators were foreign slaves. Landed property was engrossed by a small number of rich men, and the laborers employed upon it were captives, taken in war, who were shut up at night in dungeons, and who worked by day in gangs under taskmasters, like negroes in the West Indies. The Campagna, which, while tenanted by men working for themselves, those "most intelligent, most industrious, and most successful" of all improvers, had resembled Flanders in fertility and garden-like cultivation, with much more variety and picturesqueness, had been left to slaves working listlessly for rich and careless absentees, and had already begun to wear its present wild and desert aspect. Houses had been thrown down and fruit-trees rooted up; the decay of agriculture had been followed by the generation of malaria, which rendered the climate unfit for human residence; tillage was ultimately superseded entirely by pasturage, and cattle browsed on the site of many a happy homestead, and many a little town renowned in story.

Meanwhile, what became of the former inhabitants, the displaced cultivators? After their removal had cleared the ground for the operations of men of greater capital, enterprise, and skill, did they betake themselves to some new business, in which their industry, becoming more productive, proved more beneficial to the rest of the community, as well as more profitable to themselves? Did they, after their dismissal from agriculture, obtain more liberal earnings in handicraft or trade? Truly, a very different fate awaited them. When, together with their portions of land, they lost also their habitual source of livelihood, they did indeed betake themselves to Rome in search of other means of subsistence, but, finding none, they presently became dependent on charity. Thenceforward the metropolis was infested by a crowd of beggars, whom the State was compelled, for its own security, to maintain. Ten years after the death of the elder Gracchus, his brother Caius caused a law to be passed, ordaining a monthly distribution of corn among the populace, and ever afterwards, until the final destruction of the empire, the expense of providing the poor of the capital with amusement as well as food, *panem et circenses*, continued to be one of the most serious drains on the treasury. A "pauper-warren," on a scale of unexampled magnitude, was formed; but its situation was in the city, not in the country, and its foundations were laid simultaneously with the consolidation, not with the subdivision, of landed property. The progress of pauperism, not less than the decline of agriculture, might have prompted Pliny's celebrated exclamation, "*Latifundia perdidere Italiam*" — "Overgrown estates have been the ruin of Italy."

Compare the condition of this idle, dissolute, turbulent mob, with that of the Roman commons while they were still landed proprietors. It cannot be denied that even then their situation was sufficiently precarious, that they were liable to sudden reverses of fortune, and were frequently plunged into deep distress. It is equally certain, however, that their misfortunes had no connection with the size of their farms, but arose from very different and very peculiar causes. In the incessant warfare carried on with the neighboring states, their lands, lying nearer the frontier than those of the patricians, were peculiarly exposed to the ravages of an invader; and when their crops were destroyed, or their cattle carried off, they were compelled to borrow money of the patricians, whose most valuable estates were nearer the city, and who had besides some sources of revenue independent of the land. Or they might be reduced to the same necessity by the enormous taxation required to meet the expenses of war, which fell with more than ordinary weight on the lower classes; and, if any one after borrowing were unable to satisfy his creditor at the appointed time, his debt was speedily raised by the accumulation of interest to an amount which he could never hope to pay. The atrocious law with respect to bankrupts then left him no choice, but either to surrender his patrimony, or himself to become his creditor's slave. Many submitted to the latter alternative; but this very circumstance seems to show that, notwithstanding the severe calamities which occasionally overwhelmed them, the ordinary condition of the commons was sufficiently comfortable. It has been much debated by some of the most eminent political economists whether the employment of slave or of hired labor be the more advantageous; and the question has received very different answers, as indeed was no more than natural, for the truth itself is very different in different situations. The maintenance of a slave (provided his master understand his own interest) may be expected always to cost the same sum — just so much as will keep him in the most perfect state of health and strength, and neither more or less. But the wages of free labor vary with the supply, being sometimes a great deal more and sometimes considerably less than the expenses of a slave's subsistence; and in the former case only can slave labor deserve a preference. In thinly peopled countries, such as America for example, in which wages are very high, the temptation to employ slaves may be too strong for human virtue;[18]

---

[18] [Thornton failed to update this information in the 1874 edition; chattel slavery was abolished in the United States December 6, 1865 with the adoption of the 13th Amendment to the Con-

while in a densely peopled territory like England, (to say nothing of Ireland), no man would take a slave as a gift, for he could procure the more efficient service of a freeman at a much lower price. Now the wealthy Romans began very early to employ their enslaved debtors in rural labor, for numbers of such bondsmen, working on their creditors' lands, were released by the mutinous soldiers on their march from Campania towards Rome, in the famous sedition of the year 340 B.C.[19] There could have been no motive for this employment of insolvent debtors if free peasants could have been persuaded to undertake the same work on moderate terms; but the latter, no doubt, demanded higher wages than it suited the masters to give. Their little farms furnished them with full occupation, and remunerated them so liberally that they were little inclined to accept employment elsewhere. Possibly, it may be thought that these proofs of their prosperity in ordinary times, when neither impoverished by war nor ground down by taxation, might have been dispensed with; and a less elaborate argument might no doubt have sufficed to render it probable, that a man cultivating his own portion of five acres, would derive from it a much larger income than a large farmer could allow to a hired servant.

A very brief reference to Greece will suffice to show that her small proprietors of the heroic and republican periods never multiplied into a swarm of paupers. Polybius remarked that, in his time, although one of concord and comparative prosperity, afflicted neither by wars nor by epidemic diseases, population was fast diminishing, so that houses were left empty, and cities resembled abandoned hives. Strabo, who visited Greece about a century after its incorporation with the Roman Empire, was surprised by nothing so much as the scarcity of inhabitants.

---

stitution. Cf. David Christy's argument in *Cotton is King* (1855), which helped convince the American South that slavery was essential to the economic survival of the United States and the British Empire.]

[19] [The "Latin War" of 340-338 B.C.]

Messenia was for the most part deserted; Laconia contained but thirty of the hundred small towns for which it had once been celebrated; Arcadia, Ætolia, and Acarnania were solitudes. Of the towns of Doris and of the Ænianes scarcely a trace was left. Of all save three of the Bœotian cities nothing remained but ruins and names. In the reign of Trajan, according to Plutarch, the whole of Greece could not furnish more than three thousand heavy armed men the number raised by Megara alone for the Persian war.[20] Bishop Thirlwall, adopting in part the opinion of Polybius, attributes this remarkable depopulation to universal luxury and depravity of morals; but these are plagues whose contagion seldom extends beyond the wealthy classes and the inhabitants of cities. A better explanation is afforded by what Strabo says of the accumulation of property in few hands. The whole island of Cephalonia formed but a single estate, and, in continental Greece, scarcely any land was in tillage, almost the whole being occupied by vast sheepwalks, or by pastures for cattle and horses. Desolation had evidently run the same course in Greece as in Italy. Many small farms had been united to form a few enormous estates. The new landlords had expelled the remains of the ancient peasantry, and having cleared their domains of men, had supplied their places with herds of beasts. Certain modern improvers may perhaps be glad to learn that their own clearances can be justified by such illustrious precedents.

Descending from remote antiquity to times comparatively recent, we may collect from the records of our own country evidence similar to that which has been already produced. England was never, strictly speaking, a country of peasant proprietors, but always possessed among her inhabitants a considerable class of extensive landowners. Interspersed with large estates, there were, however, throughout the middle ages, a far greater number of cottage farms held on various conditions. Some were the freeholds of their cultivators; others, though scarcely less the property of the tenants, were held by servile tenure;

---

[20] Thirlwall's *Hist, of Greece*, vol. viii. pp. 460-7.

some again were leasehold, and some held at will by laborers who had obtained them in payment of their services, and in lieu of wages. So general was the tenancy of land by the English peasantry previously to the accession of the first Tudor monarch, that the converse of Goldsmith's well-known distich[21] might then have been not inapplicable. Although every rood of ground did not maintain its man, there were few rustics who were not either owners or tenants, not merely of a rood, but of several acres. Of the adequacy of these possessions to supply their occupants with abundance of the necessaries of life, we have the most satisfactory proof, and for the hundred and fifty years ending with the fifteenth century, the chain of testimony is particularly complete. Fortescue, Lord Chief Justice to Henry VI, dilates with contagious exultation on the plenty enjoyed by the lowest class of his countrymen. "They drink no water," he says, "unless it be so that some for devotion, and upon a zeal of penance, do abstain from other drink; they eat plentifully of all kinds of flesh and fish. They wear fine woolen cloth in all their apparel; they have also abundance of bed coverings in their houses, and of all other woolen stuff. They have great store of all hustlements[22] and implements of household. They are plentifully furnished with all instruments of husbandry, and all other things that are requisite to the accomplishment of a quiet and wealthy life, according to their estates and degrees."[23] Fortescue was an avowed panegyrist, and his statements might require considerable abatement if they stood alone, but their perfect accuracy is placed beyond dispute by those most unimaginative and matter-of-fact of all compilations, the statutes at large. Repeated enactments, passed during the period we are examining, use language quite as strong, and still more precise and circumstantial than that of the patriotic Chief Justice. In addition to laws designed to keep down the wages of agricultural labor, others were directed against the luxury of

---

[21] ["The Deserted Village," 1770.]
[22] [Household goods.]
[23] Fortescue *de laud. Leg. Anglise*, pp. 85-6.

the peasantry. In 1363[24] carters, plowmen, and all other farm servants, were enjoined not to eat or drink "excessively," or to wear any cloth except "blanket and russet wool of twelve pence." Domestic servants were at the same time declared to be entitled to only one meal a day of flesh or fish, and were to content themselves at other meals with "milk, butter, cheese, and other such viands." In 1463[25] servants in husbandry were restricted to clothing of materials not worth more than two shillings a yard, and were forbidden to wear hose of a higher price than fourteen pence a pair, or girdles garnished with silver. The price of their wives' cover-chief or headdress was not to exceed twelve pence. In 1482[26] a these restrictions were loosened, and laborers in husbandry were permitted to wear hose as dear as eighteen pence a pair, while the sum which their wives might legally expend on covering for the head was raised to twenty pence. This legislation, considering the fall which has since taken place in the value of money, was really much as if a law should now be necessary to prevent plowmen from strutting about in velvet coats and silk stockings, with silver buckles in their shoes, and their wives from trimming their caps with Brussels lace. It exhibits agricultural laborers in a condition which was probably never attained by the same class in any other age or country, unless, perhaps, by the emancipated negroes of the British West Indies. Yet the description applies only to the lower order of peasants — to those who worked for hire, and had either no land, or none but what was allowed them in part payment of wages. What, then, must have been the prosperity of the small freeholders and cottage farmers?

It is true that, in the midst of this abundance, the English peasantry of the middle ages ate off wooden platters, never knew the luxury of a cotton shirt or of a cup of tea, and slept on straw pallets within walls of wattled plaster, and that in some counties they used barley instead of

---

[24] 37 Edw. 3, c. 14.
[25] 3 Edw. 4, c. 5.
[26] 22 Edw. 4, c. I.

wheaten bread. But it is absurd to imagine that, because they had to put up with these inconveniences, their situation, in more important respects, was not immeasurably superior to that of their living descendants. Nothing more is to be inferred than that certain modern refinements and conveniences were unknown and uncoveted by them. Many advantages of an advanced civilization, which are now within every one's reach, were once equally unthought of by rich and poor. Our Plantagenet kings, as well as their courtiers, were fain to drink beer at every meal, and to drink it, too, out of wooden bickers; they were as ill-provided with under-linen as the meanest of their subjects; and so little did they regard what are now considered the most indispensable requisites of domestic comfort, that the bedchamber furniture of so magnificent a monarch as Henry the Eighth consisted only of a couple of joint cupboards, a joint stool, two hand irons, a fire fork, a pair of tongs, a fire pan, and a steel mirror covered with yellow velvet.[27] At this day, little, if any, grain besides oats is used in many respectable families in Scotland; and many a continental baron, whose domain stretches for miles around his princely chateau, seldom eats any but rye bread. This is mere matter of taste, and no one would think of mentioning it as a mark of social inferiority; but it would be quite as reasonable to do so as for a modern day-laborer at eight shillings a week to look back with pity on his well-clad, beef-fed ancestors, because some of his own rags are made of cotton, and because the baker, of whom he now and then buys a loaf, sells only wheaten bread.

It is also true that the peasantry of the Anglo-Norman period suffered grievously from feudal oppression, and from private and civil war; and that a bad harvest was

---

[27] *Pict. Hist, of Eng.* , vol. ii. p. 880. The Spaniards who came to England in Queen Mary's time wondered when they saw the large diet used by the inmates of the most homely-looking cottages. "The English," they said, "make their houses of sticks and dirt, but they fare as well as the king." — See Bernan's *Hist. and Art of Warming and Ventilating Rooms, etc.*; a work abounding with curious matter, of which the title gives little promise.

invariably followed by a local famine, which, aided by pestilence, its first-born son, committed ravages unheard of in later times. It is even possible that the evils arising from these sources, although only occasional, may have been as intolerable as the habitual privations of agricultural laborers of the present day; and that the latter living in peace under equitable laws, and possessing, in the extension of commerce, an assurance that their supplies of food will not be utterly cut off, have, on the whole, little cause to regret the change which has taken place in the condition of their class. This, however, is not the question. We are not balancing the advantages of rude and precarious plenty against those of civilized and uniform penury; we have only to satisfy ourselves that this plenty was anciently the portion of the English peasantry, and that the latter, in ordinary times, obtained from their lands the means of amply supplying their homely wants. This is the only point with which we are at present concerned; and surely, if any dependence can be placed on history or national records, it has been established beyond the possibility of dispute.

No argument can be required to prove that English peasant properties, though subject to the custom of gavelkind, escaped the evil of excessive partition; for consolidation, the reverse of subdivision, must have been everywhere adopted before the face of the country could be covered almost entirely, as it actually is, with large estates. To relate how the consolidation was effected, is but to repeat, with slight variations, the story already told of Palestine and Latium. In the latter part of the fifteenth century, pasturage began to be regarded as a more profitable employment of land than tillage, and, in order to afford room for its adoption on a sufficiently extensive scale, many farmhouses and cottages were pulled down, and the fields belonging to several were sown with grass and let to a single tenant. Not only were "tenancies for years, lives, and at-will, whereupon most of the yeomanry lived, turned into demesnes"[28] in this manner, but freeholders

---

[28] Lord Bacon's *Hist of Henry VII.*, Works, vol. v. p. 61.

also were ejected from their lands by force or fraud, or were harassed or cajoled into a sale of them.[29] Simultaneously with this social revolution, a new social malady made its appearance. As long as the connection of the peasantry with the land remained unbroken, England was perfectly free from every symptom of pauperism, and the supply of labor, instead of exceeding the demand, was so deficient as to induce parliament to interfere to keep down its price. But almost immediately after the consolidation of small farms commenced, legislation took a different turn, and parliament, instead of striving to curtail the laborer's honest earnings, had to exercise its ingenuity in providing for a rapidly increasing crowd of destitute, for whom no work could be found. The progress of pasturage and augmentation of farms seem not to have attracted much notice until the year 1487, when an act was passed to restrain them, and, just seven years later, commenced a series of statutes which attest the rapid spread of destitution. For a time, misled by the experience

---

[29] Massinger's Sir Giles Overreach describes very graphically one of the ways in which this might be done:

> "I'll buy some cottage near his manor;
> Which done, I'll make my men break ope his fences,
> Ride o'er his standing corn, and in the night
> Set fire to his barns, or break his cattle's legs.
> These trespasses draw on suits, and suits' expenses,
> Which I can spare, but will soon beggar him.
> When I have harried him thus two or three year,
> Though he sue in form a pauper is, in spite
> Of all his thrift and care he'll grow behindhand.
> [The best I ever heard! I could adore you.*]
> Then, with the favor of my man-of-law,
> I will pretend some title; want will force him
> To put it to arbitrement; then, if he sell
> For half the value, he shall have ready money,
> And I possess his land."

(Philip Massinger, *A New Way to Pay Old Debts*, cir. 1625, Act II, Scene i.) [*Spoken by "Marrall, a Term-Driver, a creature of Sir Giles Overreach," another character in the play. Thornton omitted this line in his quote.]

of the preceding age, parliament imagined idleness to be still the fruitful parent of the evil, and punishment its most effectual cure; no other asylum, therefore, was offered to able-bodied vagrants than the stocks, and no milder treatment than whipping at the cart's tail. After being "admonished" in this way, they were to be sent to the place of their birth, there to set themselves to work "as true men ought to do." Such were the provisions of the law of the year 1494.[30] In 1535, however, it was discovered that the aforesaid "valiant vagabonds," after returning home, could find no work to do, and the parish authorities were in consequence enjoined to collect voluntary contributions for the purpose, not only of relieving the impotent and infirm, but of enabling the strong and lusty to gain a living with their own hands.[31] In 1547, the number of beggars still rapidly increasing, in spite of the "godly acts and statutes" already directed against them, another was passed, which, though repealed two years afterwards, deserves to be mentioned, not merely on account of its astonishing barbarity, but as showing how genuine the distresses of the lower classes must have been which even such atrocious measures could not induce them to conceal. It was enacted, that every able-bodied person found loitering about should be branded with a hot iron, and adjudged to two years' slavery to the man by whom he had been apprehended, during which time he might be fed upon bread and water and refuse meat, and forced to work by beating or otherwise; that, if he ran away, he should be branded a second time, and should be condemned to slavery for life, and that if he absconded again, he should suffer death as a felon.[32] Threatened with slavery, stripes,[33] and death, men chose to run every danger in seeking to better their condition rather than pine with hunger at home, and beggars and vagabonds continued daily to increase. In 1562, voluntary alms being found insufficient for the relief of the poor, the

---

[30] 2 Hen. 7, c. 2.
[31] 27 Hen. 7, c. 25.
[32] I Edw. 6, c. 3.
[33] [Flogging.]

parish authorities were empowered to assess persons obstinately refusing to contribute.[34] Mendicancy and vagabondage continuing still unabated, in 1572[35] power was given to tax all the inhabitants of a place for the relief of its poor. Other acts followed; and, in 1601, the necessity of providing employment for the able-bodied poor by means of parochial assessments was formally admitted, the famous Elizabethan law was passed,[36] and, thanks to the abandonment of the "cottage system" — that first step, as many imagine, in the improvement of agriculture — England was saddled with a permanent poors' rate, which has now become an annual tax of some six or seven millions sterling.[37] We have now seen, that in ancient Palestine, Italy, and Greece, and in England, peasant proprietorship did not conduce to pauperism, but that, on the contrary, as long as it continued in vigor, pauperism was utterly unknown, not making its appearance until small properties began to be united. But we are not dependent upon history for our proofs of the enduring prosperity of peasant proprietors. They still form the bulk of the rural population in many territories, to any one of which we may turn with full assurance of discovering unmistakable signs of rural happiness. The *bonder* of Norway, for instance, have, from time immemorial, been owners of their respective farms, which, moreover, have always been legally liable to division among all the children of a deceased proprietor; yet the division of land has made so little progress in the course of many centuries, that very few estates are under forty acres, and very many are above three hundred acres, independently of an extensive tract of mountain pasture belonging to every farm. Some

---

[34] 5 Eliz. c. 3.

[35] 14 Eliz. c. 5.

[36] 43 Eliz. c. 2.

[37] Most writers on the subject have attributed the growth of pauperism, at the period in question, to the dissolution of monasteries by Henry VIII; but this opinion seems to be refuted by the single fact, that monasteries were not abolished till 1535, many years after the continual increase of vagrancy had become a standing topic of parliamentary lamentation.

idea of the condition of the farmers may be formed from the following particulars respecting the farm servants. These, if unmarried, are lodged in an outhouse adjoining their master's dwelling, which it resembles in appearance, neatness, and comfort; they are allowed four meals a day, consisting of oat or bean-meal, rye bread, potatoes, fresh river and salt fish, cheese, butter, and milk; and once or twice a week they have meat, sometimes fresh, but more frequently in the shape of salt beef or black puddings. At one of their meals they have also beer or a glass of potato spirits. Their money wages, in addition to all this, are about four-pence halfpenny a day. A married laborer lives on the outskirts of the farm in a cottage of his own, generally "a good log house of four rooms with glass windows," which is held on lease for the lives of himself and his wife, together with a piece of land large enough for the keep of two cows or a corresponding number of sheep and goats, and for the sowing of six bushels of corn and three quarters of potatoes. The usual rent of these tenements is from four to six dollars, and is commonly paid for by work on the main farm, each day's work being valued at a fixed rate of three-pence or thereabouts. After the laborer has paid his rent, he is allowed his food as well as the usual money-payment for every additional day's work. It need scarcely be said that a houseman, as a married laborer of this kind is called, is in a very comfortable situation; in fact, he wants few, if any, of the comforts which his master possesses; his house, though smaller, is as well built; his food and dress are of the same materials. The peasant proprietors, like their servants, are satisfied with articles of home growth, and are little desirous of foreign luxuries. They build their own houses, make their own chairs, tables, plows, carts, and harness. Their wives spin their own flax and wool, and weave their own linen and woolen cloth; almost everything they use is the produce of their own farms, except glass, pottery, iron ware, sugar, coffee, spices, and tobacco. The accumulation of so many tasks upon the same person no doubt cause them to be unskillfully performed, and marks, besides, a rather backward stage of civilization. It must not, however, in this instance, be mistaken for a sign of poverty. A Norwegian peasant does not content himself with homemade goods because he has no surplus agricultural produce to exchange for the manufactures of towns; but the nature of the climate confines him within doors for many months of the year, when he is compelled to seek some sedentary employment, if only for a pastime. Whatever were his means, and however cheaply he might buy the articles he requires, he obtains them still more cheaply if he can get them made at home, for they then cost nothing but labor, which if not so employed would be utterly wasted. In such circumstances, division of labor, instead of increasing the productiveness of industry, would condemn industry to spend half her time in idleness, and that instinctive knowledge of political economy, usually termed common sense, accordingly prevents its adoption. But although the mode of life of the Norwegian country people may be somewhat rude, it would be difficult to find a happier race; they enjoy plenty, and are content; they care little for outward show, and are exempt from the painful desire to outvie their neighbors, which makes many wretched in the midst of wealth. Almost the only thing in their condition which is much to be regretted, is the deficiency of mental culture, which prevents their turning their leisure to the best account and heightening their material enjoyments with intellectual pleasures. Would to God that laborers on large estates in other countries had as little to sigh for![38]

---

[38] Laing's *Norway, passim.* I may perhaps be here permitted to transcribe, as not altogether irrelevant, the following passage from an early work of my own, long since forgotten.

"The happiness of the Swiss and Norwegian peasantry dates from a very early period, and seems indeed to have resulted from the physical characters of their respective countries. A glance at the map of Switzerland may suffice to show that, in a territory so curiously intersected by mountains, lakes, and rivers, there can be few, if any, extensive tracts of good land, and that the first settlers must consequently have been both too much dispersed and too poor to allow of their becoming divided into the classes of masters and slaves. In Norway, the peninsula of which that country forms part, is inaccessible by land, except

The Swiss peasantry, although almost universally landed proprietors, may be divided into two classes; those who are principally or exclusively agriculturists, and those who gain a livelihood chiefly by manufacturing industry. The farms of the former, except in the cantons of Berne and Tessin, and a few other districts, seldom seems impossible that serfdom ever existed, exceed forty or fifty acres, but they are as rarely of less size than ten acres, and the poorest farmers, having rights of pasturage on the common lands belonging to every parish, can afford to keep two or three cows. Members of this class are always in the enjoyment of competence, and many of them pos-

---

at the northeastern corner, where the rigor of the climate is endurable only by reindeer and Laplanders. Its Arian colonists must therefore have approached by sea. But a pastoral people could not effect an extensive migration in boats without leaving most of their cattle behind, and, if they had waited till the winter, when the Gulf of Bothnia is frozen over and may be crossed on foot, their cattle would have perished from exposure and want of food. Most probably, therefore, the emigrants were not numerous tribes, ranged in regular subordination under their chiefs, but little bands of adventurers, all poor and nearly equal in rank; and this equality would long remain undisturbed in their new territories. Great part of Norway [sic] is merely a narrow slip between a chain of mountains and the sea, and the whole is traversed laterally, not only by numerous offshoots from the main range, but also by a succession of inlets of the sea which run many miles inland. The soil, too, even of the valleys, is for the most part sandy and poor, so that altogether there was as little room as in Switzerland for the increase of flocks and herds, or for the growth of great differences of wealth between their owners. Moreover, the need of substantial shelter for themselves and for their cattle, which in so cold a climate require to be housed in winter, must very soon have compelled the herdsmen to lay aside their wandering habits and to provide themselves with permanent habitations. The appropriation and partition of the soil must, therefore, have taken place while all the inhabitants were still free and entitled to demand their shares, the bulk of the colonists assuming in consequence, almost simultaneously with their entrance into the country, the status of peasant proprietors." *Over-Population and its Remedy*, 1846, pp. 142-3.

sess considerable wealth. Besides these, however, there is a more numerous body of smaller proprietors, whose territorial possessions consist only of a field or two, altogether not larger than an ordinary garden, and much too small for the maintenance of the family to which they belong. Here there may seem to be an instance of excessive subdivision. But the owners of these patches of land are almost invariably manufacturers rather than husbandmen; they constitute, indeed, the bulk of the manufacturing population of a country which has but two superiors in manufacturing importance. Most of the cotton and silk goods of Switzerland are produced in the rural districts of Zürich, Basle, St. Gall, Appenzel, and Argovia; and, even of those famous Swiss watches, so much admired for their delicacy and beauty, as many come from *châlets* among the mountains of Neufchatel as from the workshops of Geneva. In England, the makers of these articles would have been pent up in towns, and compelled to pass their days in close dismal factories; but in Switzerland, a happy combination of circumstances permits them to practice their business without forfeiting the use of fresh air or other advantages of a country life. Still although retaining the name, and all the privileges of peasants, they gain their living principally as manufacturers; land is valued by them as affording a means, not so much of employment as of amusement, and they require no more of it than will suffice to occupy their leisure. This affords a clue to the true explanation of the minute partition which has taken place. The ancestors of the rural manufacturers were, no doubt, originally agricultural peasants, possessing farms of suitable size; but the climate, which confined them much within doors, led them to choose some manufacturing occupation for the winter months, which, proving equally [as] or more profitable than husbandry, was eventually adopted by many as their chief pursuit. On the death of a peasant artisan, his children would very probably divide their patrimony, and each might build a separate cottage; but they would do so, not with the intention of subsisting on the produce of their respective portions, but because, independently of that produce, they possessed other means of subsistence. In the outskirts of one or two English towns, patches of garden ground are rented by a few operatives, who are not the less operatives because they amuse themselves with gardening and grow their own vegetables; neither is the smallness of their allotments regarded as a mark of inferiority in their social position. The difference between such operatives and those of Switzerland is, that the latter, besides possessing more land, and besides being owners instead of mere renters, are not confined to towns, but are spread over the whole country, and have their fields and gardens immediately adjoining their dwellings. They are manufacturers, deriving from land a small addition to the earnings of their principal occupation, and it would be strange if the accession of income so obtained were otherwise than beneficial to them. In reality, it is not merely beneficial, it may be acknowledged to be often indispensable to supply the deficiency of their other sources of revenue. Situated as they are in the center of Europe, and paying an enhanced price for the raw materials of their fabrics, they are placed at a great disadvantage with respect to manufacturers of other countries, with whom they are enabled to compete only by accepting lower wages. Their wages, indeed, would scarcely suffice for their subsistence. As their plots of land are too small to afford them a livelihood without the aid of their manufacturing earnings, so would their wages be insufficient for their maintenance without the addition of the garden produce, while both united secure to them the enjoyment of ample comfort. To this every one who has inquired into the subject bears testimony. "It is impossible," says Dr. Bowring, "to mistake the value of a policy whose results are to be traced in general content, in general prosperity. I am acquainted with no country in which prosperity has descended so low, and spread so widely, as among the laborious classes of the Swiss manufacturing districts. I was surprised to find what large proportions of them had by their savings acquired landed property; how many of them dwelt in houses and cultivated fields and gardens which their industry had made their own. In the mountains of the Jura and Appenzel, along the borders of the lakes of Zürich and Constance, everywhere, indeed, where the operatives are settled, I found in their habitations a mass of enjoyments, such as are possessed by few of similar station in other countries."[39] A weaver in Argovia, says Mr. Symons, "is almost universally the proprietor, or the son of a proprietor of land, and few householders are there in the whole canton who do not keep a pig, and generally a few sheep. Their cottages are strewed over the hills and dales, and exhibit in the interior every degree of comfort and ease. The meals of the semi-agricultural, semi manufacturing population of Zürich are as good as they themselves desire, and their clean and comfortable houses bespeak their easy circumstances. The cottages of St. Gall and Appenzel are scattered separately over the vales and hills, each standing in the midst of its little estate, with the goats or sheep, with their melodious bells around their necks, grazing on the land, which is generally pasture. The interiors of the cottages, which are built of wood, are cleanly beyond description, and are well furnished with every article of cottage comfort Appenzel is in fact the Arcadia of Switzerland, and it would be hopeless to expect any person who had not witnessed the circumstances of the peasantry, and the aspect of their abodes, to appreciate from mere description the exceeding beauty, social and scenic, which it exhibits. In the Orisons, wages are, as far as mere money goes, extremely low, and if taken as a standard of condition, would indicate a degree of poverty beneath the Irish peasant, whilst the real condition of the population is decidedly preferable to that of English farm laborers."[40] Mr. Symons sums up by expressing his conviction, "that it would require thirty shillings per week in England to place a man with a wife and three children on a footing with the average of Swiss peasants, having the same family." Mr. Macculloch objects to this as "a very exaggerated statement," but Mr. Symons appears to have anticipated the objection, for, after specifying the various articles which an Englishman might be expected to purchase with thirty shillings a week, he adds, "I fearlessly

---

[39] Bowring's *Report on the Commerce and Manufactures of Switzerland*, pp. 3-6.
[40] *Report on Swiss Handloom Weavers, passim.*

assert that this amount of comforts and necessaries, *mutatis mutandis*, is enjoyed by the bulk of Swiss artisan families, in the German cantons of Switzerland. This is an assertion which cannot be set aside by mere *ipse dixit*. They who desire to do so, can alone ascertain its validity by personally visiting the homes of the Swiss peasants, at different hours, and in various cantons. I am not afraid to submit this statement to any one who has thus qualified himself to pronounce an opinion on the subject."[41] The language of Mr. Laing, though not quite so circumstantial, is equally strong. "The peculiar feature," he says, "in the condition of the Swiss population — the great charm of Switzerland, next to its natural scenery — is the air of well-being, the neatness, the sense of property imprinted on the people, their dwellings, and their plots of land. The spirit of the proprietor is not to be mistaken in all that one sees."[42] Switzerland, however, notwithstanding the general happiness of her people, is not absolutely free from pauperism — a disease which would almost seem to be inherent in the constitution of manufacturing communities. But even the pauperism of Switzerland furnishes additional proof of the excellence of peasant proprietorship, for paupers are most rare where landed property is most divided, and are found in the greatest number in those districts which contain the largest estates. In the whole of the Engadine, the land belongs to the peasantry, and "in no country in Europe," says Mr. Inglis, "will be found so few poor as in the Engadine."[43] In the Valais, the land belongs to a few great proprietors, and, according to

---

[41] *Ibid.* p. 110.

[42] *Notes of a Traveler*, p. 354. [The note in the 1848 edition continues] Mr. Macculloch is able to oppose one fact to the mass of evidence in favor of the happiness of the Swiss Peasantry. "Le Suisse," says he, after Sir Francis d'Ivernois, "est aujourd' hui, après l'Irelandais, le people qui consommé le plus de pommes de terre." The argument involved in this statement may be arranged syllogistically thus —

The Irishman eats potatoes, and the Irishman is poor;

But the Swiss also eats potatoes;

Therefore the Swiss also is poor.

[43] Inglis's *Switzerland*, vol. i. pp. 109, 110.

Mr. Bakewell, the peasantry are among the poorest in Switzerland.[44] Inglis, however, assigns the "bad pre-eminence" to the canton of Berne, in which he says the greatest landowners reside, and which, *for this reason,* contains the greatest number of poor."[45]

The relative tendencies of large and small proprietorship to promote pauperism cannot, however, be better exemplified than by a comparison of Upper with Lower Tyrol. In the former province the inhabitants cultivate their own lands, but their properties are in general very small, not enabling them to keep more livestock than a cow and a pig or two. Inglis indeed carelessly observes, that the land of an Upper Tyrolean peasant seldom produces more than enough for the consumption of his family, and that the owner, "though in one sense independent, treading and laboring his own soil, and eating the produce of his own industry, is yet poor, and lives worse than a day-laborer in many other countries."[46] These, however, are evidently hasty conclusions, founded upon superficial observation or upon hearsay, and are directly contradicted by information subsequently obtained. Inglis, one day, took refuge from a storm in the house of a peasant of the class just referred to, and was invited to wait for dinner, which was almost ready. His host's estate consisted of no more than four acres, and he possessed only one cow, two pigs, and some poultry, yet the meal prepared for his family of six persons consisted of soup made of Indian corn and milk, a piece of boiled bacon five pounds in weight, a salad, bread two-thirds Indian corn and one-third wheat, butter, and wine of Botzen. This is expressly stated to have been the regular dinner of the house, except once a week, when fresh meat was substituted for the bacon.[47] Besides the crops raised for home consumption, a good deal of wheat and barley was sent to market; and from the proceeds, after coffee, sugar, and clothes were bought,

---

[44] *Travels in the Tarentaise, Switzerland, etc.*, vol. ii. p. 227.
[45] Inglis's *Switzerland*, voi. i. p. 223.
[46] Inglis's *Tyrol*, vol. i. p. 177.
[47] *Ibid.*, vol. li. pp. 3-7.

there remained a small surplus in money, which had gradually amounted to a considerable purse. Perhaps this may be too flattering an example[48] of the mode of life of the Northern Tyrolese, and the food of the majority may consist only of bread, Indian corn, and milk. Still it is certain that their diet, though simple, is both plentiful and nourishing, for a finer, more athletic race, does not exist. This shows very convincingly that they are amply supplied with mere necessaries; but it must be admitted at the same time, that they have not the same command over the conveniences and luxuries of life as their Swiss neighbors. We need not stay to inquire the causes of this comparative poverty, whether it proceed from Austrian misgovernment or from a want of the mountain pastures, which, in Switzerland, enable cattle to be kept at a trifling expense. We need only ascertain that it has no connection with peasant proprietorship, and in order to be satisfied on that point we have only to cross the line which separates Upper or German from Lower or Italian Tyrol. "The moment we leave Botzen and travel towards Trent, a new order of things is perceptible; the same noble-looking peasantry are no longer to be seen; poverty begins to show itself, and the air of comfort about the dwellings, and independence about the inmates, are no longer visible. All the land in Southern Tyrol belongs to great proprietors, and the peasantry have no longer an interest in the soil. It seems to the traveler, at first sight, a strange inversion of what might be expected — that in the fertile vales and finest plains in Europe, he should see so much poverty, and that on the contrary, when he journeys among mountain regions, where excessive labor forces from the soil an unwilling crop, he perceives every appearance of comfort and ease. The condition of the people in the most fertile plains of Italy, Germany, France, or England, will bear no comparison with that of the inhabitants of the Grison valleys, or of the Oberland Bernois, or of the Upper Tyrol. But the difficulty is at once explained

---

[48] I have since become enabled, by personal observation, to say that it is not at all so, and that the peasantry of Upper Tyrol live quite as well as Inglis represents them as doing.

when we learn that the former are laborers for hire, and that the latter labor their own soil."[49]

Many similar examples might be produced, but not to exhaust the reader's patience, I will, before concluding this chapter, only refer to the history and present state of the Channel Islands, respecting which I am the more desirous of mentioning a few particulars, both because they bear in a very remarkable manner on the subject under consideration, and because a recent[50] visit to the islands has enabled me to test the accuracy of some of the statements of preceding writers. Both Guernsey and Jersey, like the rest of the Duchy of Normandy, with which they were incorporated, were once subject to feudal government. The former island was distributed by William the Conqueror amongst sixteen tenants in chief, who were not only entitled to military service from their vassals or serfs, but had their tables supplied and their lands cultivated by them, and moreover, exercised over them, "la haute justice,"[51] or the right of hanging on occasion. The steps by which this order of things was subverted cannot now be traced, but it is clear that the feudal system must have been deeply undermined before the charter of King John could substitute jurats,[52] to be chosen by the people at large, for the supreme court of chevaliers who had previously exercised hereditary jurisdiction; and it further appears, from a petition presented to the Protector Cromwell,[53] that in the seventeenth century, land in Guernsey

---

[49] Inglis's *Tyrol*, vol. ii. pp. 100-4.

[50] "Recent," that is, in 1848, the date of the 1st edition of this work.

[51] ["High Justice"]

[52] [A sworn holder of certain offices, from the clause at the foot of an affidavit stating when, where, and before whom the actual oath was sworn or affidavit was made.]

[53] [Oliver Cromwell (1599-1658), English military and political leader who overthrew the monarchy and established himself as dictator of England, Scotland, Wales and Ireland under the title "Lord Protector of the Commonwealth," a short-lived totalitarian republic that lasted from 1649 to 1660. The brutality of Cromwell's conquest of Ireland has entered legend.]

Guernsey was held by the cultivators on no other condition than that of paying "chief rents, homages, services, tithes, and campart," the amount of which, though sufficiently burdensome, was, and apparently had long been, fixed and invariable. Some of these feudal dues are still exacted, though, in consequence of the fall in the value of money, and of the improvement of agriculture, they constitute at present a very inconsiderable deduction from the annual produce; but, except in so far as their right to the title; may be affected by this circumstance, the tillers are likewise in general owners of the soil, and have been so for at least two hundred years. The law of inheritance requires land to be divided among all the children of the last owner, daughters as well as sons; though it treats the latter in general more liberally than the former, and permits the eldest son, besides sharing equally with his brothers, to, take in addition his father's principal dwelling-house, and about sixteen perches of ground adjoining it. So insignificant a concession to primogeniture cannot have sensibly impeded the partition of land, for which, moreover, if any tendency to it really existed, ample time has been allowed in the course of two centuries. Is then land in Guernsey actually too minutely subdivided? and is the agricultural population redundant, and consequently poor?

When political economists speak of estates or farms as too small, they mean, either that the gross produce is less than it would otherwise be, or at least, that a smaller portion is set apart for the use of the non-agricultural classes. When they say that an agricultural class is too numerous, they mean, either that it consumes food which should be reserved for other classes, or that its own wants are inadequately supplied. We have already seen that in Guernsey neither the partition of land nor the number of cultivators is such as to produce any injurious effect on the rest of the community, for not even in England is nearly so large a quantity of produce sent to market from a tract of such limited extent. This of itself might prove that the cultivators must be far removed above poverty, for, being absolute owners of all the produce raised by them, they of course sell only what they do not themselves require. But the satisfactoriness of their condition is apparent to every observer. "The happiest community," says Mr. Hill,[54] "which it has ever been my lot to fall in with is to be found in this little island of Guernsey." "No matter," says Sir George Head,[55] "to what point the traveler may choose to bend his way, comfort everywhere prevails."[56] What most surprises the English visitor in his first walk or drive beyond the bounds of St. Peter's Port is the appearance of the habitations with which the landscape is thickly studded. Many of them are such as in his own country would belong to persons of middle rank; but he is puzzled to guess what sort of people live in the others, which, though in general not large enough for farmers, are almost invariably much too good in every respect for day laborers. The walls are often completely hidden by rose-trees, geraniums, and myrtles, which reach up to the ledge of the roof, and form an arch over the door. Every window is crowded with pots of choice flowers, which are sometimes to be found also in the little front garden, though the latter is more commonly given up to useful than to ornamental plants. Such attention to elegance about a dwelling has always been held to signify that the inmates are not absorbed by the cares of life, but have leisure and taste for its enjoyments. But beauty is not the only nor the chief recommendation of the Guernsey cottages. They are always substantially built of stone, and being generally of two stories, contain plenty of accommodation. The interior is not unworthy of the exterior. In every room, pulley windows with large squares of glass, take the place of leaded casements with diamond-shaped panes; equal attention is paid to comfort and to neatness in the fitting up; there is abundance of all needful furniture, of crockery and kitchen utensils, and flitches of bacon, those best ornaments of a poor man's chimney, are scarcely ever wanting. This picture is not drawn from one

---

[54] *Tait's Magazine* for June, 1834.
[55] [Sir George Head (1782-1855), English commissariat officer and Deputy Knight Marshal.]
[56] *Home Tour through various Parts of the United Kingdom.*

or two select models, but is a fair representation of the generality of the dwellings of the peasantry. Literally, in the whole island, with the exception of a few fishermen's huts, there is not one so mean as to be likened to the ordinary habitation of an English farm-laborer. This assertion will startle many who, using their prejudices instead of their eyes, still believe in the reality of what has long ceased to exist, except in tradition or fancy. The poets and romance writers who so highly extol the comfort and beauty of English cottages, are pseudo-enthusiasts, parading only simulated raptures. They themselves never beheld what they describe. Their descriptions are not indeed purely imaginative, for they are copies of pictures of old date, which, when first painted, were very possibly true to nature. The original artists lived while cottagers had a permanent interest in their tenements, and means, as well as taste and leisure, for adorning them. All this has long been changed. When the cottagers were deprived of their gardens, their rights of common, and their cows, they were considerately removed from their picturesque homes to others more suitable to their altered circumstances. Hear what is said of a modern day laborer's habitation, by one who will not be suspected of depreciating anything English. "There is his tenement of one or two rooms, his naked walls, bare brick, stone, or mud floor, a few wooden or rush-bottomed chairs, a deal or old oak table, a simple fireplace with its oven beside it, a few pots and pans — there you have his whole abode, goods, and chattels." And this is a sketch from "cottage life in its best estate, in its unsophisticated and unpauperized condition."[57] Yet still, in spite of the evidence of our senses, we cling to the memory of the past, as if it were a faithful representation of the present. Admiration of the dwellings of our peasantry is part of our national creed; we force ourselves to admire what we are told is admirable, and readily acquiesce in the assurance that our plowmen and cowherds are very commodiously lodged. Strangers are not always so complaisant. "Look," says a late Bailiff of

---

[57] Howitt's *Rural Life of England*, vol. ii. pp. 128-9.

Guernsey, Mr. de l'Isle Brock, "at the *hovels* of the English, and compare them with the cottages of our peasantry," and, in truth, his contempt, however strange and impertinent it may sound in English ears, would be completely justified by the comparison. It is to the Channel Islands or to Switzerland that we must look if we would see realized those pleasing poetical descriptions, the materials for which were once to be found in our own country.

The people of Guernsey are as well clad as lodged. The working dress of the men, who wear a short blue frock over their other clothes, is not indeed very becoming, but it is never ragged; and on Sundays they don a suit of broadcloth, while their wives and daughters, of course, make an at least equal display of the outward symbols of respectability.

What makes the evident affluence of these islanders a still more gratifying spectacle is its almost universal diffusion. Beggars are utterly unknown, and their absence cannot be wholly accounted for by the interdict enacted against them; for in England, where their profession is equally illegal, not a day passes without your meeting several, whereas in the Channel Islands not one is ever seen. Pauperism, able-bodied pauperism at least, is nearly as rare as mendicancy. There are two so-called "hospitals" in Guernsey, one for the town and the other for the country parishes, which, in addition to the purpose indicated by their names, serve also as poor-houses and houses of industry; yet the inmates of all descriptions in the Town Hospital, at the time of my visit, were only eighty men, one hundred and thirty women, fifty-five boys, and thirty-nine girls, and I was assured that every one of the adults was incapacitated from earning a livelihood by some mental or bodily defect, or by bad character. No one, fit for employment, had been compelled to take refuge there by inability to procure work. The same remark applies to the Country Hospital, in which I found eighteen men able to work, but who were either habitual drunkards or otherwise of such bad character that no one would employ them. The average number of inmates, of both sexes and of all ages and classes, is one hundred and forty-six. The Savings Banks' Accounts also bear witness to the general abundance enjoyed by the laboring classes of Guernsey. In the year 1841, there were in England, out of a population of nearly 15,000,000, less than 700,000 depositors, or one in every 20 persons, and the average amount of the deposits was £30. In Guernsey, in the same year, out of a population of 26,000, the number of depositors was 1,920, and the average amount of the deposits £40. Being exempt from poverty themselves, the Channel Islanders are foremost in their contributions to the relief of misery in less favored lands. In the year 1822, the inhabitants of St. Peter's Port raised by subscription about £700 for the relief of their famishing brethren in the west of Ireland, and in 1831, £600 were raised for the same purpose in Guernsey and Alderney; upon which occasion an Irish newspaper, while gratefully acknowledging the contributions received from England, "felt bound especially to notice the *transcendent* liberality of Guernsey." That island had, in proportion to its extent, done more on behalf of the famishing poor of Mayo than any other place from which relief had been furnished.[58]

It is especially deserving of notice, that the prosperity of Guernsey is not only great, but has long been steadily advancing; in other words, that the progress of population has been less rapid than the progress of wealth. In the year 1615, the number of houses in the island was 1,355, in the year 1821, it was 3,032, from which it may be inferred that the number of inhabitants had doubled in about 180 years. In 1797 the total population was 15,500, and in 1836 had risen to 24,500. But, in the petition presented to Cromwell soon after the close of the Civil War,[59] it is stated that only one-twentieth of the inhabitants had any substance; that only two or three persons had £200 a year, not ten £100, and not thirty £50 a year;[60] whereas, in 1797, the annual income of the island was assessed for

---

[58] Duncan's *History of Guernsey*, p. 304.
[59] [The English Civil War, 1642-1651.]
[60] *Ibid.*, p. 100.

the purpose of taxation at £97,691, or £6, 6s per head; and in the year 1836 at £212,440, or £8, 13s per head. Thus, in thirty-nine years population had increased fifty-eight percent, while wealth had increased one hundred and seventeen percent. It should be added, that the largest augmentation of property had taken place in the country parishes, while two-thirds of the increased number of inhabitants belonged to the town; and it moreover seems probable that the increase of population, both in town and country, was produced principally by immigration, for, at the census of 1841, the number of inhabitants, not natives, was not less than 6,517, equal to the whole addition made to the population since the year 1818, when settlers from Great Britain first began to resort to the Channel Islands. If no other example could be given, this alone might be accepted as a decisive proof that peasant proprietorship has no tendency to create a redundant and poor agrarian population, but is rather calculated to make each succeeding generation wealthier than that which immediately preceded it.

The general resemblance between Jersey and Guernsey renders it unnecessary to enter into much detail respecting the former. Land there has not been so much divided as in the sister island, owing to the influence of a law of inheritance, which might be advantageously adopted in the latter, and which permits the eldest son to take the principal dwelling-house and thirty perches of ground adjoining, besides sharing equally with his brothers in the rest of the property, and, moreover, allots to him the whole of the estate if it do not exceed four *vergées*. As the estates of the peasantry are larger than in Guernsey, so also are their dwellings — a much greater proportion of which are of sufficient size to deserve to be styled farmhouses. Some of them, indeed, have so much architectural pretension that they might almost be mistaken for the residences of independent gentlemen, if the fields of corn, parsnips, or cabbages, lying close under the parlor windows, did not show that they really belong to farmers. On the other hand, the mere cottages are very inferior in outward appearance to those of Guernsey, being commonly built of rough stone, and sometimes apparently without cement. Their inferiority, however, is probably only external, for, though I did not myself enter any of them, the well-dressed people whom I saw leaving them on Sunday were evidently not prevented by want of means from making themselves comfortable. The antiquity of the cottages may probably afford an explanation of their uninviting appearance, for most of them seem to have been built one or two centuries ago, when every peasant was perhaps his own mason, and not very deeply skilled in the art. All recent buildings, and all new additions to old ones, are in a very much better style. Mendicancy and pauperism are at present as rare as in Guernsey, and the improvement which time has wrought in the condition of the people is still more remarkable. Dr. Heylin,[61] who accompanied the Earl of Danby[62] to the Channel Islands in the year 1629, and who says, that in Guernsey he "did not see one beggar," describes the Jersey men as "more poor, and therefore more destitute of humanity," and their children as "continually craving alms of every stranger," whereas, at present, some tact would be requisite to prevent any of them from being affronted by an offer of money. Jersey seems to have been very thickly peopled at a pretty early period. Heylin, in the middle of the seventeenth century, speaks already of the "multitudes of people," whom he estimates, though very extravagantly, at 30,000; but there are good grounds for supposing that, in 1734, their number was as high as 20,000. During the next seventy years, population made little progress, for at the census taken in 1806, it was found to be only 22,855, but it has since advanced rapidly, having reached to 36,582 in 1831, and to 47,544 in 1841. As in Guernsey, however, by far the greater part of the additional number of inhabitants reside in the town.

---

[61] [Peter Heylin, also "Heylyn" (1599-1662), English ecclesiastic and author.]

[62] [Henry Danvers, First Earl of Danby (1573-1644), English soldier, courtier and politician active in James I Stuart's plantation of Ireland, Lord President of Munster from 1607-1615.]

From the map prefixed to Falle's *History*,[63] it appears that, in the year 1734, there were 354 houses in the parish of St. Helier's, and 2,594 in the eleven country parishes. In 1831, St. Helier's contained 1,917 houses, or one for every 8.5 inhabitants, and the country parishes contained 3,073 houses, or one for every 6.7 inhabitants; so that in the interval between 1734 and 1831, the population of the town would appear to have been more than quintupled, while that of the country had increased only 17 percent.

Notwithstanding the great and increasing prosperity of Jersey, there are some, even among the inhabitants, sufficiently modest to prefer the ingenious fancies of theorists to the realities of their own observation, who imagine they can see in the division of land the symptoms of approaching pauperism. Thus Colonel Le Couteur[64] declares that "the too minute subdivision which takes place, frequently drives several branches of a family to beggary; and the elder branch, by being deprived of too considerable a portion of the land, instead of being able to carry on improvements, purchase manure, or work the land properly, can scarcely extract a miserable subsistence from his estate."[65] Colonel Le Couteur's authority is deservedly very high, yet, in answer to the opinion thus expressed by him, it may be sufficient to quote a parallel passage from Falle, who, more than a century earlier, was tormented by the same groundless apprehensions. "The custom of gavelkind," says that local historian, "destroys many fine in-

---

[63] [Philip Falle (1656-1742), clergyman and historian of Jersey. His *History of Jersey* was published in 1734. In 1736 Falle presented his collection of books to the island, which, with the addition of subsequent donations, became the core of large library in St. Helier, for which he is honored with a plaque on the original building. Falle is considered a poor historian, an opinion in which Thornton seems to concur.]

[64] [This is either Amice le Couteur or Jean le Couteur, who served as Seneschals of Sark, a small (2.1 square miles) island near Guernsey, from 1785-1808, and 1808-1812, respectively.]

[65] Agricultural Survey of Jersey, in *Guernsey and Jersey Magazine* for July, 1838, pp. 238-9.

heritances by dividing them into so many small portions, which are again subdivided in the following generation, and so on progressively, till the parts of the inheritance are reduced almost to nothing."[66] Since Falle wrote, the peasantry have grown richer instead of becoming continually more impoverished, but though they should continue to advance in the same manner for another hundred years, someone will still be found to take the same gloomy view as the writers just quoted, drawing, like them, his conclusion from a few exceptional cases of minute partition, without noticing how their effects are counterbalanced by other instances of consolidation.

I refer to Alderney only in order to notice a misrepresentation of the late Mr. Inglis, which, if suffered to remain uncontradicted, might be cited in support of one of the gravest charges against peasant proprietorship. "The appearance of the cultivated district," he says, "is singular, owing to the very minute properties, and the odd way in which the proprietors have sown their crops. It is all laid out in narrow strips of different sorts of grain, and in lucerne, potatoes, clover, *etc.* These all lie in different directions, straight across and transversely, and to so great an extent has the division of property descended, that, in looking at a proprietor plowing his strip, it is difficult to see how he will find room to turn his plow."[67] This strange misstatement, for which there is scarcely a tittle of foundation, can only be explained by the shortness of Mr. Inglis's visit to Alderney, which, I was informed on the spot, did not much exceed twenty-four hours. The actual aspect of Alderney is sufficiently curious to render exaggeration or distortion of its features altogether superfluous. The dwellings of the cultivators are not scattered over the face of the island, but are collected together on a spot about a mile from the beach, forming a little metropolis of three or four streets, in which all the peas-

---

[66] Falle's *History of Jersey*, chap. ii. Not having the original work at hand, I have extracted the passage in the text from a French translation.

[67] Inglis's *Channel Islands*, vol. ii. p. 162.

antry, with the exception of some half-dozen families, reside. Close to the town is a plain of some extent, the original territory of the rustic citizens, and, between it and the sea, is a belt of what until recently was common land, but which, in the year 1830, was divided equally among all the resident inhabitants. Many of the allotments on this external belt are separated from each other by stone walls; but the central plain adjoining the town is perfectly open, without a tree, a bush, or a fence of any kind upon it, and is divided into strips, not however, too narrow to prevent a plow from turning, but varying in width from three to twenty yards, and in length from one hundred to several hundred yards. Here and there may certainly be seen a patch of potatoes or parsnips, of perhaps only a few square yards, but on inquiry it will invariably be found to belong either to the proprietor of other land, or to a shopkeeper, to whom it serves as a kitchen-garden. Of the larger strips, each belongs to one person, but does not necessarily constitute the whole of his property, for he may, and almost always does, possess one or more pieces of ground situated elsewhere. Compactness is a quality possessed by few estates, most of them consisting of scattered members lying far apart. This disjointedness seems to result from the absence of enclosures, and from the complete separation of the houses from their respective portions of land. The owner of a cottage situated amidst its own ground, would, on becoming possessed by marriage or inheritance of a detached field, endeavor to exchange it for one nearer his place of abode, more especially if he would otherwise be required to make a fence to mark the bounds of his new acquisition. But an Alderney man, whose property lies perfectly open, and who must walk some distance from home before he can reach any part of it, has not the same motive for wishing to see the whole brought near together. The inconvenience arising from the dispersion of its several portions, is not sufficient to induce him to run the risk of being over-reached in a bargain. Although separately small, the landed possessions of an Alderney man are quite sufficient, when united, for his maintenance. In fact, although *land* may be more minutely divided than in the other islands, the properties of the peasants, if by property be understood all the land belonging to one man, are considerably larger, and the proprietors live proportionably better. Considering their station, they may even be called affluent. Their houses, being arranged in rows, have no picturesqueness, but what is wanting in beauty is amply compensated in more important respects. They are too large to be termed cottages, being almost invariably two-storied erections, equal in external appearance to the dwellings of shopkeepers in English villages; and the rooms are furnished with carpets, sofas, and other articles equally rare in a husbandman's abode. Dress and diet correspond with the style of the habitations, all the habits of the inmates being marked rather by profuseness than by the parsimony characteristic of the same class in the neighboring islands. It is only fair to add, that their means of indulging in so much larger expenditure are not derived entirely from agriculture, but originally arose in part from the profits of contraband trade, which was at one time very actively carried on by them. But to whatever cause attributable, the ease and abundance in which they live are, at least, sufficient to show that Alderney is the last place in which to seek for the poverty which peasant proprietorship is said to engender.

The most specious argument that I have met with, adverse to the general tenor of this and the preceding chapter, is one urged with much force by my honored friend, Mr. Norman,[68] and by Judge Longfield,[69] who contend that "it is not for a man's interest to be a peasant proprietor."[70] In a merely pecuniary sense, this may possibly be

---

[68] [This may refer to George Norman (1823-1882), a British naturalist from Hull, England, and who may be the same person as George Norman, a pioneer in photography.]

[69] [Samuel Mountiford Longfield (1802-1884), known as "Judge Longfield," Irish lawyer and economist, first holder of the Whately Chair in Political Economy at Trinity College, Dublin.]

[70] *Papers on Various Subjects*, by George Warde Norman, pp. 154-6, 189, and 224-6; and *Tenure of Land in Ireland*, by the Rt. Hon. M[ontifort] Longfield, in Cobden Club Essays, 1st series, p. 33.

to some small extent true, though I do not think it is. Suppose a cultivator to be owner of ten acres of the sort of land which in England would be let to a large farmer at £30 an acre, and to employ in their cultivation, at £10 an acre, a farming capital of £100; his net returns, it is argued, would then be no more than £25, consisting of £15 rent and £10 interest on capital; whereas by selling the land at thirty years' purchase, for £450, he would become possessed of a capital of £550, wherewith he might rent and stock a farm of 55 acres, and make thereon, at the rate of ten percent, a net profit of £55, or more than twice what he had made while a peasant proprietor. In these calculations, however, an important circumstance is overlooked. As shown by abundant evidence, adduced from Belgium, Switzerland, and the Channel Islands, land, for which a large English tenant could not afford to pay more than £10 an acre, intelligent small farmers are, by their habit of utilizing odds and ends of time and material which the large farmer wastes, and by their use of the spade in lieu or in aid of the plow, enabled to take, at rents ranging from £4 to £6. Such then are the rates, and not a paltry £30 per acre, with which a peasant proprietor ought to be credited as rent; and according to the higher of these rates, our cultivator of ten acres of his own would obtain £60; or with the addition of profit on his capital (not at the English rate of ten, but at the rack-rented Belgian tenants' rate of only three percent), £60 altogether, or £5 more than if he had taken fifty-five acres on lease. At the lower rate of £4, indeed, his total net receipts would be only £43 altogether, or £12 less, instead of £8 more, than they would have been in the other case; but, for this difference he would probably receive adequate compensation in the increasing value given to his land — partly by the improvements wrought in it by himself, partly by the increasing prices of agricultural produce — which increased value would belong permanently to himself, whereas a tenant would, in consideration of it, have his rent raised at the end of his lease. And even though the compensation in this shape were not fully adequate, even though comparison of a small proprietor with a tenant of equal substance, should show some small balance of gain in favor of the latter, it is still to be considered that the value of landed property is not exclusively pecuniary. Just as a capitalist is, for the sake of the social distinction and political influence connected with landlordship, content to invest in an estate, which will repay him at most only three percent, money for which, on equal[ly] good security, he could readily obtain five percent, or more, so may a peasant perceive it to be for his interest to submit to some small pecuniary sacrifice for the sake of the security, the sense of independence, and the delight in labor, which appertain to the privilege of tilling one's own acres instead of those of another.

If here it be demanded, as it very fairly may, why then an English tenant farmer so seldom exhibits any desire to purchase a small farm, and why one after another of our few remaining English yeomen so readily yields to the temptation of a liberal price for his patrimony? The answer is easy. For one thing there is the expense of verifying titles to land; for another the want of successful examples of small farming in the neighborhood that might serve as types or models. The average English peasant has had no opportunity of learning what hidden treasure lies deep in the soil of Peasant Properties.

He has no suspicion of the wealth beneath his feet, waiting there for a delver to lay it open. It will not suffice to translate for him the Flemish proverb, *De Spa is de Goudmijn der Boeren*, or the Italian, *Se faratro ha il vomero d'argento, la vanga ha la punta d'oro*. Experience and observation are needed to enable him to understand how "The spade can be the peasant's gold mine," and how, "Though the plow has a silver share, the spade has a golden edge."[71]

---

[71] "You," writes Southey to Henry Taylor in January 1829, "think of the plow, I of the spade; you of fields, I of gardens; you of corn-land, I of grass-land. . . . The land on which this is going on in Germany and Holland is worse than the worst of our wastes. The spade works wonders." *Life and Correspondence of Robert Southey*, vol. vi. pp. 20, 21.

3. Effects of Peasant Proprietorship in France

Inconsistency of Evidence on this subject — Arthur Young's Description of Small Proprietors in France — Causes of their former depressed state[1] — Their condition since the Revolution — Present number of French Landowners[2] —Improbability of its having increased within the last thirty years — Average size of Estates — Erroneous conclusions of MM. Mounier and Rubichon and of Mr. John Wilson Croker[3] — Present state of the Peasantry — Evil influence of the French Law of Inheritance — State of Agriculture —Depressed condition of the Population[4] of certain Districts — Remarks on some Statements in Mr. Macculloch's "Treatise[5] on Succession to Property"

It may have been thought not a little extraordinary, that, of the examples hitherto cited in support of the arguments used in the preceding chapters, scarcely any have been taken from France, a country which, as abounding more than any other in peasant proprietors, might seem deserving of especial reference. The reason for the omission was, that the evidence with respect to France is sufficiently ambiguous and inconsistent to have led different reasoners to directly opposite conclusions. If the advocates of peasant proprietorship imagine that it furnishes fresh proofs of the correctness of their views, their opponents appeal to it with not less confidence, as affording a practical illustration of the soundness of their theory. The difference of opinion does not merely regard the inferences to be drawn from admitted facts; the facts themselves are disputed; and while their real character remains doubtful, no one can be expected to be convinced by them. It would have been mere trifling to have attempted to deduce anything from the condition of the

---

1 ["former Depression," 1848.]
2 ["French Landowners" formerly "Proprietors," 1848.]
3 ["Mr. John Wilson Croker" formerly "the Quarterly Review," 1848.]
4 ["People," 1848.]
5 ["Recent Treatise," 1848.]

French peasantry, until it had been settled what that condition is, by a cross-examination of the evidence on the subject; and it was thought more convenient to reserve that operation for a separate chapter.

It should be premised, that it is an error to suppose that peasant proprietorship in France dates only from the Revolution. As in other parts of Europe, it probably grew out of the decay of feudalism, and may have been in existence for several centuries, but at any rate it had become very general much earlier than is commonly imagined; for in the years 1787, 8 and 9, while the danger impending over the crown and nobility was suspected by few, Arthur Young found reason for supposing that one-third of the kingdom was occupied by peasant properties.[6] It must be confessed that the picture which Young draws of these little estates, is far from flattering. He speaks enthusiastically of the industry he observed upon them, but there his eulogy ends. Their cultivation he describes as "execrable." So it was indeed generally throughout France, on farms of all sizes; but Young declares, that he "never saw a single instance of good husbandry on a small farm, except on soils of the greatest fertility," such for example as that of Flanders, where, however, it does not appear to have occurred to him that the fertility he admired might be the effect of the good husbandry of which he assumed it to be the cause. The social position of the small proprietors he describes as corresponding with their agricultural skill. In Flanders, Alsace, on the Garonne, and in Beam he found many in comfortable circumstances, and in Basse Bretagne he heard that many were reputed rich; but in general, he says, they were poor and miserable, owing, in a great measure, to the equal division of land among all the children of a deceased owner. Young's honesty is unimpeachable; what he represents as having come under his own observation, he doubtless either saw, or fancied he saw. Appearances may sometimes have deceived him, but with a few unimportant deductions, his description may be accepted as substantially correct, and

[6] *Travels in France*, vol. i. p. 412.

we may believe, upon his assurance, that French peasant proprietors generally were, in his day, ignorant, unskillful, and miserably poor.

A condition, however, so opposite to that of persons of the same class in other countries, must have arisen, not from the proprietary character common to all, but rather from some circumstances peculiar to France; and Young himself unconsciously informs us what the peculiarities were. The fiscal and feudal oppression under which the peasantry groaned, would be sufficient of itself to account for their depression. Among other grievous taxes were those on land and on the profits of farming, to which they alone were subject, the clergy and gentry being exempt. These taxes, besides being very onerous, were not even of fixed amount. The rates were altered from year to year, at the discretion of the intendants[7] and their deputies, who, in assessing districts or parishes, professed to be guided by the appearance of the crops, and in assessing individuals, by the stock upon their farms. It was the interest, therefore, of every farmer, to appear to have as little stock as possible, and consequently to employ as little as possible in its cultivation, and none in its improvement.[8] The game laws were still more outrageous than those relative to the collection of the revenue. There were numerous edicts which prohibited weeding and hoeing, lest the young partridges should be disturbed; steeping seed, lest it should injure their health; manuring with night soil, lest their flavor should be spoiled by their feeding on the corn so treated, mowing hay before a certain time, or removing stubble, lest the birds should be deprived of shelter.[9] Add to this, the forced labor imposed by government, and the fines and services arbitrarily exacted by lords of manors, and it need not again be asked why the French peasantry, even such of them as cultivated their own

---

[7] [An administrative official serving a French, Spanish, or Portuguese ruler; also an administrative official in some Latin American countries.]

[8] Smith's *Wealth of Nations*. Macculloch's Edit. vol. ii. p. 196.

[9] Young's *Travels in France*, vol. i. p. 600.

lands, were in every sense of the term miserable farmers. The only wonder is that their industry could survive such manifold discouragements. From the same causes proceeded, indirectly, that minute division of land so frequently remarked by Young, and which had been carried so far that, in more than one instance, "a single fruit tree standing in about ten perches of ground constituted a farm, and the local situation of the family was decided by the possession."[10] At the time of Young's visit, France was greatly over-peopled in the only sense in which that phrase is ever appropriate; that is to say, the supply of laborers greatly exceeded the demand. The connubial improvidence, invariably attendant on wretchedness like that to which the peasantry had been reduced, had had the usual effect of increasing their numbers. "The swarms of people were incredible."[11] The inheritor of the smallest scrap of ground had scarcely an alternative but to attempt to subsist upon its produce. To sell it would in general have been to deprive himself of his only means of livelihood; for he could not hope to obtain employment as a hired laborer. It was natural, then, that the sons of a peasant proprietor should divide his farm amongst them, and settle down each on his separate portion. Very natural too, that although a man's property were barely sufficient for his own support, he should take a wife to participate in his indigence. Why not? The usual dissuasive from such matrimonial indiscretion could not influence him. If he had been brought up in the enjoyment of something like competence, he would have feared to lose the comforts he had been accustomed to; but, having been early habituated to privations seemingly as bad as they well could be, he might look with equanimity on a chance so infinitesimal as that of their growing worse, and have no dread of their continuance. There seems no reason to doubt that in France, under the old government, peasant proprietorship was attended by all these evils; but it is not on that account to be condemned. What its advocates contend for is, that peasant properties, sufficiently large when cre-

---

[10] *Travels in France*, vcl. i. p. 402.
[11] *Travels in France*, p. 404.

ated to afford their owners a competent maintenance, are at least as likely as larger estates to preserve the same average size for an indefinite period; but it is not denied that peasant proprietors are affected by misery in the same manner as other men, or that, when reduced to poverty by wicked laws, poverty will extinguish in them the virtue of prudence. Peasant proprietorship did not obtain a fair trial in France until the worst abuses of tyranny and feudalism were swept away at the Revolution, and its history since that period is consequently deserving of especial attention. The evil with which Young imagined it to be fraught, was attributed by that writer to the practice of the partition of an estate among all the deceased owner's children, and he strongly urged the enactment of a law placing certain restrictions on the division of land. Without such a law, he imagined that the most dreadful consequences must inevitably ensue, and that the populousness of France would eventually "exceed the populousness of China, where," he says, "the putrid carcasses of dogs, cats, rats, and every species of filth and vermin are sought with avidity, to maintain the life of wretches born only to be starved." It need not be said that no such law has been passed, but that, on the contrary, what was before a custom, has now become an obligation, and that one-half at least of all property, whether real or personal, must, on the owner's death, be equally divided among his children. Moreover, to the large body of peasant proprietors who previously occupied one-third of the kingdom, were added, in the course of the Revolution, one million two hundred and twenty-two thousand more, among whom were divided a considerable proportion of the forfeited lands of the clergy, of corporations, and of emigrants.[12] Let us inquire, then, what effect time has wrought in the condition of these small proprietors, and whether the lapse of nearly half a century has brought them any nearer to the dismal fate which we are assured is awaiting them.

---

[12] Mourner, *De l'Agriculture en France*, vol. i. p. 78. See also, as to the extent of forfeited land actually sold, Lavergne's *Économie Rurale de la France*, p. 25.

For the last thirty[13] years a succession of witnesses have been asserting Young's prediction to be in course of fulfillment. The Duc de la Rochefoucault,[14] on revisiting, after the Restoration, what had once been his estate of Liancourt, found it parceled out into a number of properties, most of which, he says, occupied less than two-thirds of an acre; and he adds that these properties, small as they were, were always subdivided by the heirs of the last owners. M. de Bonald[15] represents the *morcellement* — the piecemealing — of the land in the south of France, as proceeding in a geometrical ratio. He describes a farm as divided first among all the last owner's children, and, at the end of a second generation, among as many sets of his grand-children, every one of whom is so much attached to his little fragment of patrimony that he would work the flesh off his bones in striving to procure a wretched subsistence from it, rather than resort to a profession in which he might earn a more abundant livelihood with less trouble. M. Rainneville,[16] referring to the north of the kingdom, denounces with more vehemence than perspicuity of metaphor, the "division whose fatal action devours the soil of the fields with afflicting rapidity." M. Bosc[17] declares that he has noticed in Lorraine numbers of fields only four yards long by two broad, reduced to that size by the passion of co-heirs for dividing every piece of ground, however small. Mr. Birkbeck[18] speaks of the country people as "poor from generation to generation, and growing continually poorer as they increase in numbers, by the division and subdivision of property;" and M. Lafitte as-

---

[13] The reader is requested to bear in mind that this chapter was first printed in 1848.

[14] [François de Alexandre Frédéric duc de la Rochefoucault-Liancourt (1747-1827), French social reformer.]

[15] [Louis Gabriel Ambroise, Vicomte de Bonald (1754-1840), French counterrevolutionary, philosopher and politician.]

[16] [Alphonse Valentin Vaysse Rainneville (1798-1864), French agricultural writer and social commentator.]

[17] [Louis-Augustin Bosc d'Antic, also, Louis Augustin Guillaume Bosc (1759-1828), French botanist, zoologist, entymologist.]

[18] [Morris Birkbeck (1764-1825), English born American pioneer and publicist.]

serts that a considerable portion of them eat neither bread nor meat, but feed solely on coarse roots, and have no other covering but rags.[19] Finally, Messrs. Mounier[20] and Rubichon[21] assert the great body of the peasantry to be on the brink of starvation; and this opinion, having been adopted by a leading contributor to the most dignified of English periodicals, has been accepted as an article of faith by a large proportion of English readers.[22]

Happily it is not necessary to put every one of these witnesses to the question. All, save the two last-named, profess to describe the state of affairs previously to the year 1827; Messrs. Mounier and Rubichon alone, whose book was published in 1846, treat of things as they are, and we may therefore confine our scrutiny to them and to their English expounder. These have given us, not only their opinions, but also the statistical reports and tables upon which those opinions are founded, and have thus furnished us with the means of testing the soundness of their judgment. Their representations, as they may prove to be true or false, will confirm or refute the statements of their predecessors. According to the latter, the division of land had not only been carried too far, but was proceeding with accelerated speed; the agricultural population was daily becoming more numerous and poor. To prove that their reasonings were false, it will be sufficient to show that since they wrote, things have not become worse; that land is not more divided, nor pauperism more general. If it shall, moreover, appear that during the interval, the

---

[19] The statements of the several writers quoted may be found more at length in Mr. Macculloch's edition of the *Wealth of Nations*, vol. iv. pp. 466-470.

[20] [Jean Joseph Mounier (1758-1806), French politician and judge.]

[21] [Maurice Rubichon (1766-1849), French economist and co-author with Mounier of *De l'agriculture en France, d'après les documents officiels*, 2 vols. (Paris: Guillaumin, 1846), cited by Karl Marx in *Das Kapital*.]

[22] See *Quarterly Review*, No. 157, Art. 7. The writer of the article was understood at the time to be the late Rt. Hon. John Wilson Croker.

average size of estates has increased instead of diminishing, or that, instead of deterioration, a very sensible improvement has taken place in the condition of the peasantry, their refutation will be still more complete. But in either case it will be evident, either that they were misled by superficial observation, or that they began to theorize without having first laid a sufficient foundation of facts.

France, in 1835, contained 33,326,573 inhabitants, composing about seven millions of families, of whom, according to M. Mounier, nearly five millions and a half (5,446,763) were families of landed proprietors. This last statement, however, is nothing more than a guess, for nothing certain is known on the subject. What is known, is the number of properties assessed to the land-tax, which in the same year was 10,893,528, or almost exactly double the supposed number of proprietors. All the lands or buildings possessed by the same person in one commune, are assessed as a distinct property; but many persons possess many such properties in different communes. It has been assumed, that, on an average, every proprietor possesses two, and in order to obtain the number of proprietors, the whole number of properties assessed has been divided by two. A result so obtained is evidently worth nothing, and it is accordingly disregarded by M. Mounier's own coadjutor, M. Rubichon, who is content to reckon the proprietary families at four millions, and the whole number of agricultural families at 5,200,000, or at three-fourths of the entire population.[23] That the second of these estimates, although so much reduced, is yet far beyond the truth, will instantly appear, on reference to the statistical tables of houses, of which very considerably more than one-fourth are situated in towns containing not less than 1,500 inhabitants,[24] so that, if every resident in towns of smaller size and in the rest of the country were engaged in husbandry, the number of agricultural families would still be much less than M. Rubichon imagines. Even if his estimate were correct, and if the inhabitants of

---

[23] *De l'Agric. en France*, tom. i. p. 117. See also p. 266.
[24] *Systemes de Culture*, par M. Hippolyte Passy, p. 163.

the rural districts were really thrice as numerous as those of towns, the proportion of the rural to the whole population would be found to have diminished within the last sixty years; for, in 1793, the inhabitants of the towns were 5,709,270, while those of the country were 20,521,538; or much more nearly four times than three times as numerous as the former.[25] It is obvious, however, that notwithstanding this change in the proportion between the agricultural and other classes, the absolute number both of agriculturists and of landed proprietors may have greatly increased; and those who maintain that this is really the case are able to point to one fact, which at first seems strongly to favor their conclusion. This is the great increase which has taken place in the number of *cotes foncières*, or properties assessed to the land-tax. In the year 1815, the number was 10,083,751; in 1826, 10,296,693; and in 1835, 10,893,528. Thus, in the interval between 1815 and 1826, there was an annual increase of 21,294, and in the next decennial period an annual increase of 59,683; so that the number has not only been continually advancing, but has advanced with continually increasing rapidity. It further appears, that in the eleven years ending with 1826, the increase took place among the properties most lightly taxed, while the number of properties paying as much as one-thousand francs fell off considerably; and it has thence been not unnaturally inferred, that the multiplication of the smaller properties was the effect of the division of large ones. M. Passy[26] has, however, furnished us with a more satisfactory explanation of the

---

[25] Arthur Young's *Travels in France*, vol. i. p. 479. One reason why the agricultural population has been so much overrated is, that all the proprietors are commonly counted as cultivators (Macculloch, *Geog. Diet.* vol. i. p. 853); whereas, according to Châteauvieux, only 50,000,000 acres, or considerably less than one-half of the cultivated land, are cultivated by the owners, the rest being held by tenant farmers. Another circumstance deserving of notice is, that as the same tenant often holds of several proprietors, the number of estates must much exceed the number of farms.

[26] [Hippolyte Passy (1793-1880), French political economist.]

phenomenon. Among other ways and means of meeting the extraordinary expenses of the year 1815, was an addition to the land-tax, which caused most estates to be placed in the register in the class above that to which they had previously belonged. When the war taxes were removed, the old rates of assessment were resumed, and from the highest class of all, consisting of estates assessed at one thousand francs and upwards, more than four thousand were withdrawn to be placed in the class immediately below. As a proof that this was the true cause of the reduction of the highest class, it may be mentioned that since 1826, and more particularly since 1835, the number of estates of every class, without exception, has increased, and that the increase has been greatest in the highest class. Between 1835 and 1842, the estates rated at 1,000 francs and upwards increased in number 22.4 percent.

Those rated at from 500 to 1,000 frs. increased 11 percent.

"	"	100 to 500	"	10.3	"
"	"	50 to 100	"	9.8	"
"	"	30 to 50	"	8.8	"
"	"	20 to 30	"	7.4	"
"	"	10 to 20	"	6.6	"
"	"	5 to 10	"	3.2	"
"	below	5	"	4.5	"

Now, if it were the subdivision of estates which had occasioned the augmentation of their number, what one class had gained another must have lost; but as an increase has taken place in every class without exception, it has probably proceeded from other causes;[27] unless, indeed, the average size of the estates of the aggrandized

---

[27] It is moreover to be noted, and that very particularly, that the ratio of numerical increase was greatest in the class of largest properties, and small by degrees, and beautifully less, as the area adopted for classification diminished. It is only in the lowest class of all that the ratio is slightly higher than in the class immediately above it. If, then, division of area was the cause of multiplication of number, it would seem that in France the larger estates are, the more liable they are to be divided.

class has meantime diminished. The information supplied by M. Passy enables us to discover what those causes were. Among the *cotes foncières* are included houses and all other buildings, of which, between 1826 and 1835, there were placed on the register 321,226, which were either newly constructed, or had been omitted in former assessments; and of these, M. Passy reckons that three-fifths have little or no ground attached to them beyond the sites on which they stand. The construction of such buildings increased the number of *cotes foncières* without occasioning any perceptible partition of cultivable land.[28] During the same period, Crown lands to the value of nearly five millions and a half sterling were sold,[29] and communal lands of unascertained extent were divided. Add to the effects of these operations the permanent division of house property in towns by co-heirs, and it will be easy to understand how the whole increase in the number of *cotes foncières* may have taken place without any sensible diminution in the size of landed estates. M. Passy mentions some other facts, which are too significant to be omitted. For some years past, a new survey and valuation of land has been in progress in France, and, in thirty-seven cantons scattered throughout the kingdom, the operation has been completed. At the previous survey in 1810, there were in these cantons 154,266 *cotes foncières*. There are now 163,277, the difference being equal to an increase of five percent, while the population has increased at the rate of 19 percent. But not only do the *cotes foncières*, at present, bear a smaller proportion to the mass of inhabitants than at the date of the last survey; the small addition which has been made to their number may be accounted for entirely by the progress of building. The number of *cotes foncières* is, at present, greater by 9,011 than in 1810; but in the same interval, an addition has been made to the population of 120,000, for whom at least 22,000 new houses must have been built.[30] If we suppose that these new houses have led to the creation of

---

[28] Passy, *Systemes de Culture*, pp. 162-170.
[29] Mounier, *De l'Agric. en France*, tom. i. p. 110.
[30] Passy, *ut supra*, pp. 171, 174.

less than one-half the same number of *cotes foncières*, they may still suffice to convince us that landed property, properly so called, is not at present divided among a greater number of owners than it was thirty-seven years ago.

But although the partition of landed property ceased long ago to make any sensible progress, it may, perhaps, have advanced too far before its course was stopped. Estates may already be too minutely divided; the majority of proprietors may not possess nearly enough of land for their proper maintenance, and, if destitute of any other means of livelihood, may be pining in extreme indigence. That such is actually the situation of the great mass of the French peasantry is unhesitatingly affirmed by Messrs. Mounier and Rubichon, and by their English reviewer, Mr. Croker, all of whom affect quite arithmetical precision in the details which they bring forward to justify the assertion. There are 10,893,528 *cotes foncières*, or rated properties, and there are supposed to be about half this number, or 5,446,763 distinct proprietors. So says Mr. Croker, who, however, in the very next sentence, forgets the distinction he had just drawn between properties and proprietors, and finding that of the former there are 5,163,000 taxed at less than five francs, imagines that there must be the same number of persons taxed equally lightly; and he adds, that as the French land-tax is on an average equal to ten-pence the English acre, there must be upwards of five millions of proprietors whose average holdings are under five acres.[31] The conclusion to which his own premises should have brought him is, that the class of proprietors he is speaking of consists, not of five millions, but of two millions and a half, taxed, not at five, but at ten francs, and possessing on an average, not five, but ten acres. The credit of this mistake[32] belongs exclusively to Mr. Croker himself; into the next he only follows

---

[31] [Note in the 1848 edition: "*Quarterly Review*, No. 157, pp. 211, 216."]

[32] ["blunder" in the 1848 edition, in which Mr. Croker is referred to as "the Reviewer."]

his leader. M. Mounier informs us that there are 2,602,705 proprietary families whose income is supposed not to exceed fifty francs; whereupon, Mr. Croker, having first generously increased by one-half the supposed income, cannot suppress his astonishment and scorn at the idea of 2,600,000 families (families of proprietors, too!) having but sixty shillings a year to live upon; and he protests that the "poorest day-laborer would earn four times as much."[33],[34] But, surely, Mr. Croker might have known or guessed that the value of the produce of five acres must be somewhat more than sixty shillings — somewhat more than the bare price of the grain that would have been required to sow that acreage with wheat — but both he and Mounier confound the rent for which land might be let, with its gross produce, and — first reducing rent to a ridiculously low figure — imagine that a peasant proprietor receives only rent. They forget that he unites in his own person the characters of landlord, tenant, and laborer, and takes for his own use the shares of all three, or the entire produce of his fields. If the great body of the peasantry cannot subsist in comfort, although holding their lands on such terms, their inability must proceed from some other cause than the smallness of their holdings. Mounier's own figures, rightly understood, assign to the poorest two and a half millions of proprietors an average approaching nearer to ten than to five acres; and a much better authority, M. de Châteauvieux,[35] estimates the average holdings of the 3,900,000 poorer proprietors at eight acres and a half.[36] French agriculture is confessedly very defective, but unless a French peasant obtains less from an acre than an English allotment-holder sometimes does from a rood, the owner of eight acres and a half must, at

---

[33] [Note in the 1848 edition: "*Quarterly Review*, No. 157, p. 210."]

[34] [A sentence is deleted here from the 1874 edition: "A writer who can put forth such stuff as this must either be very dull himself, or must count upon an extraordinary share of dullness in his readers."]

[35] [Frédéric Lullin de Châteauvieux (1772-1841), French political commentator.]

[36] Mounier, *ut supra*, tom. i. p. 265.

the very least, have an income of £40, instead of forty or sixty shillings. It is true that if eight acres and a half be the average extent of the smallest class of properties, many must be larger, and very many smaller; perhaps not far from a million of an acre or half an acre, or even of only a few square yards. There are many cottage gardens in England of no greater size — why not also in France? — and why should the French, any more than the English cottager, be supposed capable of subsisting upon the produce of such a scrap of ground? Why should not he also be a day-laborer, depending upon wages for the chief, part of his subsistence?[37] The Quarterly Reviewer imagines that no one would employ him, for that the generality of his neighbors are in the same condition as himself, each tilling his own allotment, and, instead of hiring extra labor, wishing himself to be hired. Indeed! Let us turn again to the tables of M. Mounier. The cultivable land of France is 114,000,000 acres. The *cotes foncières* of less than five francs are 5,163,494, supposed to represent just half that number, or 2,581,747, of united properties of less than ten acres each. Their aggregate area can scarcely be more than 22,000,000 of acres, leaving 92,000,000 of acres belonging to larger proprietors, and divided into farms, of which, if the average size be as low as thirty acres, there must be more than three millions. Suppose that one-half of the poorest class of proprietors are not fully employed on their own lands, and must seek additional occupation elsewhere; it will be hard if they cannot obtain it, when for every person occasionally requiring work, there are more than two farms occasionally requiring laborers. If we prefer the calculations of M. de Châteauvieux, we shall have 3,900,000 proprietors of eight and a half acres each,

---

[37] [Cf. "In France most of those who labor for hire in agriculture are themselves owners of certain plots of ground, which just enable them to subsist without working for anyone else. When these laborers come to offer their services to a neighboring landowner or farmer, if he refuses them a certain rate of wages they retire to their own small property and await another opportunity." Alexis de Tocqueville, "Influence of Democracy on Wages," *Democracy in America* (1835, 1840), II.3.vii.]

and of a total area of about 33,000,000 of acres, leaving about 81,000,000 of acres to be divided into 2,700,000 farms of thirty acres. Even then, supposing one-half of the poorer proprietors to be insufficiently employed at home, there would, for every two persons requiring work, be three farms on which they might obtain it.

That the condition of the French peasantry, whether proprietors or field laborers, if not yet perfectly satisfactory, has been steadily improving for many years past, is evident from the testimony of all who have themselves examined it. The opposite opinion is maintained by those only who have made their researches in books, instead of amongst the people. Mr. Croker considers it quite certain that the small landholders are in great distress, because, in the ten years ending with 1835, about one-fourth part of the whole landed property of the country was sold; whereas sales of land are really the most obvious and effectual means of counteracting the evil tendency of the French law of succession. During the same ten years, a fourth part of the land likewise passed into new hands by inheritance or gift, the new owners by inheritance being, of course, in the first instance, much more numerous than those whom they succeeded. Most of their shares were only fractions of the estates of their predecessors, and, being too small to afford them what they considered a suitable livelihood, were sold and annexed to other properties. Yet these sales, which prevented the further *morcellement* of land, and the enlargement and consequent impoverishment of the agricultural class — these very sales are declared to be signs of the poverty which they really prevented. A similar construction is placed, without much more reason, on the extent to which landed property is mortgaged, the interest payable in consequence being equal to one-third of the estimated rental of the kingdom. This would be a startling fact if the proprietors had become so deeply indebted from the difference between their ordinary income and their ordinary expenditure. It would then be obvious that their resources had not been sufficient for their permanent support, and that, in order to provide for immediate necessities, they had been compelled to make use of their capital, and so to ruin their prospects for the future. But the Reviewer himself admits, though he does not see the importance of his admission, that the debts were incurred before the debtors became proprietors, or rather in order to enable them to become proprietors. A large proportion of the landowners obtained their property by purchase, and their debts are a part of the purchase-money still remaining unpaid. In this there is not the smallest ground for uneasiness. In France, as in other countries abounding with small estates, it is usual for a person who cannot afford to buy a piece of ground outright, to buy a certain interest in it, leaving it still charged with an annual payment to the last owner, until by industry and thrift he shall have saved enough to free it from all encumbrances. Until that time arrives, he, in fact, holds the land by payment of a fixed rent,[38] the very best possible tenure by which he could hold it, except that of an unembarrassed proprietor. The French mortgagees are, for the most part, tenants of this description, paying interest or rent, whichever it may be called, at an average rate of four shillings an acre, which, being no more than an English farmer frequently pays for poors' rates, can scarcely be deemed sufficient to reduce a French peasant to pauperism.

Again, Messrs. Mounier and Rubichon, poring over rows of figures, and comparing the amount of agricultural produce of the whole kingdom with the number of inhabitants, believe they have ascertained that a Frenchman's daily average allowance of food is rather less than two ounces of meat and fifteen ounces of bread or its equivalents; and, without being stopped for a moment by the marvelousness of this result, jump to the conclusion that their own nation is the worst fed in Europe. Very different was the opinion of the aged cultivators and workmen consulted by M. Clement in different places, all of whom, without a single exception, agreed that the classes of the

---

[38] ["Fixity of rent" was one of the demands of the National Land League in Ireland, formed five years after the publication of the revised, 1874 edition of this book.]

population who have only their wages, and are consequently the most exposed to indigence, are now much better fed, lodged, and clothed, than at the commencement of the century.[39] Very different is the language of one who has traversed great part of the Continent on foot, and whose evidence is the more valuable, because, having no favorite theory to support, and being little more than a keen and shrewd observer, his impressions are always perfectly unbiased. "With a tolerably intimate knowledge," says Mr. Inglis, "and distinct recollection of the lower orders of France, I am inclined to assert that, upon the whole, the French peasantry are the happiest of any country in Europe."[40] While passing through Languedoc, Inglis particularly remarked the "very enviable situation" of the laboring class. Upon every estate large enough to require them he found one or more small separate houses, in each of which two or three farm servants were accommodated. These people had commonly a garden and a bit of land for Indian corn, and were supplied by their master with as much bacon and wine as they required, besides receiving enough of wages for clothes, etc. A day laborer received two francs. The people appeared to be well off, and paupers were rare. He did not see one miserable between Carcassonne and Toulouse.[41] No special allusion is here made to small proprietors; but in a district in which they are intermixed with hired laborers, their condition is always the best of the two. The cultivators are observed to be most prosperous in those parts of France in which the largest proportion of them are proprietors. Mr. Henry Bulwer[42] remarks, that by far the greatest number of indigent is to be found in the northern departments, where land is less divided than elsewhere, and cultivated with larger capitals.[43] Mr. Birkbeck, noticing that on the road from St. Pierre to Moulins, "the lower classes appeared less comfortable," found on inquiry that "few of the peas-

---

[39] Recherches sur l'Indigence, par A. Clement, pp. 84, 85.
[40] Switzerland and South of France, vol. ii. p. 269.
[41] Ibid. p. 80.
[42] Afterwards Lord Balling.
[43] Monarchy of the Middle Classes, vol. ii. p. 107.

antry thereabouts were proprietors"[44] Mr. Le Quesne,[45] who, when asking the causes of the smiling productiveness of Anjou and Touraine, received for answer that the land was divided into small parcels, noticed that the houses of the country people there were remarkable for their neatness, and indicative of the ease and comfort of their possessors. They are built, he says, of fine white stone, and besides being more numerous, are far superior in appearance to those of Normandy, where estates are larger, and where the laborers on those estates commonly live in miserable mud cottages, with heaps of dung and filth in front.[46] Yet even in the districts in which small properties so much abound, there would seem to be no lack of larger farms to afford work to such cottagers as are not fully employed at home. Inglis, in his walks through Touraine, was overtaken by a countryman who said that he had land enough of his own to supply him with bread, and to enable him to keep a cow and a couple of pigs, and that he was accustomed to earn, in addition, from twenty-five to thirty sous a day by working for others. These sketches are taken at random from different parts of a country of which Mr. Macculloch, in 1823, prophesied that in "half a century it would certainly be the greatest pauper-warren in Europe, and, along with Ireland, have the honor of furnishing hewers of wood and drawers of water for all other countries in the world." Well might Mr. Laing, as, in his tour through France he read this lugubrious prediction, "look up from the page and laugh" to see around him on the rivers, canals, and roads, in steamboats, iron suspension bridges, new factories, and coal works — numberless proofs of the progress of industry and wealth under the very system so prematurely denounced.[47] Mr. Macculloch's own favorite witnesses, Messrs. Birkbeck and J. P. Cobbett, testify against him whenever they descend from the oracular tripod, and in-

---

[44] Birkbeck's *Tour in France*, p. 30.
[45] [This may be Charles Le Quesne (1811-1856), historian.]
[46] Le Quesne on the Commerce of Jersey; *Guernsey and Jersey Magazine*, vol. iii. p. 110.
[47] Laing. *Notes of a Traveler*, p. 53.

stead of prophesying what was to be, are content to describe what actually was. "There is no advancement in French society," exclaims Mr. Birkbeck; "no improvement nor hope of it;" yet shortly before he had said, "I have inquired, and everybody assures me that agriculture has been *improving rapidly* for the last twenty-five years; that *the riches and comforts of the cultivators of the soil have been doubled* since that period, and that vast improvement has taken place in the condition and character of the common people. On my first landing I was struck with the respectable appearance of the working class; I see the same marks of comfort and plenty wherever I proceed. *I ask for the wretched peasantry*, of whom I have heard and read so much, but I am always referred to the Revolution; it seems they vanished then. The laboring class here is certainly much higher on the social scale than with us. Every opportunity of collecting information on this subject confirms my first impression, that there are very few really poor people in France. In England, a poor man and a laborer are synonymous terms; we speak familiarly of *the poor*, meaning *the laboring class*; not so here."[48] Mr. Cobbett's comparison between France and England is equally favorable to the former. He *heard* that unless the law of inheritance were changed, "society would become degraded in the extreme," but all that he *saw* would have warranted more cheering anticipations. He was surprised to find that the "laboring people or peasantry had usually cows of their own, sometimes one, sometimes two or three," besides pigs; and he could not help seeing that their dress was "better than that of laborers in England," and that their breakfast of cabbage soup, bread, and wine, was a thousand times better than the "cold potatoes and tea" with which people of the same class in this country often prepare for a hard day's work. He saw besides, "a great many beggars, but not more of them," he acknowledges, "in the country parts of France than he would have seen in England if traveling along the same high-road;" and he adds, "there is this important difference between

---

[48] *Tour in France*, pp. 1-22.

the appearance of beggars in France and England; a very large portion of our beggars are neither aged nor infirm, while in France there is scarcely any object of this description that is not old or in some way incapable of earning a living. The greater part of the English beggars beg because they cannot get employment, and the beggars of France beg because they are unfitted for employment. It is the state of society in England which creates the beggar, while in France it is his inability to render society any service."[49]

Compare the statements quoted above, or any other account of the present or recent state of France, with the pictures drawn — not by Marshal Vauban,[50] who, in Louis the XIV's time, estimated that three-fifths of the inhabitants were either beggars or on the verge of beggary — not by Arthur Young, who, at the commencement of the Revolution, found the peasantry half-starved, and distress and misery everywhere prevailing — but with the descriptions given since the Restoration, of a people fed with roots and clothed in rags. The comparison admits of only two alternatives. Either things were not nearly so bad in M. Lafitte's time as that writer believed, or they have

---

[49] *Ride through France*, p. 210. "It is, however, certain that with the exception of some departments which are suffering from exceptional causes, such as inundations or failure of crops, the general aspect of the French rural population shows a marked improvement in the last twenty years. Every house is better built and better arranged than the old cottages. The blue linen blouse is not the only garment of the peasant, winter and summer, but it is worn over good woolen clothing. The bread of the common people is whiter and purer, and the consumption of meat increases. Five and twenty years ago, in a small market town of Normandy which we have sometimes visited, there lived but one butcher, who earned a precarious subsistence from the neighboring gentry. In the same town there are now nine persons living by the sale of meat. The same progress is even more striking in Touraine, Picardy, and the environs of Paris. But this progress in wellbeing has not led to any corresponding increase of population." *Edinburgh Review*, April, 1837.
[50] [Sébastien Le Prestre, Seigneur de Vauban (1633-1707), Marshal of France and military engineer.]

marvelously improved since. Either the pauperism said to be inseparable from peasant proprietorship did not even then exist, or it has since disappeared, although its alleged cause still retains all its vigor. The assailants of peasant proprietorship may choose between the horns of this dilemma. By whichsoever they may prefer to be transfixed, their perplexity will serve equally to refute their unfounded charges.

One more remark before we leave this part of the subject. Land in France sells much better when offered in small than in large lots. According to the Marquis Garnier,[51] a farm which would let for about £200 a year, could not be sold entire for more than twenty-five years' purchase; whereas, if divided into several lots, it might sell for forty years' purchase. This, whatever else it may prove, proves likewise that peasants of the lower grades outbid their betters, which they could not do unless, besides gaining enough for their ordinary expenses, they were able to save money. It is true that purchases of small estates are not commonly completed at once, but that part of the price is left to be paid off by installments; but the credit thus given to the purchaser shows the confidence reposed in his ability to obtain a good deal more than a livelihood from his land, and the preference given to him over his wealthier competitors, shows also how firm and how general is the belief that small farms are more productive than large ones. Land is the bank in which the peasantry invest their savings. They are the highest bidders for it; but, as they cannot afford to buy much at a time, it must, when offered for sale, be divided into small lots, in order to be brought within their reach.

Enough has now been said to show that the effect of peasant proprietorship in France, as elsewhere, has been very different from that of promoting pauperism; that the average size of the properties which in that country are termed small, by way of distinction from large or middle sized, is more than eight acres, and that their average

---

[51] [Marquis Germaine Garnier (1754-1821), French political economist.]

size has remained without sensible diminution for more than thirty years, during which period the people have been steadily advancing to a higher social position. Their actual situation will suffer little from comparison with that of the most favored nations, and experience justifies the strongest confidence that their prosperity will be permanent at least, if not progressive. This result, too, has been obtained notwithstanding the operation of a law of inheritance, whose natural tendency is to increase the number, and to diminish the possessions of landowners; but peasant proprietorship has diffused general competence, competence has engendered prudence, and prudence has counteracted the influence of the law. Not that the law has been rendered altogether harmless. It has not been followed by the fatal consequences expected from it, but it has produced an evil of a somewhat different character, which, though of secondary importance, is still exceedingly serious. This is not the multiplication but the division of estates. The number and the average extent of landed properties have undergone little alteration, but instead of being compact, an estate is frequently composed of several detached portions. These *parcelles*, as they are technically called, are to the number of properties as twenty to one, so that unless *parcelles* belonging to the same person, although entered separately in the register, are sometimes contiguous, every estate must, on an average, consist of twenty fragments in twenty different places. This is in part the direct effect of the law, which not only assigns to every child a certain proportion of his parent's property, but permits him to insist on having a share of every separate field; but the law acts still more powerfully in an indirect manner, by multiplying sales. The mischief arising from it can scarcely be exaggerated. The expensive litigation and ill-will, occasioned by the partition, the loss of ground in the numberless paths connecting the *parcelles*, and the loss of time in passing from one to another, the mutual trespasses of cultivators whose slips of ground, are sometimes so narrow that the animals employed in plowing one cannot avoid trampling on the adjoining one; the consequent disputes and law-suits — all these are commented on by Mounier and his colleague with great but not unjust severity. But these evils, although justly attributable to the French law of inheritance, are not its necessary consequences. Such partition as that alluded to, however legal, would be impracticable except in a country open and unenclosed. Thus, it is usual in Alderney, where fences are rare, but is unknown in the other Channel Islands, where, although peasant proprietorship and gavelkind equally prevail, every field is enclosed with hedges. It was once common, likewise, in the open plains of Germany, until experience of the inconveniences arising from it, led to its prohibition, and it might, of course, be put a stop to by the same means in France also. As long, however, as the practice continues, it must present formidable obstacles to the progress of agriculture, which, accordingly, must be confessed to be in a very backward state. But that it was ever in a more forward condition does not necessarily follow, nor yet that it is better on large than on small farms, although both propositions are affirmed more zealously than discreetly by Messrs. Mounier and Rubichon. In support of their assertions, they produce tables, which their reviewer pronounces "the most minute and accurate ever made in any country," and from which he draws the astounding conclusion, that "the average produce of the whole territory may be about 10s per acre," or only 2s more than the rated, and 2s less than the supposed real rent. In justice, however, to the French authors, this must be acknowledged to be another error of their commentator's, and to be three times as absurd as what they have said themselves. According to them, the value of the average gross produce of an acre is 30s; but of this estimate also no more need be said, than that it is founded upon the same tables as those which represent the daily average ration of each individual of the whole French population, (an average, of course, infinitely above that of the laboring classes,) to be no more than fifteen ounces of bread or vegetables, and one ounce and three-quarters of meat. Arguments resting on so frail a basis are not entitled to the compliment of examination, but one or two facts may be mentioned in opposition to the conclusion at which they are directed. In 1794, the cultivated area of France was estimated by Arthur Young at 108 millions of acres. According to Châteauvieux, it is now 114 millions, implying an addition of about 5½ percent. Population has meantime advanced from 26 to 33 millions, or at the rate of about 27 percent. If these estimates be correct, the original area of 108 millions of acres, which formerly maintained only 26 millions of inhabitants, now maintains 31 millions, and feeds the larger number much better than the smaller was fed before the Revolution. France was never a large importer of provisions, and is less so now than ever, many articles of food which were once admitted free being now subject to heavy duties. How then can an additional population of five millions be fed by the produce of the same territory, unless the land be better cultivated than formerly? It is evident that, in spite of the great and manifold disadvantages under which the peasantry labor, in spite of the *parcellement* of individual estates, in spite of the continuance of the old customs of *vaine pâture* and *parcours*, whereby at certain seasons the cattle of all the inhabitants are let loose to graze over a whole district, the characteristic industry of proprietors, hampered as it is, has yet been so vigorously exerted, as to create an increase of nearly one-fifth in the produce of the soil.

So much for the alleged decline of French agriculture generally. The next subject for comparison is the relative cultivation of large and small farms. M. Rubichon finds that in the forty-two northern departments, there are 10,079 properties paying a land-tax of 1,000 francs or upwards, while in the forty-three departments of the south, there are only 3,282 of such properties; further, that in the north the average rate per hectare is about three francs, and only two francs in the south. Whence, as the rate of land-tax is regulated by the produce of the soil, he concludes that those parts of France are the most productive in which there is the greatest number of rich proprietors.[52] The truth of this proposition is unassailable, but its converse is equally true. There are more of large properties in the north than in the south, by about 6,800, but in

---

[52] Mounier, *ut supra*, vol. i. p. 116.

the north the number of properties of the smaller class is also the greatest by more than a million, whence it appears, that those parts of France are the most productive in which there is the largest number of small properties. So far the balance is equal between the two parties; it does not appear whether the superiority of northern agriculture is attributable to the prevalence of large or of small proprietors. But sentence must be passed in favor of the latter, when it is considered that they outbid the former not only as tenants,[53] but as purchasers. If they merely paid a higher rent, it might be supposed that, like Irish cottiers, necessity compelled them to submit to any terms, however unreasonable, in order to obtain land; but they can likewise pay a higher price, which they could not do unless their business were relatively more profitable, and more favorable to saving than that of larger farmers. Among the supposed signs of the decay of French agriculture, one is the alleged diminution of the number of sheep and cattle. With respect to sheep, it is generally admitted that small farms are unsuitable for the management of them, and it is probable enough that sheep-farming, which, as Young informs us, was very ill understood even before the Revolution, was still less practiced in the period immediately following that event, and after the domains of the clergy and nobility had been distributed among forty times as many owners as before. As long as the average size of estates was decreasing, the number of sheep may also have decreased, but during the last thirty years at least, the former has remained nearly stationary, and it may fairly be presumed that the latter has undergone as little variation during the same period. At any rate, much stronger proofs of its having recently declined are needed than those produced by M. Mounier, who, in the whole kingdom, has only been able to discover two

---

[53] According to M. Passy, the average rent per hectare of large, middling, and small farms, is in France, 75, 85, and 140 francs respectively. *Systemes de Culture*, pp. 102, 103.

communes in one of which seven flocks have disappeared in thirty years, and in the other, five flocks in six years.[54]

Small farms do not lie under the same disadvantage with respect to the breeding of horned cattle; on the contrary, when well managed, they are peculiarly adapted to it. In England, there are seldom more than ten or twelve head of horned cattle on a farm of a hundred arable acres; but a Flemish farmer of fifteen acres, of which only seven or eight are under green crops, will keep six beasts stall fed.[55] Yet in France, the national stock of cattle is said to have diminished since the Revolution, and the assertion, unlike most of those put forth by the same parties, is not a mere assumption, but receives countenance from the unquestionable fact that the supply of beef to several towns bears a smaller proportion than formerly to the population, and that the price has likewise risen considerably. The supply has increased, but not so much as the number of inhabitants, In Paris, for instance, the consumption of meat was 150 lbs. for each person in 1789; but in 1841, the average had fallen to 121 lbs.; of beef, the consumption per head is said to have fallen from 105 lbs. to 54 lbs., and the price to have risen 16 percent, in seven years. Mr. Mill has given a satisfactory explanation of these phenomena, without ascribing them to the substitution of small for large farms, which should naturally have produced effects directly opposite. "In Paris, before the Revolution, there was, comparatively speaking, no production at all, but only distribution; the population consisted of the great landlords, the court and higher functionaries paid by the State, the bankers, financiers, government contractors, and other moneyed classes, with the great and small dealers and tradesmen needful for supplying these opulent customers, and few laborers beyond those who could not be wanting in so large a town. In such a city the rich must have borne an unusually high nu-

---

[54] Mounier, *ut supra* , vol. ii. p. 125.
[55] *Flemish Husbandry*, p. 80.

merical proportion to the poorer consumers."[56] But Paris has since become one of the chief seats of French manufacture, and the addition of one-third to the population is no doubt principally owing to the augmentation of the laboring and poorer classes. As the poor eat much less meat than the rich, such a change in the numerical proportion between the classes would occasion a corresponding reduction in the average consumption per head of the whole population. This would be the case even if the demand continued to be adequately supplied, a supposition, however, which is inconsistent with the rise of price that has taken place. But this rise of price does not necessarily imply a decrease in the number of native cattle. The increasing demand of towns can only be met by supplies brought from a distance, and at an expense continually increasing; and in order to convey increased supplies to inland towns, like Paris and Lyons, to which, before the discovery of steam navigation and the construction of railways, cattle could only be brought by tedious land journeys, the increase of expense must have been considerable. Again, France was formerly a large importer of foreign cattle, which, until 1814, were admitted free; but, in that year, a duty of three francs on every head of cattle was imposed, and, in 1822, a sudden increase of the duty to 55 francs nearly put a stop to the importation. "Moreover, the octroi or town custom duty, now so burdensome, did not exist at all in 1789, and has been largely increased at various periods, both in Paris and most other towns, since its first establishment." These three causes seem to be quite sufficient to account for the enhancement of price without attributing it to a diminution of the national stock of cattle, a supposition which, although it cannot be completely disproved, for want of sufficient evidence, is contradicted by such partial evidence as is procurable. We have no means of comparing the present number of cattle existing throughout France with that existing at a remote period, but we are able to make such a comparison in particular

---

[56] *Morning Chronicle*, Jan. 16, 1847. The article quoted was shortly afterwards reprinted by Mr. Mill in his *Principles of Political Economy*, vol. i. Appendix.

districts. For the Département de l'Eure, for instance, a very careful statistical report was drawn up in 1800, from which and from investigations made in 1837, it appears that in the interval, the quantity of livestock increased exceedingly; horses increasing in number from 29,500 to 51,000; horned cattle, from 50,000 to 105,000; swine, from 36,000 to 49,000; and sheep, from 205,000 to 511,000.[57] It maybe objected that this Département is one in which large farms are more numerous than in most parts of France; but it appears that large and small farms are intermixed, and that the relative proportions have not perceptibly varied since the commencement of the present century. Those, however, who may nevertheless think that the large farms alone are entitled to the credit arising from this increase of livestock, may be induced to change their opinion by a statement of some particulars respecting the commune of Vensat, in Auvergne, one of the provinces in which, if anywhere, *morcellement* of land has been carried to excess. The arable land of that commune was occupied in 1790 by thirty-seven farms. The present number of farms is not stated, but the number of properties is 591. But in 1790 there were only 300 horned cattle, and from 1,800 to 2,000 sheep; there are now 676 of the former, and 533 of the latter; so that it has gained 376 oxen, and lost 1,300 sheep; or, as ten sheep are reckoned by French agriculturists to be equivalent to one cow or ox, its real gain may be stated at 246 oxen.[58] A still more satisfactory account is given of the *arrondissement* of Fougères, by its Sous-préfet M. Bertin, who tells us that, between 1813 and 1844, horned cattle multiplied from 34,500 to 51,900; sheep, from 6,300 to 11,000; swine, from 9,300 to 26,000; and horses, from 7,400 to 11,600.[59] It may be added, that, in the Département du Nord, cattle are most abundant in those districts in which farms are smallest. The *arrondissements* of Lille and Hazebrouck, besides a greater number of horses, maintain, respec-

---

[57] Passy, Changemens survenus dans la Situation Agricole du Département de l'Eure, p. 12.
[58] Passy, *Systemes de Culture*, p. 119.
[59] Bertin. *Notice sur la Baronie, etc.* de Fougères, p. 390.

tively, fifty-two and forty-six oxen on every 250 acres, while the *arrondissements* of Dunkerque and Avesnes, in which the largest farms are situated, maintain only forty-four and forty respectively.[60]

General descriptions are seldom at once both literally accurate and sufficiently distinct, nor is the aspect of a large country ever so uniform that in many places deviations from the prevalent character may not be detected. Taking a comprehensive survey of France, we have seen that the number of landed proprietors has long remained nearly stationary; that cultivators deriving a livelihood from their own fields have in general land enough for their maintenance in comfort; and that the condition of the peasantry and of the other laboring classes has for many years been steadily improving. But the truth of this statement is not incompatible with the existence of many exceptional cases. That peasant proprietorship is a wellspring of poverty is a notion utterly groundless, but to represent it as a palladium against indigence would be only a few degrees less absurd. Its tendency is assuredly both to give and to secure to the agricultural classes the possession of competence, but its influence may be counteracted by numberless opposing causes. Men are not mere machines, to take invariably the course prescribed for them; self-will is sometimes more than a match for self-interest, and, even if they were willing to be guided by prudence, they could not always provide against extraordinary accidents. Instances, no doubt, occur of a peasant's sons who will not acknowledge the necessity of selling their little patrimony, and who, persisting in their efforts to gain a living, each from the patch of ground which has fallen to his share, have to struggle desperately for subsistence. But in opposition to such acts of folly are to be set cases of more than ordinary thrift and foresight, which counteract the effects of the former, and maintain undiminished the proportion of the prosperous to the unfortunate. The examples of poverty, however, are not all isolated. Both in France and in some parts of Germany,

---

[60] Passy, *Systemes de Culture*, pp. 118, 119.

the peasantry of entire villages are sometimes reduced to severe and long-continued distress. The causes of their misfortunes are probably somewhat different in every instance, and cannot be precisely determined without a knowledge of many local circumstances, but a reasonable conjecture may be hazarded as to their most usual character. When the cultivators are only tenant-farmers, their embarrassment may arise from a fall in the market price of their produce. If, in England, the cheapness consequent on an abundant harvest is invariably accompanied by a cry of "agricultural distress," and if English landlords, making a virtue of necessity, are frequently obliged to take the praises of the county newspapers in payment of their irrecoverable dues, it is not very wonderful if something of the same kind should sometimes occur in France, and if there also arrears of rent should occasionally remain long unpaid. It may be thought, however, that cultivators of their own lands should be comparatively unaffected by fluctuations of the market; that, selling no more of their produce than what remains after their own consumption is satisfied, they should at all times be equally well supplied with the necessaries of life, and should suffer from no other deficiency than that of the less indispensable articles which they are obliged to buy. But, besides that many of the so-called peasant proprietors of France have not completed the purchase of their property, and are more properly tenants at a fixed rent, they frequently employ only a small portion of their farms in raising provisions. Notwithstanding the superior productiveness of their mode of husbandry when applied to grain or to esculent vegetables, their superiority over larger farmers is shown still more decisively in crops requiring more minute and constant attention. In many districts they find it most profitable to cultivate hemp, or flax, or hops; in others their chief dependence is on their vineyards, or orchards, or plantations of olive or mulberry trees. The crops thus obtained are more valuable than corn or roots, but they are also more liable to failure, and the demand for them is much more irregular. The proprietor must sell in order to buy necessaries, and, if unfavorable weather have lessened the quantity or injured the quality of his produce, or if a change of taste or fashion, or a superabundant supply, or an alteration of custom-house regulations have lowered the price, the money he obtains may be insufficient for his wants, and he may be compelled to borrow in order to live. A succession of bad seasons will plunge him deeper and deeper into difficulties, and a continuance of the causes which have lowered prices may ruin him irrecoverably. Many owners of small vineyards in the neighborhood of Paris have suffered much within the last thirty years from the competition of the vine-growers of the south; owing probably to some similar cause, some of the smaller proprietors in the *arrondissement* of Fougères are obliged to borrow seed for sowing their fields; and, since the accession of Nassau to the Zollverein,[61] and the consequent abolition of the monopoly they formerly enjoyed, some of the inhabitants of at least one village in that Duchy have been compelled to surrender their lands to their creditors.[62] But would these disasters have been escaped by larger farmers similarly situated, or would not they have been equally affected by a permanent depreciation of their produce? Their losses might not indeed have been so extensively felt. When they ceased to fulfill their engagements to their landlords, they would have been removed to make way for fresh tenants at reduced rents, who might have continued to employ as many laborers as their predecessors; whereas, where properties are much divided, the owners are themselves both farmers and laborers, and their misfortunes are those of the whole agricultural body. But this does not prove that peasants are necessarily more secure as hired servants than as proprietors. It proves only, if it proves anything, that they should not trust to the sale of their produce for the means of subsistence, but should raise their own provisions; but it would be difficult to show why this obligation should be imposed upon them more than

---

[61] [The Zollverein was a Northern German customs union established in 1818 that eventually provided the foundation for German unification under Prussia in 1871.]

[62] Passy, *Systemes de Culture*, pp. 72-75; Bertiru Notice sur la Baronie, *etc.* de Fougères, p. 336.

upon artisans and handicraftsmen, and the multitudes of other laborers who live by the sale of their work.

The foregoing pages were written before the publication of the "Treatise on Succession to Property," by Mr. Macculloch, who, in the Chapter on Compulsory Partition, treats at some length of peasant proprietors, and particularly of those of France. What he there says on the subject (though he avails himself of the opportunity to retract or modify one or two of his early opinions) is for the most part a repetition either of statements made in former works by himself, or of the fallacies of Messrs. Mounier and Rubichon, and has already been brought before the reader's notice. One of his arguments, however, is sufficiently novel to deserve a distinct examination. It is drawn from the dearth of the year 1846-7, the distress consequent on which was, according to Mr. Macculloch, "wholly confined to the countries in which subdivision has been carried to excess — that is, to Ireland, France, parts of Belgium, and of Rhenish Prussia;" whence it is inferred that, "even in the best years, occupiers of small patches have but little produce to part with; and that, in unfavorable years, they are themselves, as well as those who depend on them for supplies, usually involved in the greatest difficulties."[63] Here premises and conclusion appear to be equally erroneous. The distress of the period referred to was not confined to countries of small farms, nor are the peasantry of such countries peculiarly disqualified for contending with the calamities of adverse seasons. It is true, that during the recent scarcity, England suffered less than some of her neighbors; but it is not true that no countries suffered except those in which land is minutely divided. The dearth extended over almost the whole of Western Europe, from the Baltic and North Seas to the Mediterranean and Atlantic; and from the unexampled price to which bread rose at Lisbon, would seem to have been still more acutely felt in that capital of a kingdom of large farms than at Paris or Brussels. Neither was the comparative exemption of Britain owing to the excellence

---

[63] Macculloch on *Succ. to Prop.* pp. 130, 131.

of her agricultural arrangements; it is to be ascribed entirely to the fact of her having escaped one of the visitations that afflicted her neighbors. In common with them she suffered from the failure of the potato, but the loss in her case was partially compensated by an abundant wheat harvest; whereas, in theirs, it was aggravated by a deficiency of all grain crops, especially of rye. Having thus less to bear she was able to bear it better; but there is no reason to suppose that she would have exhibited greater patience if subjected to the same trial. Whenever on former occasions her wheat crops have actually failed, the peasantry have suffered at least as grievously as those of other countries; and it is indeed difficult to understand how the fact of their being hired laborers, instead of small landowners, should enable them to bear up better against their difficulties. The latter, unless their farms be unusually small, raise in ordinary years more produce than they require for their own consumption, and in bad seasons can, if they please, retain the whole for their own use instead of sending any to market; so that the worst evils of scarcity must be felt, not by themselves but by their customers, the nonagricultural part of the community. Even if their farms be so small as in ordinary years to produce no greater quantity of provisions than they themselves require, their position is still at all times at least as good as that of the hired laborer. If in a bad year they obtain only half a crop, they must place themselves on half rations; but the laborer at the same time receiving his usual wages, would not, on account of the rise of prices, be able to buy more than half his usual allowance of food, nor indeed nearly so much; for, as is well known, the price of provisions always rises much more than in proportion to the deficiency of the supply. The comparative security against want enjoyed by small proprietors and by laborers may be estimated from the degree of their dependence on public charity. Thousands of English laborers are supported during a part of every year at the public expense; and it is the aid which they derive from the poors' rates that prevents them, in periods of distress, from breaking into open violence more frequently than they actually do. The French peasantry, on the other hand, are in general self-dependent; and the interference of the government last year,[64] in order to procure for them additional supplies of food, was a step almost without precedent. What amount of money may have been expended for this purpose is not very generally known; but it was certainly nothing like ten millions sterling, to which sum it must nevertheless have reached in order to correspond with the amount annually expended on the relief of the poor of the much smaller population of England. Yet the condition of peasant proprietors is pronounced to be peculiarly unfortunate, because, on an occasion of extraordinary exigence, such as does not occur once in a century, exertions were required for their relief, very inferior to those which are annually made in a country where peasant proprietors are scarcely known.

Besides, if we had more minute information respecting the distress recently experienced in France, we might very possibly find that among the multitudes fed at the public expense were very few peasant proprietors, and no great number of peasants of any description. It is certain that the sympathies of the government were principally excited by the clamors of the populace of the capital and other large towns, and it is likely enough that in this as in many other instances, Paris and France have been confounded, and that distress has been hastily assumed to be national, which, if analyzed, would have proved to be much more urban than rural. It may be recollected that during the last winter the tranquility of the usually contented and peaceable Channel Islands was partially disturbed, and that food riots took place in Jersey. The rioters were, however, exclusively townspeople, and the greater part of them were laborers on the public works. The peasantry not only took no part in the tumult, but never seemed to suffer anything more than inconvenience from the unusually high price of provisions. Scarcely an instance occurred in any of the islands of the owner of a piece of ground, however small, condescending to apply for parochial relief.

---

[64] 1847.

In one province, however, of one of the countries mentioned by Mr. Macculloch the distress was certainly felt most acutely in the rural districts. In Flanders, it was the very small landholders who suffered most; nor has their distress disappeared with the causes which for awhile aggravated its symptoms. Although the dearth of 1846-7 has been followed by a plentiful harvest, many of the Flemish peasants are still in great want; pauperism and mendicancy are making progress amongst them, and the Belgian legislature has for some time been anxiously debating by what means these plagues can be arrested. Of course, this state of things is triumphantly referred to as corroborating the doctrines of the opponents of peasant proprietorship, although peasant properties cultivated by their owners are in Flanders rather the exception than the rule, and though it does not really deserve to be cited as testimony even against small farming. Under this latter system the Flemings have confessedly flourished for ages, yet no sooner does a calamity befall them, than what had previously been regarded as the source of their prosperity, is pronounced to have occasioned their ruin. For ages, they have lived in competence on small farms, which have been transmitted from generation to generation without diminution of size; yet the occupation of these farms is suddenly discovered to have always contained the germs of pauperism. By those who are unwilling to believe that effects so directly opposite can have proceeded from the same cause, a more reasonable explanation may be easily found. Land has long been more minutely subdivided in Flanders than in other parts of Belgium. Among the farmers properly so called — that is to say, among those holding land sufficient for the occupation and maintenance of a family — are interspersed many smaller occupiers, whose territorial possessions correspond closely with what in England are called cottage allotments; and it is this class whose condition has lately undergone so deplorable a change. But these men could never be properly called husbandmen. Their situation closely resembled that of the rural artisans of Switzerland. The produce of their plots of ground formed only a small part of their means of subsistence; the spade enabled them agreeably to vary their employments, but their chief dependence was on the wheel or loom. Most of them were spinners of thread, or weavers; and, as long as the articles made by them kept up their price, their earnings were sufficient for their decent maintenance; but latterly they have been subjected to a rivalry with which it is in vain to struggle. Their manual labor has had to compete with steam, and has of course been outdone — the factory has been raised at the expense of the cottage. The rural spinners and weavers have thus been deprived of their principal resource; but theirs is evidently a case, not of agricultural, but of manufacturing distress. Their connection with the land may, and no doubt does, alleviate their misery, but cannot in any conceivable manner have helped to produce it. If they had been landless operatives, they must, in losing their occupation, have lost everything. As it is, they are saved from utter destitution by the possession of their plots of land. In either case they must have been reduced to poverty; but it is surely a strange perversion of the truth to impute their ruin to the very cause which prevents it from being complete.[65]

---

[65] So far as Flanders is concerned the distress adverted to in the text arose from temporary causes, and has now (1874) completely disappeared. Taking a walk last summer in the neighborhood of Ypres with a well-known Belgian economist, I inquired how pauperism is provided for in his commune. "There is none," was the reply, "either here or in any of the purely rural communes. Nowhere in Flanders, outside the great towns, will you see a beggar holding out his hand. It is very different in Namur and some of the other provinces." This is quite in accordance with my own subsequent experience.

4. Social Effects of Peasant Proprietorship; The Subject Resumed

Confirmation by M. de Lavergne of views set forth in preceding Chapter — Praises of Peasant Proprietors applicable to such only as till their own lands — No other Landlords so grasping as Peasants who let their land — Tendency of Peasant Proprietorship to lapse into Petty Landlordism — Examination of Colonel Mure's argument to that effect

Except that here and there some slight corrections have been made, a word or two changed, a sentence or two erased or introduced, and a few notes added, the last two chapters have been reprinted as they were originally written. They present what at that time seemed to me to be the entire truth of the case, and what I still believe to be all truth; but I am now aware that some additional remarks must be added to make that truth complete.

In respect to the special phenomena exhibited by France, I have little, if anything, to qualify. M. de Lavergne's valuable work on the Rural Economy of that country[1] was published in 1860,[2] and it is not a little satisfactory to me to find the views I had put forward twelve years previously confirmed as to every essential point by so high an authority. M. de Lavergne[3] shows that French population, instead of advancing with the rapidity apprehended by numerous prophets of evil, slackened its pace very remarkably during the decade immediately subsequent to the latest date to which I had occasion to refer. Between 1815 and 1846 the annual rate of increase had averaged 200,000; from 1847 to 1856 its average was only 60,000.[4] In no less than twelve out of fifteen northeastern

---

[1] [*Économie rurale de la France depuis 1789.*]

[2] [De Lavergne previously published *Essai sur l'Économie Rurale de l'Angleterre, Écosse, et Irlande* in 1854.]

[3] [Louis Gabriel Léonce de Lavergne (1809-1880), French economist, politician and writer.]

[4] *Economic Rurale de la France*, p. 47. A serviceable supplement to M. de Lavergne's treatise is a paper by Mr. Cliffe Leslie on

departments to wit — in Haute-Saone, Meurthe, Bas Rhin, Meuse, Vosges, Jura, Côte d'Or, Yonne, Haute-Marne, Doubs, Ardennes, and Moselle — the number of inhabitants had even decreased within five years, and that, by no less than 212,695, one-fourth of the decrease moreover being due to excess of deaths over births.[5] But indeed it has now become superfluous to insist that no fear was ever more misplaced than that of France becoming a "pauper-warren." Her danger in regard to population is now perceived to be of an opposite character. "La plupart des Normands," says M. de Lavergne, "n'ont pas lu Malthus, mais ils pratiquent instinctivement ses conseils," and it is well understood that a similar remark would be perfectly applicable to the bulk of the French peasantry.

M. de Lavergne does not profess to state with any precision what changes took place, during the decade in question, in the numbers either of the wholes body of landed proprietors, or in the various classes of which that whole body was made up. It is not, however, at all likely that, with a total population so nearly stationary, with so insignificant an addition to the number of persons among whom the land could possibly be divided the landowners could have increased to any extent beyond what the reclamation of land previously waste would fully account for, without help from any supposititious subdivision of land already occupied. M. de Lavergne does, however, point out that, whereas in 1789, out of a total population of 26,500,000, 20,500,000 were rural and only 6,000,000 urban, in 1861 out of a total of 36,000,000, 15,000,000 were urban and no more than 21,000,000 rural,[6] the rural

---

the "Land System of France" in the first series of Cobden Club Essays.

[5] Lavergne, *ut supra*, pp. 174-5. Seven other departments in other parts of France are mentioned, which had lost altogether 257,627 inhabitants between 1790 and 1856, but whether any part of this loss took place within the last ten years is not stated.

[6] In one place M. de Lavergne, after giving 50,000 as the number of large proprietors in 1861, and 500,000 as that of the middling-sized, reckons the small proprietors at no less than 5,000,000,

population having thus remained nearly stationary for 70 years. He bears witness, too, to the accelerated improvement, due mainly to the simultaneously increasing productiveness of the soil, which, during the latter portion of the same period, had been going on in the material condition of the cultivators, and calculates that of the 100 percent, added to the wages of agricultural laborers between 1789 and 1856,[7] 80 percent, were added subsequently to 1815.[8] Also he adverts to a cause which for some years past has sensibly checked the sale of rural estates, and which is likely to have henceforward more and more influence of the same kind the recently awakened willingness of the country people to invest their savings in the public funds and railway and other stocks. Together with the incalculable evil of Louis Napoleon's sway, there will have been some enduring good if, by his ingenious expedient of *emprunts nationaux*, he shall have taught the French peasantry other uses for their spare francs besides that of tempting their neighbors to part with strips of their petty patrimonies.

Apart, however, from any special reference to France, the credit given to peasant proprietorship in general, requires some not unimportant qualifications. Even that particular virtue which most frequently accompanies such proprietorship, is not its invariable characteristic.

---

and seems to admit that they had increased in number by 1,200,000 since 1815 (pp. 49-51). I suspect, however, that this must have been a slip of the pen on his part; for the statement, independent of other objections to it, is irreconcilable with the following on page 454. "500,000 fermiers avec leurs familles, 500,000 metayers, 2,000,000 de journaliers et domestiques, les une et les autres petits proprietaires pour la plupart, avec 2,000,000 de proprietaires ruraux independands, telle est à peu près la decomposition de notre population rurale." The million of fermiers and metayers had previously been described as tenants of a "million d'exploitations" belonging to the large and middling landowners, so that, these tenants being abstracted, there would remain less than 4,000,000 of landowners of every degree, large and small.

[7] Lavergne, *ut supra*, pp. 417 and 420.

[8] *Ut supra*, p. 58.

"Wealth," M. de Lavergne remarks, "as well as poverty, is contagious," and so too are the industry which alone can create the one and the laziness which, in husbandry at least, has commonly the other for its punishment. A man who, tilling his own fields, is his own employer, and is assured of having for his own use the whole fruit of his labor, has the strongest possible incentive to exertion; still, if the majority of his neighbors are in the habit of taking things easily, he is only too likely to follow their example, while no one can be reasonably expected to trouble himself to raise more produce than he expects to find demand for. Perhaps it may be for the first of these reasons that the few isolated specimens still to be found in our midland and southern counties of the old yeoman class — men tilling and living upon their own three or four scores of ancestral acres — often contrast rather unfavorably than otherwise with the tenant-at-will farmers with whom they are intermingled. It is not in human nature for these latter to take extraordinary pains in order to suggest to their landlord the expediency of raising their rents; and it is the practice of these which the yeoman adopts as his industrial standard, while ambition to play the part of a squireen[9] is apt to prevent his acting very steadily even up to that. It may have been for the second reason that Wordsworth, in the pleasing picture he has drawn of the "statesmen" of Cumberland and Westmorland, was unable to add to the other praises he has bestowed on his favorite peasantry, that of model cultivators.

Besides, no one of the praises passed upon peasant proprietors must be understood to be applicable except on one obvious condition, that, namely, of the peasants being themselves the cultivators of the fields they own. Peasants who let their land to be cultivated by others are, of all landlords, the most griping. Their one object in that capacity is to obtain the highest possible rent; and they never hesitate to accept the utmost that competition causes to be offered, unless from doubt whether the of-

---

[9] ["Little squire," a pejorative term in Ireland signifying a small landowner or tenant who gives himself airs above his station.]

ferer may be able to pay. They have nothing of the sense of patronage which, in England, is invariably felt by hereditary owners, and, even by recent purchasers, of extensive domains; nothing of the intelligent self-interest or kindly sympathy by which these are so often prompted to cooperate with their farmers in costly improvements, or to build model cottages for laborers, or to contribute largely to schools for the village children. They are themselves of the same social class as the cultivators who hold of them; their dealings with these are regarded by them purely as matters of business, and they have no more notion of letting their lands for a farthing less than can be screwed out of the tenants, than the tenants have of taking less than the market price for their milk and butter. Neither, if they had any taste for such liberality would they fancy themselves able to afford to indulge it; for, with them as with other people, to live is the prime necessity, and the rent of a score or so of acres, however high the rate, is not much to live upon. Every penny is of consequence, and accordingly every obtainable penny is sternly exacted. Anything but satisfactory, therefore, is the condition of the actually cultivating class, wherever, on the one hand, landed property is minutely divided, and, on the other, is not occupied by its owners. Such is the case throughout Flanders generally, and more especially in the Pays de Waes; and quite saddening are some of the details given by M. de Laveleye with respect to Flemish tenant farmers. Rents, according to official statistics, increased, between 1830 and 1846, 21 percent, in Western, and 30 percent, in Eastern, Flanders; and the augmentation, instead of slackening, became accelerated between 1846 and 1860, so that the total average rise was 40 percent, in thirty years, although during the same period corn advanced in price only 3 percent. And still the rise of rent goes on; the certainty of its taking place every ninth year, at the expiration of the lease, meanwhile filling the farmer with anxiety and poisoning his existence. By continual sacrifices and unintermitted toil he has almost doubled, within the space of a single generation, the net produce of his fields; but it is only very transitorily indeed that he is permitted to benefit by the additional fertility he has created, the effect of which, so far as he is concerned, speedily becomes simply an enhancement of the demands upon him. So he distrusts everyone who asks him for information on the state of agriculture, and replies with reluctance to questions on the subject, dissembling the productiveness he has contrived to communicate to the soil, for fear of its being discovered that the farm which his management has so much improved, can in consequence bear a proportionably heavier rent.[10]

Is there, then, inherent in peasant proprietorship any tendency to degenerate into this worst and most offensive form of landlordism? Colonel Mure,[11] in some able letters addressed by him to the Editor of the *Times*,[12] has forcibly contended that there is. He sees a glaring example of such degeneracy in Flanders, and he considers the same result inevitable in every country having its land parceled out among a multitude of small owners, and being at the same time subject to the law of equal division of property among the children of a deceased owner. He argues that, "in such circumstances, as generations succeed each other, and population increases, and with it competition, the proprietor finding it impossible without excessive labor to extract from the land a fair return for his capital, and unable to resist the temptation of high offers, soon learns to prefer the ease and petty power of the landlord to the toil of the husbandman." If I thought Colonel Mure right in this view, I should at once throw up my brief; peasant proprietorship should have no advocate in me. It would, in my eyes, be no compensation for the evil of a system which condemned the bulk of the agricultural population to such sorry fare as black bread and potatoes, that it caused twice as much milk and butter as would be forthcoming under another system, to be supplied for the nourishment of the rest of the community. Whenever the

---

[10] Laveleye. *Économie Rurale de la Belgique*, pp. 71 and 72, also 233, c. 8.

[11] [William Mure of Caldwell (1830-1880), British soldier (Lieutenant-Colonel in the Scots Fusilier Guards) and Liberal Party politician.]

[12] In December, 1869, and January, 1870.

laborer is worthy of his hire, it is plainly desirable that the hire should be worthy of the laborer, particularly when the labor to be recompensed is agricultural, upon which, as its basis, rests whatever of comfort or luxury any class enjoys. But, in order to be able to agree with Colonel Mure, it is necessary to look nowhere but in the direction in which he points. In the Channel Islands, in France, in Switzerland, in the Rhenish Provinces of Germany, nay, even in Belgium elsewhere than Flanders, we shall not find that any large proportion of the petty landholders are village shopkeepers, or attorneys, or the like. The vast majority are their own tenants, occupying and tilling their own fields; and, so far from finding it impossible without labor more "excessive than formerly to extract from the land a fair return for their capital," finding, on the contrary, that "as population increases," and with it the price of every kind of produce, the reward of their labor likewise goes on increasing, and with it the inducement to continue tilling their land instead of selling it. To make Flanders an exception to this general description some special influences must of course have been at work, and it is not very difficult to conjecture what they were. From the earliest times the Flemish peasantry have been accustomed to combine industrial pursuits with husbandry. As defined by the English chroniclers of the twelfth and thirteenth centuries — who saw their sovereigns bringing over colonists from Flanders to settle on their domains — every cultivator of that country was a man knowing how to make cloth and to handle arms.[13] In regard to cloth many of them do so still, though the majority of weavers are now congregated in villages; almost every one of them, however, hiring, if not owning, a few perches, at least, of garden ground. To villagers of this sort who had prospered in their various callings, land might naturally seem the most suitable bank wherein to invest their savings, and thus may have arisen those petty non-resident landlords with whom the Pays de Waes unhappily swarms. But men's notions on the subject of

---

[13] Laveleye. *Econ. Rurale de la Belgique*, p. 13.

investment will no doubt ere long change in Belgium, in the same manner and for the same reasons as M. de Lavergne informs us they are already changing in France; and, whenever it becomes generally understood that the highest rack-rents realizable from land are lower than dividends from funded and other equally good securities, a general transfer of petty freeholds may be expected to take place, from burghers who are not themselves disposed to cultivate, to peasants who are.

5. Moral Effects of Peasant Proprietorship[1]

Honesty, Sobriety, and Loyalty of Small Proprietors — Their Educational Advantages — Excessive Parsimony and Bigotry — Means of Correcting these Defects[2] — Cruelty to Animals involved in the most approved mode of Peasant Farming[3]

Unless the preceding pages have been written in vain, peasant proprietors may now, perhaps, be acknowledged to deserve the praise of industry and foresight; but, to complete their portraiture, others of their characteristics must be mentioned, and (since even they are not altogether faultless monsters) some defects as well as excellencies must be included in the list. Among the latter, honesty, sobriety, and loyalty, duly combined with independence of spirit, are preeminent, as might indeed have been expected, for circumstances could scarcely be more favorable to the development of those virtues. Honesty, in the most common if not the most exalted acceptation of the term, signifies little more than respect for the rights of property, and none are so likely to pay such respect as those who have property of their own which they wish to see respected. Where there is no feeling there cannot well be sympathy. An Arab meeting you in the desert will bid you undress, because your aunt (his mother) is without a garment, and because so dutiful a son as himself is, of course, little better provided. If he had been accustomed to wear good clothes, he would be more scrupulous about stripping a cousin so unceremoniously. Nowhere does the national reputation for probity stand higher than in England, and nowhere is it better deserved. Among so commercial a people mutual confidence is indispensable; the quality on which alone confidence can securely rest has (in nice accordance with the principles of political econ-

---

[1] [Chapter 4 in the 1848 edition.]

[2] ["these Defects" formerly "the Defects of their Character," 1848.]

[3] ["Cruelty to Animals involved in the most approved mode of Peasant Farming" added to the 1874 edition.]

omy) come forward to meet the demand, and the puritanical spirit which still influences us so strongly, both for good and evil, has helped to strengthen and foster it. But, although certainly one of our national virtues, honesty is no longer a characteristic of the poorest classes of our countrymen. Take a rustic, for example — a man working at fourteen or fifteen pence a day, and himself the son of a day laborer, not more liberally remunerated. Perhaps he has received some sort of education, and at a National or Sunday school may have been made acquainted with the Divine commandment against stealing. He does not presume to dispute the authority of the precept, but he is not convinced of its justice. It meets with no echo in his breast. Why should he not steal? He may be answered that he should do to others as he would have them do to him; but he has himself no fear of being robbed, for he has nothing worth taking, and, having scarcely ever experienced the feelings of ownership, he cannot readily understand them or the pain occasioned by their violation. The law offers him nothing, save a protection which he does not require, while it forbids him from benefiting at other people's expense. He is strongly tempted, therefore, to evade it whenever he can do so with impunity. He is too closely watched to have many opportunities of the kind, but he is likely to avail himself of such as occur. He will break down fences for firewood, take tithes of all fruit-trees within his reach, and appropriate to his own use whatever waifs and strays may come across his path. These are trifles; but as straws show how a stream flows, trifles will serve well enough to mark a man's disposition, and to declare whither it would urge him if freed from restraint. English field laborers are probably understood by none better than by their own employers, and what the latter think of them may be inferred from one of the most common objections to cottage allotments, which farmers are opposed to, because, they say, it would be impossible to distinguish between the produce which an allotment-holder had raised and that which he had plundered. It is far otherwise in countries in which the same persons are cultivators and owners of the soil. A peasant proprietor may be said to feel, as well as to understand, his moral obligations. His anxiety to preserve his own rights from invasion informs him that his neighbors are similarly solicitous, and he knows that unless he abstains from molesting them, he cannot reckon upon their forbearance. He teaches his children the same wholesome lessons. In England, if you catch an urchin in your garden filling his pockets with apples and pears, you may perhaps box his ears before dismissing him; but your choler will have been excited principally by a sense of personal injury, for the offence is of too common occurrence to move your indignation very greatly by its intrinsic turpitude. It may possibly remind you of some events of your own schoolboy days, and that "boys will be boys," may be the most serious of your moral reflections. But in France and Germany, the fruit on the wayside trees is left untouched by boys and beggars, and, in the Channel Islands, many a tempting orchard is not much more effectually barricaded than used to be those of Cimon the Athenian. In the same islands, what robberies take place are for the most part committed by strangers, the purer natives being very rarely in fault. Of 2,107 offenders of all descriptions tried in Jersey, in the ten years ending with 1845, only 670 were natives of that or the neighboring islands, 1,264 were English, Scotch, or Irish, and 173 foreigners.[4] Distribute the tenth part of 670 among a population of 33,000, and there will be annually but two offences cognizable by a court of justice for every thousand of the native inhabitants.

Mr. Macculloch employs a somewhat arbitrary process in order to convict small farmers of dissipated habits. They cannot, he argues, have full occupation at home, nor can they obtain employment from their neighbors; they must consequently, perforce, be often idle, and, as

"Satan finds some mischief still
For idle hands to do,"

---

[4] Report on the Criminal Laws of Jersey, by the Commissioners, Messrs. Ellis and Bros.

they must, from sheer listlessness, have frequent recourse to the bottle, when a train of consequences will ensue which only the pencil of a Cruikshank[5] can adequately delineate. To be sure, a man who must work with his own hands for his living and yet wastes half his time, cannot well have a vast sum from his earnings to spare for liquor; but this is treated as only a slight impediment to the indulgence of his propensity. "The small farmer," we are told, "must have his porter and gin, as well as the extensive farmer," and need not be prevented by emptiness of purse from drinking as becomes his rank. "The want of time and opportunity," it seems, "still more than the want of money, prevents a hired laborer from aping the conduct of his employers;" but a small farmer, however penniless, has at least time enough at his disposal, and can therefore get as drunk as a lord whenever he pleases.[6]

Here is a curious tissue of gratuitous assumptions. It is first decided that small farmers have not have enough to do; next, that forced inactivity makes them lazy; and finally, that they while away their hours of idleness by getting drunk; whereas, in reality, they are the most hard-working of mortals, and having no unoccupied leisure, have no need to resort to the pastime so considerately proposed for them. In their fields and gardens, their out-houses, looms or workshops, they find wherewithal to fill every vacant minute, whether in summer or winter, and idleness offers them neither temptation nor excuse for dissipation. Not that their sobriety is without merit, as being the result of necessity. Provided they hold their land by a secure tenure, incessant diligence commonly rewards them with the competence they deserve; and, busy as they are, they could, no doubt, if so disposed, steal a minute now and then to take a dram; but they value money too highly to squander it on intemperance, either in meat or drink. Their fault is rather to be too sparing in

---

[5] [George Cruikshank (1792-1878), British caricaturist. Noted for the illustrating the works of his friend, Charles Dickens.]
[6] Compare *Statistical account of British Empire*, vol. i. p. 451; and *Encyclop. Brit.*, vol. vii. p. 389.

their diet. What most frequently sends a man to the ale-house is the discomfort of his home. The ill-paid day laborer flies from his dreary hovel and the wan looks of his wife and children, to his snug seat in the chimney-corner of the inn parlor, and the merriment of his boon companions; but the peasant proprietor, or leaseholder, has a blazing hearth and a neat parlor of his own, and sitting there, with his family about him, has no wish for a change of scene or company. That a British writer should impute habits of intoxication to small occupiers of land is the more extraordinary as no peasantry on earth are so strongly addicted to the vice as the landless laborers of his own country. The French *paysan* or German *bauer* can spend a holiday in dancing and singing, and yet return from the village wake as decorously as he went to it; but, with an English rustic, festivity and beer-swilling are synonymous terms. And the system which has so degraded the descendants of the "noble yeomanry," once "the honor and strength of England," is held up for admiration!

It is wonderful how long a time must elapse before changes in national characteristics are generally acknowledged. Yeomanry, as a class, have long been almost entirely rooted out from amongst us; but they are spoken of as familiarly at agricultural dinners as if they were still as numerous as ever. We walk between two lines of hovels scarcely good enough for cows of any tenderness of nurture, and we are called upon to admire the convenience and beauty of English cottages, by an imaginative companion whose thoughts have strayed from the objects before him to the "peasant nest" and picturesque huts,

"All hidden in a sylvan gloom, some perched
On verdant slopes from the low coppice cleared,"[7]

---

[7] [This may be a quote from "An Evening in Furness Abbey" by John Wilson of Ellerey (1785-1854), Scottish lawyer, literary critic, author and professor of moral philosophy at Edinburgh University (1820-1851). This is not certain — Thornton appears to have lifted the quote from William Howitt, *The Rural Life of England*. London: Longman, Orme, Brown, Green & Longmans, 1840, 411, an overly maudlin, if not saccharine panegyric on

described by Cowper and Wilson. So, likewise our agricultural laborers are occasionally eulogized for their proud self-reliance and frankness of demeanor, just as if they still held it disgraceful to accept parish relief, or could always by their own exertions avoid that shameful necessity. In times past, when none who chose to work were in danger of want, they were indeed distinguished by the qualities referred to; which, however, it would be too much to expect from men who must receive as a favor employment at eight or nine shillings a week who have little or no work in the winter, and no substitute for it — no cow, no pig, no garden stuff — whose present subject of anxiety is the difficulty of obtaining outdoor relief, and whose future prospect is that of ending their days in the workhouse. Independence of spirit and manner cannot reasonably be sought except among those who are assured of a livelihood, and no peasantry have such just ground for confidence on that score as those who cultivate their own lands. Deriving their support from their own resources, they can indulge in the pride of self-dependence, and scorn the idea of owing their subsistence to charity. Neither desiring the favor nor fearing the enmity of their richer neighbors, they can accost them without servility. Not that the possession of property, in giving them independence, renders them insubordinate; while it permits them to respect themselves, it teaches them also to respect the laws.

A mere day laborer, half-employed, and wretchedly paid, who is compelled to apply to the neighboring landholders for a livelihood, and obtains from them only a miserable subsistence, not unnaturally regards his employers as oppressors, takes every opportunity of showing his spite against them by wanton aggressions, and is ever ready to listen to the harangues of seditious demagogues, But a peasant proprietor has no such cause for envy or animosity against the owners of larger estates, but is rather disposed to join with them in repelling any attack

English country life in the chapter titled "Cottage Life," and the attribution, buried under a layer of purple prose, is unclear.]

on their common rights; he is deeply interested in the preservation of tranquility, and proportionably fearful of civil convulsions, in which he might lose his all. He molests no one who does not molest him; and, as for politics, provided neither his privilege? nor his prejudices be attacked, he cheerfully leaves them to those who have more taste and capacity for their discussion. Throughout western Europe, from the Polar to the Mediterranean seas, wherever there are peasant proprietors there likewise is an orderly and loyal rural population. In the Channel Islands, Norway, Belgium, Switzerland, and Germany, there are no rick-burners, no breakers of thrashing machines, no riots among the country people, and no secret disaffection. The peasantry are thriving and content, and sincerely attached to the laws under which they enjoy so much happiness. Even France presents no exception to the truth of this remark. Popular outbreaks are certainly of frequent occurrence there, but they do not take place in the rural districts. The glories of the last Revolution,[8] and the glory or the shame of the many subsequent attempts to imitate it, belong not to France, but to Paris; and within the capital and a few more of the principal towns the revolutionary spirit is almost exclusively confined. The French peasant "is no politician; he leaves it to the inhabitants of cities to settle state affairs. He receives, indeed, with goodwill the blessings of political freedom when they are tendered to him, and congratulates himself upon being '*un Français*' but such matters do not occupy his mind, and, if the question were whether he should attend a political meeting or a village festival, he would stick a nosegay in his breast, and a ribbon in his hat, and seek the village green."[9] The countryman whom Inglis questioned on the subject, no doubt spoke the sentiments of his class when he said, that "all governments were alike to him so that they kept at peace, and allowed him to live at home."[10]

---

[8] When this was written, the last Revolution was that of 1830.

[9] Inglis, *Switzerland and South of France*, vol. ii. p. 271.

[10] *Ibid.* p. 286.

Among the incidental advantages possessed by small proprietors, should be mentioned one enjoyed by them in common with small tenant farmers and allotment holders, *viz.*, the facilities which their social situation affords for the moral and technical training of their children. The latter, instead of being suffered to run wild, or instead of being locked up to keep them out of harm's way, are almost constantly under the eyes of their parents. They follow their father to his work, and think it as good as play to perform the light tasks he assigns them. Gardening, and the care of poultry and animals, favorite occupations with all children, afford them at once exercise and amusement, and afford also uses for offal and other refuse which would otherwise have been thrown away; and these pursuits are not the less cheerfully followed because they are perceived to be profitable, to lighten the common toils and to increase the common stores. The girls, besides, help their mother indoors, and in the same pleasant and unconscious manner are initiated into the mysteries of housekeeping, and taught the important secret how to make home happy. Such constant cooperation of all the members of a family tightens the bonds of affection and promotes domestic harmony, and more directly favors the adoption of early habits of industry and frugality, and imparts early instruction in those particular kinds of information which are most likely to be practically useful in after life. Perhaps I should be accused of riding my hobby [horse] too hard if I were to add, that the importance of this domestic education is strikingly exemplified in domestic servants, who were certainly not quite so universally regarded as "the greatest plague in life," when the class from which they are chiefly taken consisted not of mere hired laborers, whether agricultural or manufacturing, but of persons who partook more or less of the character of cottage farmers.

Perfection is unattainable on earth, and peasant proprietorship, like everything else of human institution, has its dark side; but it was not, perhaps, to be expected that its most usual defects should be those least consistent with its acknowledged excellences. Extremes, however, meet, and virtues, carried to excess, run into the opposite vices; and thus it is that the frugality of small proprietors, though the firmest support of their independence, not unfrequently passes into meanness, and sometimes even oversteps the barrier of honesty. The habit of saving by long practice becomes a pleasure, and finally a passion, not over-scrupulous about the means adopted for its gratification. The Jersey peasantry (differing in this, far as the poles asunder, from their countrymen of higher rank) are said to be so far inhospitable as to be unwilling to give anything, however trifling, to a stranger without payment; and, according to Inglis, although generally far above stealing and incapable of a breach of truth, they are not proof against the temptation of overreaching in a bargain. The same ubiquitous traveler tells us how, while walking from Lachen to Glarus, he was beset by beggars in the shape of children, who left their play to assume the whining tone of practiced mendicants, while their parents stood by encouraging them to ask for alms which they did not need; and how, in some parts of the Grisons, "where the inhabitants are accustomed to see strangers, you cannot pass a hamlet without being assailed by children, while the parents, richer, perhaps, than you are, stand at the door with an air of Grison independence."[11] He adds some anecdotes of the petty frauds practiced upon him, in explanation (not, of course, in extenuation) of which it may however be mentioned that peasant proprietors are still more prone to impose on themselves than on others, often cheating themselves even of their just allowance of food. Whatever be their pecuniary circumstances they very frequently condemn themselves to Lenten fare. Those of Norway, Belgium, and Switzerland, are exceptions to the rule; but in Jersey, even the better sort of farmers do not, or at least till within the last twenty years, did not, use meat except as an occasional luxury; their standing dish was a soup made of cabbage, lard, and potatoes, and this, with bread and butter, furnished the material of every meal. The German *bauers* also live

---

[11] Inglis, *Switzerland*, vol. i. pp. 63, 139.

chiefly on soups and puddings, and so likewise do the French. Now, mere abstinence from meat would be by no means remarkable, for meat neither is nor can be much used by the working classes of any thickly peopled territory, nor is it indispensable to the attainment of the highest degree of bodily vigor, for nowhere can more athletic frames be found than those fed with maize and milk in the Tyrol, or with potatoes and milk in some of the least wretched parts of Ireland. Provided the diet of a people be sufficiently plentiful and nourishing, it does not very much matter of what it is composed. But the peasantry of some of the countries referred to above are so much more careful of their pockets than their stomachs that they stint the latter even to the injury of their health and strength. Physicians attribute to low diet the prevalence both of dyspepsia and rheumatism among the country people of the Channel Islands. Inglis, who had often inspected the flower of the Jerseymen while going through their militia exercises, says he saw few fine, well-grown forms amongst them, and no one who has crossed the straits of Dover can have failed to notice within what diminutive bodies are compressed the gigantic souls of the French soldiers. This is a matter of national concernment. "La destinée des nations," says the author of the *Physiologic du Gout*, "dépend de la manière dont elles se nourissent;" and a philosophic eye might perhaps, distinguish, in the combats of Agincourt and Waterloo, a conflict of adverse principles the triumph of fibrin over gelatine and ozmazome of roast beef over frogs and *soupe maigre*. If peasant proprietors always restricted themselves to hermit's fare, they would not only pay too dearly for the advantages of their position, but would always be in danger of being deprived of them by such of their neighbors as used a more generous diet. One of those resolute theorists who are never at a loss for facts to suit their purpose, goes so far as to affirm that subjection to a foreign yoke has been their lot in all ages. Nations *à petite culture* (small cultivators), says M. Tapies, have always been invaded and conquered by nations *à grande culture* (large cultivators); a remark which needs no other reply than an expression of astonishment that it should have been made by a countryman of the small cultivators who, within living memory, overran two-thirds of continental Europe. It cannot be denied that peasant proprietors do, in certain circumstances, become excessively penurious, but only, it should seem, when no examples of liberality are placed before them. Left to themselves, they contract niggardly habits; but intercourse with the classes above them appears to cure them of those defects. In England, people of all ranks have always been famous for their love of good cheer, and the peasantry, as long as the possession of land gave them the means of indulging their tastes, were not less celebrated as trenchermen than their betters. The reason of this was, that in England the gentry, instead of congregating in towns as in most continental countries, resided on their estates, and keeping open house and a plentiful table, set an example of profusion which was imitated by their inferiors according to their ability. It may be worth mentioning that in Guernsey, the smaller of the two principal Channel Islands, and the one in which the residences of the rich are most scattered, extreme parsimony is much less frequent among the laboring class than in Jersey, and the mode of living is more expensive. Even in Jersey, the fare of the country people has sensibly improved since the formation of good roads and the progress of commerce have brought them into more frequent communication with the inhabitants of the town.

Most of the other failings with which peasant proprietors, as such, are sometimes justly chargeable, seem to proceed from the same source as their inordinate parsimony. Ignorant self-sufficiency, coarseness of mind, and rudeness of manner, are natural to those whose days are spent in incessant bodily labor, and who are cut off from intercourse with classes enjoying more leisure and more abundant means for intellectual cultivation. Wherever, as in the greater part of Germany, the gentry live entirely in towns, and abandon the rural districts to a laboring peasantry, the latter, seeing none superior to themselves, form their standard of excellence from their own practice, to which they become absurdly bigoted, while they conceive a stupid prejudice against all customs which differ from their own. Wholly absorbed in material cares, they remain in ignorance of the higher gratifications of which man is capable; they cannot aim at elegance and refinement of which they have no examples, nor sympathize with sensibilities which they do not understand; they continue through life plodding and dull, and their demeanor answers to the obtuseness of their nature. Education by itself is not calculated to have much effect in humanizing them. They may have been taught to read, but they have little time and less inclination for availing themselves of the acquirement. In their brief intervals of leisure they are too much exhausted by toil to seek for recreation in intellectual exertion. The civilization of the lower orders of society can scarcely originate amongst themselves, but must rather descend from the ranks above. The rich are too often unmindful of their duties, but they have an important office to discharge. To them it belongs to encourage science, literature, and art, to diffuse the blessings of knowledge, to exhibit in their own persons the advantages of mental cultivation, and to set examples of intelligence, delicacy, liberality, and good taste. These are their peculiar functions, the discharge of which is scarcely less necessary for the attainment of the legitimate objects of human society than the performance of the labors by which it is fed and clothed; but the fulfillment of these duties is impossible unless the rich are intermixed with the other classes, and if a class so numerous as the agricultural is isolated from the rest, and consists wholly of members who must work with their own hands. But this is an arrangement of society very different from that which it is the object of these pages to recommend. By the preceding vindication of small farmers and small proprietors, it was not implied that all farms and all estates should be small. Very little reflection will show that disparity of ranks and fortunes is essential to the welfare of mankind. If a community in which there are many indigent cannot properly be called happy, the happiness of a community in which there are none rich enough to command and to avail themselves of leisure, cannot be of a much more exalted character than that of cattle. To secure the welfare of agricultural laborers it seems indispensable that they should not be entirely dependent on the hire of their services, but should be owners or tenants of pieces of land sufficient to afford them occupation and subsistence when they cannot procure employment elsewhere. It is also desirable, at least, that of the holdings large enough to be entitled farms some should be small enough to lie within reach of a mere laborer's ambition, and stimulate him to exertion by offering him hopes of rising above, his actual station. But it is not less desirable that there should also be many farms so extensive as to require the superintendence of men of considerable wealth and proportionate instruction, who would avail themselves of the discoveries of science, and effect improvements in agriculture, and would also serve as models for their humbler neighbors in their modes of life and general habits of thinking, as well as in the conduct of their business. All peasants should be landholders, but all landholders should not be peasants. In the agricultural, as in all other classes, the interests of the members would be best promoted by a just gradation of ranks.[12]

A moral blemish not yet adverted to, but much too serious to be left unnoticed, is the cruelty to animals involved in the species of husbandry in vogue on the best managed small farms. The reproach hereby implied does not indeed attach exclusively to small farmers; on the contrary, none are more obnoxious to it than the agricultural magnates in this and other countries under whose auspices high farming has been carried to the loftiest pitch and widest extension. Our own most eminent stockbreeders have almost ceased to be graziers. When going over their premises, you see little or no pasture, and look in vain for the comely, many-hued cattle, whose diffusion over the flowery meads imparts to the ordinary English landscape one of its most characteristic charms. On asking what has be-

---

[12] Part of this paragraph has been ludicrously falsified by time, and the remainder but ill expresses my present sentiments. I have, however, left the whole standing for the sake of its possible historical value as a specimen of what, a quarter of a century ago, passed for rather advanced thinking.

come of them, you are led into a spacious hall, built usually of open planking, with mats that can be raised or lowered at pleasure for protection against sun, wind, or rain, and with holes in the floor for the droppings of the animals to fall through into a tank below; there are stone troughs full of pure water, and other troughs continually replenished with sliced roots, bruised beans, crushed oil-cakes, chopped hay and straw, barley meal and oatmeal all more or less cooked; there is good ventilation, light enough for seeing, exemplary cleanliness, coolness in summer, warmth in winter; in short, all the arrangements for fabricating milk, meat and manure seem at first sight perfect. Nevertheless, after visiting one of these factories, you are apt, like M. de Lavergne, to feel that you have had your fill of meat for some days to come. For there, each in his narrow stall for ever pent, the poor beasts are doomed to pass their whole existence from the cradle to the grave, never stirring out till marched off to the slaughter and to final entombment in human sarcophagi. It is bad enough to have to reflect — or to have to banish the reflection — that we are by the conditions of our nature condemned to assume the relation of beasts of prey towards so many beasts of the field, insomuch that, if these had minds to speak and tongues to speak them, any moralists among them would be fully warranted in execrating us with all the horror and disgust with which we are accustomed to declaim against man-eating tigers and alligators. And then to think of that habit of the more refined of us, of sentimentalizing over the innocent-looking creatures destined in due season to be served up to us in the guise of quarters of lamb and fillets of veal! Is it not much as if Polyphemus, with the captive Odysseus in his cave, had, before making a meal of a handsome cabin-boy, gone into aesthetic raptures over his soft eyes and delicate complexion? Of course, however, there is no use in rebelling against physical necessity. E'en let us then submit, with as much of reluctance as may be needful for the stilling of our consciences, and resignedly kill and eat, seeing that if we would live, we must at any rate kill, even though we did not eat what we had killed. Still, until the proper season for killing arrive, we may at least abstain from torture, and vouchsafe to the respited lives such alleviations as may be consistent with their primary obligations of subserving human appetites; all the more, leaving to sheep and oxen what emotional enjoyment they are capable of deriving from the balmy air and the sun's light and warmth, because, being but brutes, they are destitute of our rational and imaginative capacities. Granted for argument's sake, that a good deal more meat may be manufactured in prison cells than can be grown naturally under the open sky, and that denser human multitudes may be nourished in consequence, the command on mankind to increase and multiply is not after all so imperative that all other injunctions emanating from the same source must give way to it. Really, to listen to the insolence with which the prerogatives of the lords of creation in respect of the subject races are sometimes asserted, is almost enough to tempt one to wish that the doctrine of metempsychosis could come again into fashion, and so selfishness be enlisted on the side of humanity. For with whomsoever it was an article of faith that there are no bodies into which their own souls might not possibly transmigrate after death with them, also, there would possibly be more scrupulousness as to the sort of experiments they tried on the vilest bodies; they would think twice before sanctioning by example practices of which they might chance to become ere long the subjects, and would grow shy of skinning eels alive, or of thrusting liver complaints down the throats of geese, or of consigning, oxen to durance not many degrees less vile than Caspar Hauser's.[13] In the absence, however, of such moral deterrent, a hygienic apprehension may be suggested as not unlikely to come effectively home to men's business and bellies. If

---

[13] [Caspar or Kaspar Hauser (cir. 1812-1833) was a boy who in 1828 appeared in Nuremberg, Germany, claiming at first to have been raised locked in a private house, and later to have been raised in a dungeon completely isolated from all human contact. Hauser changed his story many times. There were a number of alleged attempts to murder him, all under suspicious circumstances without witnesses. He died of a stabbing that police believed may have been self-inflicted.]

there be one grain of truth in sanitary science, it is manifestly impossible for cattle to keep their health, shut up from birth to death in dusk or darkness, without a solitary whiff of heaven's breath or a glimpse of sunshine to cheer them, with only three square yards to turn in for exercise, and with nothing to do in order to kill time, but to be perpetually gorging their unstinted supplies of unctuous provender. Continuance from generation to generation in such a regimen, cannot but occasion fatty degeneration of heart, liver, and lungs — of every organ and every tissue — vitiating every secretion, and impregnating milk and meat with germs of disease, sure, on transfer to the hotbed of a human stomach, to shoot up forthwith into rankest development. No prophet is needed to warn us that murrain among cattle, pestilence among cattle-eaters, must sooner or later be the result; nay, with a view to the greatest happiness of the greatest number, almost were it to be desired that both epidemics should come at once, and once for all, if so and not otherwise, the surviving men and beasts could obtain for themselves and for posterity, guarantees — these for tolerably humane treatment, those for the wholesomeness of the animal part of their diet.

Perpetual stabling, however, as the practice above inveighed against may be called — *stabulation permanente* being its continental designation — although nowhere else carried to such unmitigated excess as in the establishments of great English agriculturists, is no original device of theirs, but has been borrowed by them from the Flemish peasantry, of whose system it is, indeed, pretty generally esteemed to be a chief excellence and almost essential feature. And, no doubt, it would be impossible for the cultivator of ten or twelve acres to feed four or five kine on the produce of only a moiety of his land, if, instead of growing roots and artificial grasses to be brought to them from the field, he were to let them loose in the field to graze natural herbage. Even of pasture as rich as that of the Vale of Aylesbury, fully three acres would be needed to keep a cow in grass and hay throughout the year; nor, even if she were tethered, according to the

Guernsey custom, instead of being allowed to range over the meadow, could much less than two acres suffice. But although, if cattle are to be kept in a numerical proportion to land at all like that of Flanders, the greater part of their food must be brought to them, it does not follow that it must be brought to them in the stable. No farm in the Pays de Waes, however small, is without an orchard or other patch of grass to which the cattle are led out every morning for an hour's airing; and to tether them there for the best part of the day, with their fodder strewed around, would cost nothing that would not be repaid ten times over by improvement in their condition. If small farmers will not be persuaded that their livestock must have air, light, and a modicum of locomotion, until a good many of the poor beasts sicken for want of those essentials of salubrity, the sooner the sickening takes place the better. Eventually, it cannot fail to come, if practices, so eminently calculated as the one in question to bring it on, be persevered in. No system, agricultural or social, resting on a basis so unnatural as permanent stabulation can permanently endure; and pity 'twere if it could; nor should peasant proprietorship itself receive advocacy in these pages, if it really stood in need of such support.

6. Ireland, Past, Present, and Future, as Viewed in 1848[1]

Wretchedness of the Irish Peasantry — Its Causes —Historical Sketch[2] — Changes required in the Tenure of Land — Necessity of retaining[3] the Small Farm System in Ireland — Examination of various Proposals for improving the Condition of the Irish[4] Laboring Class — Impossibility of providing the Peasantry[5] with adequate Employment except on Small Farms — Plan for the formation of a Proprietary Peasantry on the Waste Lands[6]

Ireland, even more commonly and with more confidence than France, is appealed to as testifying strongly against small farms and small properties. The "cottage system," it is said, has there been tried on a very extensive scale, and has utterly and lamentably failed. Five-sixths of all the farms in the island are less than fifteen acres in extent, and nearly one-half are less than five acres; yet in no part of Europe is agriculture more defective, or the peasantry more idle and thoughtless, or so miserable and ill-disposed. What reply can be made to a statement the truth of which is too notorious to be disputed? Simply, that to Irish farms are wanting certain conditions without which no farms, whether small or great, nor their occupiers, can be expected to flourish. There are no bounds to the tenant's liabilities,[7] and no security against his ejection.[8] That Irish holdings should have been supposed capable of furnishing any argument against peasant proper-

---

[1] [Chapter 5 in 1848; "as Viewed in 1848" added to the 1874 edition.]

[2] ["Historical Sketch" formerly "Sketch of their History," 1848.]

[3] ["retaining" formerly "continuing," 1848.]

[4] ["Irish" added from the 1848 edition.]

[5] ["the Peasantry" formerly "it," 1848.]

[6] ["Conclusion" deleted in the 1874 edition.]

[7] [Similarly, before the Limited Liabilities Act of 1855, shareholders in joint stock companies were individually liable for the debts of the corporation.]

[8] [The "Three Fs" demanded by the Irish National Land League (1879-1881) were "Fair Rent, Fixity of Tenure, and Free Sale."]

ties, is only one among many examples of the profound ignorance which prevails respecting Irish affairs. Ireland is one of the few countries in which there neither are, nor ever were, peasant properties. From the earliest appropriation of the soil down to the present day, estates have always been of considerable size, and though these estates are now cut up into many small holdings, the actual occupiers of the soil, far from being landowners, are not even leaseholders, but are rack-rented tenants-at-will. In this single phrase may be found a complete explanation of all the evils of their condition, and all the defects of their character. They are indolent, because they have no inducement to work after they have obtained from their labor wherewithal to pay their rent, and to save themselves from starvation. Whatever additional produce they might raise, would only subject them to additional exactions. They are careless of the future, because they cannot, by taking thought, improve the gloomy prospects of the morrow; they are reduced to the verge of destitution, because they are permitted to retain no more of the fruits of their labor than will barely suffice for their subsistence; and they set at naught all other laws, divine or human, partly in obedience to the first law of nature, that of self-preservation, and partly because familiarity with misery has rendered them desperate.

Before we proceed further it may be well to inquire how it is that Irish cottiers are unable to make better bargains with their landlords. In other countries in which the property of the soil is not vested in the peasantry, the latter nevertheless obtain possession of it without submitting to terms altogether unreasonable. Even where leases are not granted to them, they do not suffer the landlord to fix his own rent. They will not consent to pay more than they deem the land to be worth, as a means of employing their capital and labor. But in Ireland, they dare not venture to reject any demands, however outrageous. Whatever rent may be asked they readily promise to pay, perfectly heedless whether they shall be able to fulfill engagements which the necessities of their situation leave them no choice but to undertake. In a country in which farms are in general too small to afford employment for hired labor, a peasant has scarcely a chance of being able to gain a livelihood unless he obtain possession of land; and in Ireland, the competitors for land are so numerous that the price paid for the use of it has reached a degree of exorbitancy unheard of elsewhere. Such keen competition clearly shows that population is excessive; that is to say, that the laboring class is too numerous in proportion to the amount of employment for it; but it would be a mistake to regard this redundancy of population as a consequence of the prevalence of small farms. The progress of population has, indeed, been extraordinarily rapid since the period when nearly the whole territory was given up to pasturage, and since the immense grazing farms, by which it was formerly occupied, have been brought under tillage, and divided amongst more than half a million of cottage holdings. But population, in becoming more dense, has not perhaps become much more excessive. Ireland was certainly never before so populous as at present; that is to say, it never before contained so great a number of inhabitants, but it has long, perhaps, been nearly as much over-peopled; that is to say, the number of inhabitants has long been nearly as much disproportioned to the means of subsistence. The prodigious strides which population has made of late years have rendered the destitution of the poor more obvious than before, but it is doubtful whether they have rendered it much more severe. The mass of the people has always been subjected to such extreme privations, that although the number of sufferers is now far greater, the sufferings of individuals have not been much aggravated. A very hasty retrospect may serve to display the grounds for this opinion.

From the earliest times Ireland has been noted for the excellence of its pastures. Its level surface, overspread with the most luxuriant herbage, presented a wide field over which the cattle of the first settlers might freely range, and multiply at an exceedingly rapid rate. Their owners became proportionably wealthy, but the possession of great wealth by individuals implies a corresponding disparity of ranks in the community. The authority of the leader of a tribe may have depended on his personal character or on accidental circumstances, but whatever may have been the political position of the chief with respect to his fellow-herdsmen, the latter, no doubt, exercised almost unlimited power over their servants and dependants. It is, indeed, a recorded fact, that these retainers did, after a while, degenerate into absolute bondsmen, who were attached to the manor on which they dwelt, and, under the name of "betages," were as completely at the disposal of their lords as the serfs of continental Europe. The pastoral occupation of the primitive Irish was not laid aside as soon as they had divided their new country amongst them, and had stationed themselves on particular spots, but continued to be practiced by their descendants for many generations. The principal obstacle to change was, probably, at first, the nature of the climate, which, Mela says, was as unsuitable for grain as it was favorable to the growth of grass;[9] and this was, perhaps, the sole reason why, so late as the twelfth century, the people could still be represented as despising husbandry, and as not having departed from their ancient pastoral mode of life.[10]

When greater intercourse sprang up between them and more civilized nations they might have been taught the advantage of cultivating the soil; but, unfortunately, in the long period of anarchy which succeeded to the conquest by Henry II, the incessant warfare between the English colonists and the natives acted as an effectual bar to agriculture, for both parties thought it wiser to keep their property in the shape of flocks and herds, which could easily be removed to a place of refuge, than in corn stacks or standing crops, which must have been left to the mercy of a successful invader. Cattle thus continued to be the principal produce of the country; so much so, indeed,

---

[9] Pomp. Mela, de Situ Orbis, lib. iii. cap. 6. So likewise the poet Spenser; "A great soyle for cattle, and very fit for breed; as for corne it is nothing natural." View of Ireland.

[10] "Gens agriculture labores aspernans, a primo pastorali vivendi rnodo non recedens," says Giraldus Cambrensis.

that they were often used as a medium of exchange, and that, even in the beginning of the sixteenth century, the Book of Ballymote[11] is said to have been purchased for 140 milch cows,[12] and that in 1595, when Hugh MacMahon[13] wanted to get a promise to be settled on the forfeited estate of his brother, 600 cows was the bribe he offered. Many years later, we find the poet Spenser lamenting that "all men fell to pasturage and none to husbandry," and recommending that an ordinance should be issued to compel every one who kept twenty kine to keep one plow going likewise.[14] It is not likely that agriculture made much progress during the reigns of Elizabeth and of the first two Stuarts, or during the Protectorate, periods marked by the rebellion of the Earls of Tyrone and Tyrconnel, the massacre of the Protestants at the instigation of Roger Moore,[15] the equally bloody invasion of Cromwell and the confiscation of five-sixths of the island; and, if it did, it must have been thrown back as much as ever after the Revolution of 1688, when a twelfth of the land again

---

[11] [A miscellany composed in the late 14th century, named for the parish of Ballymote in County Sligo. It contains, among other things, a description of the ages of the world, a history of the Jews, lists of Irish kings, fragmentary accounts of the fall of Troy, passages from the *Æneid*, rules for Irish versification, the "Book of Rights" (*Lebor na gCeart*), and the only surviving copy of "the Scholar's Primer," *Auraicept na n-Éces*, attributed to Virgilius Maro Grammaticus in the 7th century.]

[12] Moore, vol. i. p. 191. *Plowden's Hist. of Ireland*, vol. i.

[13] [Brian Mac Hugh Og. His brother had been hanged by the English authorities in Dublin in 1591 and had taken possession of Monaghan, one of the events that precipitated the Nine Years War (1594-1603).]

[14] Spenser's *View of Ireland*. Dublin, 1763, p. 230. In another place, Spenser speaks of its being an "use amongst them to keepe their cattle, and to live themselves, the most part of the yeare, in boolies pasturing upon the mountaine and waste wilde places, and removing still to fresh land as they have depastured the former . . . . driving their cattle continually with them, and feeding only on their milk and white meats."

[15] [Roger O'Moore, more commonly Rory O'Moore or Ruairí Ó Mórdha (*cir.* 1600-1655), titular king of Laois, principal organizer of the Irish Rebellion of 1641.]

changed masters, and in the reign of Queen Anne, when a series of penal acts was directed against the Roman Catholics. These atrocious laws, amongst other monstrous provisions, forbade papists to purchase lands, or to hold them by lease for more than thirty-one years, or to derive from leasehold property a profit greater than one-third of the rent. The great majority of the people, being Roman Catholics, were thus, in effect, restrained from all practice of higher agriculture, and the proprietors of estates had really little option but to let them to the few capitalists who could legally compete for them, and who could not, of course, properly superintend the management of the immense tracts which fell into their hands, except by keeping them almost entirely under grass. This they were, moreover, tempted to do during the first seventy years of the eighteenth century by the extraordinary demand of England for grazier's produce, landlords at the same time doing their best to prevent any other use of the land, "everywhere," says Swift, "by penal clauses prohibiting their tenants from plowing."[16] So general and so prolonged was the neglect of tillage, that in the year 1727 a law was made to compel every occupier of 100 acres to cultivate at least *five* acres; but the injunction seems to have been little regarded, and, until about forty years later, little additional land was brought under the plow.

From the earliest times, then, until late in the last century, Ireland was almost entirely a grazing country. Now, it is true that, in pastoral communities which have little commercial intercourse with more civilized nations, every class of persons is commonly sufficiently supplied with the necessaries of life. In such circumstances, a rich herdsman may have literally no means of getting rid of his superfluous wealth, except by maintaining a large retinue of servants, and he is naturally liberal enough of the milk, cheese, flesh, hides, and wool, which would be wasted if he did not give them away. But Ireland, from a very remote period, has carried on a considerable export trade,

---

[16] *Proposal for the use of Irish Manufactures.* See also Plowden's *Hist, of Ireland*, vol. ii. pp. 137-8.

and the owners of the soil have always possessed in foreign countries a market for their surplus produce. It was therefore the interest of the primitive Irish herdsmen to restrain the consumption of their servants, and to confine it within narrow bounds. When the servants became serfs, they were not, according to the custom in more agricultural countries, provided with portions of land to cultivate for their own support; for the estates of their lords, however extensive, could scarcely be too extensive for pasturage. They lived on such fare as their masters chose to provide, went half-naked, and slept under trees, or the scarcely better shelter of branches cemented together with mud. When they became enfranchised, they gained nothing but personal freedom. Their condition in most other respects remained unchanged. Froissart[17] describes them as living in forests, in huts made of boughs, like wild beasts.[18] There was so little demand for labor that most were still glad to serve for a bare subsistence, and the few who were permitted to be tenants of land obtained little more from their farms. "Irish landlords," says Spenser, "do not use to set out their lands in farm, or for terms of years, but only from year to year, and some during pleasure; neither, indeed, will the Irish husbandman otherwise take his land than so long as he lists himself. The reason hereof is that the landlords used most shamefully to rack their tenants, laying upon them coigns and livery at pleasure, and exacting of them, besides his covenants, what he pleaseth."[19] Spenser goes on to speak of the farmhouses, which he calls "rather swine-sties than

---

[17] [Jean Froissart (*cir.* 1337, *cir.* 1404), French chronicler, important source for the first half of the Hundred Years War.]

[18] Johnes's *Froissart*, Edition of 1839, vol. ii. p. 578.

[19] Of coigne and livery, which Sir John Davies says "consisted in taking of horsemeate, mansmeate, and money of all the inhabitants of the country at the will and pleasure of the soldier," he proceeds to speak as follows; "It is said in an ancient discourse of the Decay of Ireland, that though it were first invented in Hell, yet if it had been used and practiced there, as it hath been in Ireland, it had long since destroyed the very kingdom of Beelzebub."

houses;" and of the farmer's "beastly manner of life, and savage condition, lying and living together with his beasts in one house, in one room, in one bed that is clean straw or rather a foul dunghill."[20] Matters were not at all mended in 1672, when Sir William Petty[21] made his survey, and estimated that out of 200,000 houses then existing in Ireland, 160,000 were "wretched, nasty cabins, without chimney, window, or door-shut, even worse than those of the savage Americans." Neither was any improvement visible fifty years later, when we find Swift continually speaking of the "farmer screwed up to the utmost penny by the agents and stewards of absentees, and the revenues employed in making a figure at London;" of "the enormous rents paid by cottagers for their miserable cabins and potato plots;" of "the rise of rents squeezed out of the very blood, and vitals, and clothes, and dwellings of tenants, who live worse than English beggars;" of rents that still grew higher upon every lease that expired until they have arrived at their present exorbitancy.

From these premises it may be inferred that the present misery of the Irish peasantry is of no recent origin, but has been from time immemorial an heirloom in the race. The number of laborers has always been greatly in excess of the demand for labor, and the remuneration of labor has consequently never been much more than sufficient to procure the merest sustenance. This was as much the case when Ireland was one vast grazing farm, and contained few inhabitants beside cattle and their attendants,

---

[20] Spenser. *View of Ireland*, pp. 125-7.

[21] [Sir William Petty (1623-1687), English economist, scientist, and philosopher. He carried out the "Down Survey," 1654-1656, published as *Hiberniae Deliniatio* in 1685, and is one of the best sources for information on 17th century Ulster. Petty is credited with developing the idea of the "velocity of money," which eventually led to Irving Fisher's formulation of the Quantity Theory of Money, M x V = P x Q, where M is the quantity of money, V is the average number of times each unit of currency is spent in a year, P is the price level, and Q (sometimes T) is the number of transactions in the economy. See Irving Fisher, *The Purchasing Power of Money*, 1911, 1931]

as now that the face of the country is cut up into potato gardens, and dotted with cabins, each containing a separate family. The inhabitants have always been as numerous as the country in its actual circumstances could support, and population has only advanced in proportion as the limits set to it have been widened. How much soever population may have varied in amount at different periods, it has always been nearly equally in excess of the sphere of employment[22] and means of subsistence; and

---

[22] A serious omission in the text is that of any allusion to the factitious narrowing of the sphere of employment due to the almost incredible selfishness and insolence of British commercial legislation in former days. It must be difficult for any Englishman, without deep shame, or for any Irishman, without bitter indignation, to read the story of this class of Ireland's wrongs as told by Lord Dufferin in the following effective passages:

"From Queen Elizabeth's reign until within a few years of the Union, the various commercial confraternities of Great Britain never for a moment relaxed their relentless grip on the trade of Ireland. One by one, each of our nascent industries was either strangled in its birth, or handed over, gagged and bound, to the jealous custody of the rival interest in England, until at last every fountain of wealth was hermetically sealed, and even the traditions of commercial enterprise have perished through desuetude.

"The owners of England's pastures opened the campaign. As early as the commencement of the sixteenth century, the beeves of Roscommon, Tipperary, and Queen's County undersold the produce of the English grass counties in their own market. By an act of the 20th Elizabeth, Irish cattle were declared a nuisance, and their importation was prohibited. Forbidden to send our beasts alive across the Channel, we killed them at home, and began to supply the sister country with cured provisions. A second Act of Parliament imposed prohibitory duties on salted meats. The hides of the animals still remained, but the same influence soon put a stop to the importation of leather. Our cattle trade abolished, we tried sheep-farming. The sheep-breeders of England immediately took alarm, and Irish wool was declared contraband by a Parliament of Charles II. Headed in this direction, we tried to work up the raw material at home, but this created the greatest outcry of all. Every maker of fustian, flannel,

the multiplication of the people, much as it has increased the mass of misery, has not, perhaps, sensibly aggravated the misery of individuals. The chief difference is that, whereas people were once starving on a short allowance of meat, they are now starving on a short allowance of potatoes. Abundance of the former they never knew, nor of the latter, except during one short period. This brief interval of comparative plenty commenced soon after the middle of the last century, when the increase of tillage increased the demand for farm servants; but the increase was too gradual to produce any material or permanent effect. In

---

and broadcloth in the country rose up in arms, and by an act of William III the woolen industry of Ireland was extinguished, and 20,000 manufacturers left the island. The easiness of the Irish labor market, and the cheapness of provisions still giving us an advantage, even though we had to import our materials, we next made a dash at the silk business; but the silk manufacturer proved as pitiless as the wool stapler. The cotton manufacturer, the sugar refiner, the soap and candle maker (who especially dreaded the abundance of our kelp), and any other trade or interest that thought it worthwhile to petition, was received by Parliament with the same cordial partiality, until the most searching scrutiny failed to detect a single vent through which it was possible for the hated industry of Ireland to respire. But, although excluded from the markets of Britain, a hundred harbors gave her access to the universal sea. Alas! a rival commerce on her own element was still less welcome to England, and, as early as the reign of Charles II, the Levant, the ports of Europe, and the oceans beyond the Cape were forbidden to the flag of Ireland. The colonial trade alone was in any manner open, if that could be called an open trade which for a long time precluded all exports whatever, and excluded from direct importation to Ireland such important articles as sugar, cotton, and tobacco. What has been the consequence of such a system, pursued with relentless pertinacity for two hundred years? This: that debarred from every other trade and industry, the entire nation flung itself back on the land, with as fatal an impulse as when a river, whose current is suddenly impeded, rolls back and drowns the valley it once fertilized." *Irish Emigration*, pp. 129-132. "Ireland," says Swift, "is the only country I ever heard or read of, which was denied the liberty of exporting their native commodities and manufactures wherever they pleased." *Short View of the State of Ireland.*

the year 1762, the Irish parliament granted high bounties on the inland carriage of grain, and in 1783 and 1784 granted further bounties on its exportation, and prohibited its importation from abroad; and the rise of price which took place in consequence was further promoted by the demand for foreign corn in Great Britain after the commencement of the war with France, and by the abolition in 1806 of all restrictions on the corn trade between this country and Ireland. Inducements were thus given to landholders to substitute tillage for pasturage, and, as the tracts held by single graziers were in general much too extensive to be cultivated by the actual tenants, they were divided into farms of more convenient size, and let to such persons as were willing to undertake them. There was not, however, capital enough in the island to meet the requirements of this revolution in husbandry, and most of the new race of farmers were so poor that they could not pay their laborers in any other way than by assigning to them pieces of ground to build cabins upon, and to cultivate for their own subsistence. Together with the farmers, therefore, a considerable body of cottiers sprang up, and in this manner the bulk of the peasantry were converted into occupiers of land; but the conversion was effected much less suddenly than is commonly supposed. Although the inland carriage bounty caused a good deal of pasture to be broken up in a few counties, yet, after it had been several years in operation, the proportion of tillage to pasturage over the whole island was still not more than one to ten; and it is certain that the Acts of 1783 and 1784 caused only an inconsiderable tract to be brought under the plow. The inconsiderable increase in the exportation of grain, which may be regarded as an exact measure of the increase of cultivation consequent upon those Acts, shows that the latter likewise was inconsiderable. The quantity of corn exported from Ireland was 211,979 barrels in 1783, and 648,884 barrels in 1789, showing a difference in seven years of 436,905 barrels, or about 266,000 quarters; and this quantity, divided by seven, gives about 38,000 quarters as the annual ratio of increased exportation. But to produce 39,000 quarters of corn, not more than 15,000 acres can have been required, and one thousand men are quite as many as can possibly have been required to cultivate 15,000 acres in the ordinary manner. In each of the seven years, then, ending with 1789, additional employment was created for no more than a thousand laborers at the very outside. But such an increase of employment in the midst of a population of nearly four millions, could not perceptibly raise the price of labor, nor enable the peasantry to live perceptibly better than they had always been accustomed to do. The usual rate of wages was sixpence a day; but, after the necessary deductions for Sundays, holidays, and bad weather, there remained only about 270 working days in the year, and of these the laborer was generally obliged to give up 60 to his master in payment for his cabin and garden, and 60 more in payment for the grazing of a cow. His actual cash earnings were therefore not more than three pounds fifteen shillings. His allotment of land, which was generally an acre or an acre and a half, might indeed have supplied the deficiency of his money wages; but as it was held at will, and as its extent was regulated by the slovenly mode of tillage commonly practiced, the rent would no doubt have been raised if the tenant had made the land more than ordinarily productive. He only troubled himself, therefore, to obtain from it as many potatoes as he needed, and with these, and with milk, he was at that period abundantly supplied; insomuch that Arthur Young was struck with the contrast between the scanty meals of an English cottager, and the exuberance of an Irishman's potato bowl, to which every member of his family, wife, children, pig, and poultry, enjoyed free access. Plenty of food was, however, the sum total of the Irish peasant's advantages, even in this his shortage of gold. While reveling at a succession of potato feasts, his clothing was little else than rags, and his cabin was the same miserable hovel as at this day, consisting generally of only one room, without chimney or window, and with walls, which, if artificial, were built of mud and straw, but which were sometimes merely the sides of a broad ditch, united at the top by a roof of thatch or sods overgrown with weeds, on which the pig might occasionally be seen grazing.[23] Thus the increased remuneration of the laborer did not raise his standard of comfort by suggesting to him new enjoyments and new wants, but merely gave him ampler meals, and enabled him to feed his children better. The addition to the resources of the peasantry was just sufficient to give a fresh impulse to population, which advanced so rapidly, that, although the extension of tillage continued to increase the demand for labor, the supply of laborers fully kept up with it, and prevented it from working any beneficial change in the condition of the people. The partition of grazing farms, and multiplication of cottage holdings, enlarged the field of employment; but the enlargement was effected so gradually, that time was allowed for the number of seekers for employment to increase in the same proportion, and the same keen competition raised the rent of land which had formerly depressed the rate of wages. Thus, from the very first, land was procurable by the peasantry only on terms which forbade their deriving much benefit from the possession, and to this defect in their original tenure may be ascribed all the evils which have resulted from the introduction of the cottage system into Ireland. Population could not indeed have reached its present amount but for the general distribution of land among the peasantry but, neither, in all probability, would it have done so if the peasantry had obtained the land on advantageous terms. If their conversion into landholders had sensibly improved their condition, the benefit might probably have been permanent; for their indigence and their improvidence might have been simultaneously lessened. From the peculiar manner in which the change was brought about, it failed to relieve

---

[23] Young's *Tour in Ireland*, vol. ii. App. pp. 25-27. The exact words are worth transcribing. "Mark the Irishman's potato bowl placed on the floor, the whole family upon their hams around it, devouring a quantity almost incredible; the beggar seating himself with a hearty welcome, the pig taking his share as readily as the wife, the cocks, hens, turkeys, geese, the cur, the cat, and perhaps the cow, and all partaking of the same dish."

that ancient and inveterate poverty which is not less the cause than the effect of the redundancy of population in Ireland; otherwise it might have produced effects the very opposite of those which have actually proceeded from it, and have established the prosperity of the peasantry on a firm basis, instead of merely increasing the number of participators in their misery.[24]

It is a conclusive proof that the occupation of land by the Irish peasantry does not of itself contribute to their misery, that it is precisely where the distribution of land amongst them is most general that population is least redundant, and the condition of the people most tolerable. In Ulster, the number of farms not exceeding five acres in extent, and the proportion of inhabitants occupying land, are greater than in any one of the other three provinces; yet in Ulster, the competition for land is less keen than in the rest of Ireland, and in Ulster only is the English tourist occasionally reminded of the happiest parts of his own country, by the comparative neatness of the white-washed cottages, and by the appearance of the comparatively well-dressed and well-fed inmates. It is true that Ulster is the most densely peopled portion of the whole island, but population has not there outrun subsistence in the same manner as in the other provinces, and the inhabitants, though much more numerous, have long preserved the same proportion between their numbers and their means of livelihood. The reason of this is, that they have always enjoyed something approaching to a comfortable subsistence. The terms of their tenure of land do not leave them just so much only of the produce as may suffice to keep them from starving. They are not mere tenants in the ordinary sense of the word, but possess a proprietary right which limits that of the landlord, and restrains his power of raising the rent, or ejecting the actual occupant. This

---

[24] It is highly gratifying to me to find my friend Professor Cairnes, in the interesting *Fragments on Ireland*, included amongst his recently published *Political Essays*, not only adopting all the foregoing views, but elucidating them by valuable sidelights of his own.

"tenant-right," as it is called, which is peculiar to the north of Ireland, has probably grown out of the privileges conceded to the English and Scottish emigrants by whom Ulster was colonized in James the First's reign, to induce them to settle in so barbarous a region. Although founded solely on prescription, its operation is almost as effectual as if it were recognized by law, and its value to the possessor is self-evident. It stimulates him to exertion by securing to him a larger portion of the produce of his additional labor, and enables him to procure some few of the conveniences as well as the mere necessaries of life. The natural desire to retain these advantages is only another name for prudence. A cottier's sons possess still greater facilities in Ulster than in Munster or Connaught for dividing their father's holding, yet they have long been much less in the habit of effecting such a partition. If they saw that they could not maintain themselves on their respective shares without sacrificing the few comforts they had been accustomed to, they naturally sought for some other means of livelihood. The cottage farms have consequently been transmitted from one generation to another without diminution,[25] and the agricultural population has advanced only in proportion to the increase of means for its support. The only county in Ulster to which this description does not apply is Donegal, in which, as the indigenous Celtic inhabitants were never extirpated, tenant-right has not been introduced except partially, and in an imperfect shape. The peasantry of that county, ever since they became occupiers of land, have been kept as poor as their brethren in the most wretched districts of Connaught, and their numbers consequently have in-

---

[25] In the north of Ireland, Arthur Young, in 1776, found that ten acres were considered a large farm, and five or six a good one. (*Tour*, vol. ii. App. p. 21). Farms had been reduced to that size because the tenants, being rather weavers than farmers, required no more land to furnish them with a competent livelihood; but having once reached that limit, they did not afterwards fall below it, being at this day quite as large as they were seventy years ago.

creased as fast, and the partition of their holdings been carried as far.

If it be objected that the prosperity of Ulster is, after all, only relative, and that anywhere but in Ireland it would receive a very different name, it may be replied, that tenant-right is a very inadequate substitute for the protection of leases or ownership. It has no legal sanction, but derives all its validity from custom; and, having grown up by slow degrees, was no doubt at first stoutly contested by those to whose pretensions it was opposed. If, wherever even this imperfect security exists, the condition of agriculture and of the peasantry is far better than in other parts of Ireland, may it not be fairly concluded that, with more complete security, the superiority would be proportionably more striking? Is it not likewise reasonable to suppose that, in order to place the peasantry of the other provinces on a level in all respects with those of Ulster, nothing more is required than the concession to them of equal rights? Yet with these grounds for presuming that the small farm system of Ireland needs only to be modified in order to become a source of national prosperity, nothing short of its utter abolition is insisted on. The consolidation of small farms is continually declared to be an indispensable preliminary to the improvement of Irish agriculture, or to the regeneration of the Irish people. This sentence is surely somewhat arbitrary. The present race of cottiers, exhausted and disheartened by merciless exactions, and liable as they are to have their rents raised, or to be themselves ejected at a moment's notice, are confessedly, for the most part, wretchedly poor and shockingly demoralized. The fact is decisive against rackrents and tenancies-at-will; but does it prove anything against small leasehold farms, or small properties? Because small farmers cannot thrive without security of tenure, therefore security of tenure is to be refused them. Why not add that, because hunger cannot be appeased without food, therefore a hungry man should not be permitted to eat?

Not only, however, are not small farms the cause of Irish misery; not only is their preservation quite compatible with the improvement of Ireland; their continuance (though on a different tenure), and a considerable increase to their number, are perhaps the only means by which the manifold disorders of that country can be radically cured. Whatever may have been the original source of the wretchedness of the Irish people, its proximate cause is evidently a deficiency of employment;[26] the supply of labor so greatly exceeds the demand, that multitudes have not adequate means of gaining a livelihood. This being the nature of their present distress, no scheme for its relief can have complete success which does not furnish them with adequate occupation, and it may not be difficult to show that, for the agrarian population of Ireland, adequate occupation cannot be afforded except on small farms. This will appear from a hasty examination of the various schemes proposed. By a large class of reasoners, the deficiency of employment is held to be a necessary consequence of deficiency of capital, and to be incapable of being supplied except by the introduction of additional capital; and, as capital will not enter a country in which life and property are unprotected, the first step towards improvement is declared to be the repression of that spirit of outrage which makes Ireland the terror of all who have anything to lose. For this purpose, either coercion or conciliation may be tried. But four or five millions of famishing desperadoes must be almost exterminated before they can be dragooned into loyalty. If force only is to be used, force must create a solitude before it can establish peace.[27] Still less can be expected from conciliation, if by that term be understood merely the redress of political grievances. Most of these causes of complaint have already been removed, without removing anything of that bitterness of feeling which they were supposed to have

---

[26] [Cf. Dr. Harold G. Moulton's identification of production and employment as the two chief factors in an economic recovery, *The Recovery Problem in the United States.* Washington, DC: The Brookings Institution, 1936, 114.]

[27] [An allusion to Tacitus's comment, put in the mouth of Calgacus, a British chieftain, in *Agricola* about the devastation wrought by Roman conquests.]

engendered, and the redress of the monster grievance which remains, however desirable on other accounts, would assuredly not have a much more soothing effect. Should the church of the majority be at once reinstated in her ancient position, and again endowed with the wealth of which she has been plundered, her clergy would be almost the only gainers. The mass of the people would remain as destitute as ever, and would have as little reason to submit quietly to their dismal lot. The priests, indeed, when in the receipt of liberal stipends, and when no longer dependent on voluntary contributions, would, besides being no longer so eager to promote improvident marriages for the sake of the fees, cease to have the same motives for affecting to sympathize with the evil passions of their hearers, and might rather exert themselves for the maintenance of order. Their influence has, however, been exceedingly overrated. With a few disgraceful exceptions, the Roman Catholic clergy are not accused, even by their most virulent calumniators, of openly countenancing violence. Many have used their utmost efforts to allay the violence of the people, and almost all are so far mindful of their sacred obligations as to remain at least quiescent; if they do not labor very earnestly to prevent crime, they do not directly encourage it. In truth, such encouragement would be superfluous. Where the materials for spontaneous combustion exist in such abundance, no torch is needed to kindle them. The flames burst forth as freely without any extraneous aid. The outrages by which life and property are endangered in Ireland result naturally from the wretchedness and desperation of the people. The law is disobeyed because, to the multitudes who have nothing to lose, it affords no protection, while it withholds from them everything they covet. Self-preservation is the first law of nature, and they who cannot keep their lives by any other means must fight for them. To an Irish cottier a writ of ejectment is equivalent to a sentence of starvation, and he not unnaturally endeavors to retain possession of his land by sending a bullet through the head of every competitor. It is the fear of destitution that goads him on to crime. In such a temper he is doubtless more easily led away by factious demagogues, and more morbidly alive to national insults; but, independently of such additional excitement, he finds in his own reflections but too many stimulants to aggression and assassination. As, then, the lawlessness of Ireland does not originate in priestly instigation, so neither could it be repressed by priestly authority. As long as the peasantry continue on the verge of starvation the most persuasive eloquence will fail to keep them quiet. There will be no peace, even though the priests take upon them the office of peacemakers. Their counsels will be disregarded until their hearers are tolerably fed, and that cannot be until work is found for such as require it. For this first essential, no conceivable substitute can suffice. Education would avail as little as clerical authority; it could neither give the people food, nor reconcile them to the want of it. Poorlaws may possibly be mentioned as providing for the first of these alternatives; but poor-laws create nearly as much distress as they relieve. What they give to one section of the laboring class they take from another; whatever is levied for poor-rates is subtracted from wages. Besides, the gratuitous maintenance of one-third of the Irish people cannot be seriously proposed. A compulsory provision for the poor, in order to be of any avail, must be intended to have only partial operation, and to be combined with measures which shall enable the great mass of the poor to earn their own livelihood. But such measures, it is said, require additional capital. If so, we have before us a complete circle of difficulties, impregnable at every point. The country cannot be tranquilized until the people are employed, nor the people employed until capital be introduced, and capital will not enter until tranquility be established. So that the end proposed must be accomplished before the requisites for its accomplishment can be procured!

But it may be urged that, although private speculators are unwilling to venture their money in such a country as Ireland, capital might be furnished by government, and expended on public works in the construction of roads, railways, canals, and bridges, on drainage, or on the embankment of rivers. Such measures might be adopted with a view to two distinct objects. The first and most obvious would be that of affording facilities for the development of the resources of the country; but it might also be expected that the works, while in progress, would furnish occupation for the multitudes who had been previously unemployed. We need not stop to inquire whether the enormous expenditure requisite for this purpose would be incurred by any government. Undeterred by this, or any other objection, let us suppose, for the sake of argument, that government had undertaken to provide occupation for all who required it; that the peasantry were all in the receipt of good wages, and either too busy, or too well pleased at being paid for idling, to think of mischief; and that, tranquility and confidence having been established, British speculators had crossed the Channel, with as large an amount of capital as the country could absorb. In what manner could this capital be applied? Partly, perhaps, in fisheries and manufactures; but the former could not afford regular occupation, except to the inhabitants of the coasts; and the tendency of the latter seems to be less to attract surplus hands from other occupations, than to encourage the growth of a fresh population for themselves. A future generation of Irishmen might perhaps consent to become operatives, but the existing race would exclaim as loudly against being shut up in factories as in workhouses; and even if they were more tractable, few manufacturers would much like engaging, for their delicate machinery, hands that had only been used to the spade and pickaxe. The only occupation immediately suitable for an agricultural population is agriculture; and, if the Irish peasantry are to be adequately employed, they must be principally employed in farming. Let us suppose, then, that the greater part of the newly imported capital had been entrusted to scientific agriculturists, who, overcoming all the obstacles which have hitherto impeded such operations, had removed the present class of cottiers, and, consolidating their holdings, had divided Ireland into farms of the same size as those of England. Let us next calculate what proportion of the peasantry could obtain employment on these enlarged farms. The extent of land in Ireland, either already cultivated or capable of cultivation, may be stated at 18,000,000 of acres, which, at the rate of one for every twenty-eight acres,[28] the proportion usual in England, would furnish work for 642,000 male adults. But of one million and a half of families, constituting in 1841 the entire population, nearly 1,000,000 were chiefly engaged in agriculture; and of 2,400,000, the total number of male adults, 1,600,000 were similarly engaged. When, therefore, the new farms had absorbed all the labor they required, there would remain nearly 600,000 families, comprising 3,000,000 of individuals, who, after the termination of the works undertaken by government, would be without work of any kind. The revolution effected in agriculture would have deprived them of their former occupation, and manufactures, as we have seen, would offer them no adequate resource. It is true that those who recommend the extinction of the cottage system, and the adoption in Ireland of the English mode of farming, acknowledge that those measures must be accompanied by others for the promotion of emigration, and are not dismayed even by the necessity of transporting across the Atlantic a colony of 2,000,000 of human beings. The eminent names appended to a recent scheme for that purpose, and the ability with which it is drawn up, forbid its being mentioned otherwise than in terms of respect; but it may, without disparagement, be pronounced of too startling a character to be adopted by any government without much more mature deliberation than the urgency of the case will allow time for. The plan of improving the condition of the Irish peasantry by the consolidation of farms might therefore be at once rejected, if only on account of its requiring, as supplemental to it, a scheme of emigration on so vast a scale.

There remains no resource but that of small farms. So far as Ireland is concerned, the question is not whether small or large farms are preferable, abstractedly considered. The former do actually predominate, and have

---

[28] This is the proportion of land to male adult laborers; but of agricultural laborers of both sexes and of all ages, there is one for every twenty-four acres.

raised up a population for which they alone can furnish occupation; to what objections soever they may be open, their abolition is nevertheless impracticable; if they be an evil they are a necessary evil, and the only wise policy is to make the best of them. Subjoined [on page 173] is a table, showing the distribution of the cultivated area, and of the agricultural population of Ireland: —

This table shows, that of 974,000 agricultural families, only 40,000 are altogether without land, and that more than 500,000 occupy farms of eight acres or upwards. Eight acres are quite enough to enable an intelligent tenant family, paying only a fair rent, to obtain a competent maintenance; so that occupiers of this class, in order to be enabled to thrive, require only a secure tenure, or, in other words, the security of leases, with such conditions as would ensure to them a fair remuneration for their expenditure of money and labor. Without such leases, wherever the cultivators are not owners of the soil, it is impossible that agriculture can flourish and wise landlords are as ready to grant as tenants are anxious to receive them; but landlords are often but short-sighted judges of their own interests, and with the view of quickening their perceptions, it has been proposed to make rent irrecoverable without a lease. The late Mr. O'Connell,[29] by whom this expedient was recommended,[30] acknowledged it to be a violent remedy; but a more serious objection is, that it would probably have little effect upon the disease. The value of leases depends entirely on their provisions; and the Legislature, although it might require them to be granted, could not pretend to regulate the demands for rent, or the other conditions to be imposed upon tenants.

---

[29] [Daniel O'Connell or Dónal Ó Conaill (1775-1847), Irish political leader, known as "The Liberator" and "The Emancipator" for his fight for Catholic political emancipation and repeal of the Act of Union of 1800.]

[30] Arthur Young had long before suggested, as a necessary step towards improvement, that "the meanest occupier should have a lease, and none shorter than twenty-one years." (Tour, vol. ii. App. p. 24.)

NUMBER OF PERSONS HOLDING MORE THAN

AND NOT MORE THAN

Cultivated Area in Statute Acres.	Number of Families chiefly employed in Agriculture.	Total Number of Persons holding land.	Number holding not more than one Acre.	1 acre / 2	2 acres / 3	3 acres / 4	4 acres / 5	5 acres / 6	6 acres / 7	7 acres / 8	8 acres / 9	9 acres / 10	10 acres / 20	20 acres / 50	50 acres / 100	100 acres / 200	200 acres / 500	500 acres / 1000	1000 acres / 2000	2000 acres / 3000	3000 acres / 4000	4000 acres / 5000
13,838,782	974,188	935,448	135,314	50,355	35,951	45,363	50,281	36,630	42,665	31,610	41,596	35,408	187,582	141,819	45,394	17,121	6,393	1,179	286	46	13	3

Number whose holdings are greater than 5000 Acres . . 6

Number of Persons holding in Joint or Common Tenancy . . 30,433

N.B.—*This Table is altered from one inserted in Captain Kennedy's most able Digest of Evidence on Occupation of Land in Ireland—a work which cannot be too carefully studied by all who would obtain a knowledge of the actual state of that unhappy country.*

Thus the only lease to which the landlord would consent might be such as either the tenant would not accept, or such as would fetter without protecting him. As a substitute for leases, the propriety of establishing tenant-right throughout Ireland has, of late, been a good deal discussed. If by the term be meant the qualified proprietary right enjoyed by the peasantry of Ulster, the beneficial effect which would result from its extension to the other provinces will scarcely be denied by an advocate for peasant proprietorship. The equity of such a measure is, however, a different question. The tenantry of the midland and southern provinces are, in general, tenants-at-will, removable at the landlord's pleasure; and to give them, with what conditions soever, permanent possession of land which they previously held by so slight a tie, would be an invasion of the rights of property from which even Stein and Hardenberg — the boldest innovators of modern times — would have shrunk, and which will certainly not be attempted by the statesmen of a country in which reverence for vested interests is carried to the verge of superstition. If, on the other hand, nothing more be meant than that an ejected tenant should be entitled to compensation for substantial improvements, the advantages of a law to that effect would probably be more than counterbalanced by the endless litigation to which it would give rise. The only unobjectionable way of enabling tenants to obtain reasonable terms from their landlords, is to diminish the competition for land, by lessening the number of competitors. There are at present in Ireland nearly half a million of farms large enough, if held on leases and at fair rents, to maintain the actual tenants in plenty and comfort; and there are about 400,000 smaller holdings, comprehending more than a million of acres, which might be consolidated and redistributed into 130,000 farms of eight acres each. Moreover, the farms of more than twenty acres each are 202,260 in number, comprehending about fifteen millions of acres, which would furnish occupation for about 120,000 families, in addition to those of the occupiers. Thus, of the whole number of agricultural families, which in 1841 was 974,000, but which must have been considerably reduced by the famine and pestilence of the last two years, and does not probably now exceed 950,000, about 750,000 might obtain a competent livelihood from the land actually under cultivation, if relieved from the competition of the 200,000 families remaining. These last constitute a redundant population, which must be withdrawn from a field of employment in which, while they have not room to work themselves, they are always in the way of their neighbors. But whither can they be removed? Emigration cannot dispose of such multitudes, nor would they readily betake themselves to the sedentary occupations of towns. The employment afforded to them must be agricultural, and must be procured in Ireland, yet not on the land already under cultivation. Where, then, can they be provided for? The question admits of but one answer — They must be transferred to the waste lands.

Of such lands, Ireland contains 6,290,000 acres, of which 2,535,000 are said not to be worth the cost of improvement; but 1,425,000 acres are acknowledged to be improvable for tillage, and the remaining 2,330,000 for pasture. These wastes are scattered over the whole island, but it fortunately happens that they are most extensive in those counties in which there is the largest amount of destitution. In Mayo, for example, there are 170,000 acres of waste land fit for cultivation; in Galway, 160,000; in Donegal, 150,000; in Kerry, the same number; and in Cork, 100,000; while in all Ulster, exclusive of Donegal, there are only 269,000; and in the whole province of Leinster, only 186,000. Altogether, there are 1,425,000 acres classed as arable; and these, with the addition of 175,000 acres of land, which, though represented as only fit for pasture, is really, as shall be presently shown, well deserving of tillage, would suffice for 200,000 allotments, of eight acres each.

The waste land of the best quality is, however, far from being fit for immediate cultivation. Some of it may only require to be pared, burned, and limed, but much is bog or moor, which requires to be thoroughly drained, and to have the sub-soil mixed with the surface mould and with lime; but these, and all other preliminary operations, might be performed at very little expense by the persons for whose ultimate benefit they were designed. The proposed grantees are at present without employment, and, unless some such measure as that under consideration be adopted, without any prospect of it. They are now, and they must for an indefinite period continue to be, supported at the public expense, and it would be much cheaper to keep them usefully engaged than to maintain them in idleness. It would therefore be good economy to take them forthwith into pay, and to employ them in draining and sub-soiling the wastes selected for reclamation. After the completion of these preparatory operations, the next step would be to mark off districts suitable for the settlement of collections of families, which would vary in size according as the colonies were intended to constitute separate village communities, or to be united to communities previously existing, Each district should be divided into lots corresponding in number to the number of settlers, and the latter should be further required to construct a cottage, according to an approved plan, on every lot. Every family should then be placed in possession of one of the cottage farms, and be made perpetual lessees at a fixed rent, and on certain other conditions, which will be more particularly described hereafter; and having been furnished with tools and some farming stock, should be instructed that, after the next harvest, they would have to provide for their support by their own industry.

Before we proceed to inquire what further measures would be necessary to ensure the success of this great social experiment, one or two apparent objections to it must be answered. One, which will take most people aback, is the enormous expense which would be required. To maintain two hundred thousand families for many months, to purchase land for their occupation, and to supply them with materials for building, and with farming implements and stock, would certainly cost an immense sum. But the cost of an undertaking, however great, would not justify its rejection, provided its advantages could be shown to be commensurate; more especially if, as in the present instance, great part of the expenditure were inevitable in any circumstances, and the further outlay were calculated to prevent the recurrence of demands which would otherwise be perpetual. Two hundred thousand destitute families must be fed at the public expense, whether they be set to work or be suffered to remain idle, and must continue to be so fed until they are placed in a position to provide for themselves. The present cost of maintaining them is an annual tax, which must be levied until redeemed, and exemption from it would be cheaply purchased at many times its amount. At how low a price its removal might be effected in the mode indicated above will appear from an examination of the various items of expense.

It would be necessary, in the first place, to buy up the proprietary rights possessed by private persons over the waste lands required. Of the perfect competence of the Legislature to enforce the sale of such rights there can be no question. An authority which compels individuals to part with their most valued property on the slightest pretext of public convenience, and which permits railway projectors to throw down manor-houses, and to cut up favorite pleasure-grounds, need not scruple to insist upon the sale of boggy meadows, or upland pastures, with the view of curing the destitution and misery of an entire people. But upon this point it is the less necessary to dwell, as the right of parliament to dispose of the wastes has been asserted in the most explicit terms by the first Minister of the Crown.[31] The compensation to be made by the proprietors would depend on the present produce of the land. The average value of this cannot at present exceed two shillings an acre, so that £2 an acre, equal to twenty years' purchase, would be a very liberal payment for the fee-simple. The expense of thorough drainage would scarcely reach £4 an acre, and that of sub-soiling would not exceed 30s.[32] A cottage with its appurtenances, suitable to a farm of eight acres, might be built for £40,[33] and the farmer on

---

[31] Lord J. Russell's *Speech on the State of Ireland*, Jan. 25, 1847.
[32] *Digest of Evidence* on Occ. of Land, pp. 82-83.
[33] *Digest of Evidence* on Occ. of Land, p. 139.

entering might manage to get on without an advance of more than £20. The whole outlay may, therefore, be stated as follows:

Purchase of 1,600,000 acres, at £2 per acre	£3,200,000
Expense of drainage and sub-soiling, at £5 10s	8,800,000
Construction of 200,000 cottages, at £40 each	8,000,000
Advances to 200,000 cottiers of £20 each	4,000,000
	£24,000,000

From which must be deducted the cost of maintaining 200,000 families, or 1,000,000 individuals, for the two years during which the operations might be expected to last. This, at £5 per head, would be £5,000,000 annually, or for two years, £10,000,000; which, subtracted from £24,000,000, would leave £14,000,000. At this low price, less than three years' purchase, the public would be relieved from the necessity of an annual payment of £5,000,000. The operation, viewed merely as a financial feat, would establish the reputation of the minister by whom it was achieved. The transfer to the waste lands of the destitute portion of the Irish peasantry has here been treated as the only feasible scheme for placing them in a satisfactory position, public works of other descriptions, as well as emigration, having been previously examined, and rejected as incapable of effecting the grand object. Otherwise the reader might be reminded that, according to the estimates of Mr. Godley, the transport to Canada of 200,000 families would occasion a certain loss of £6,000,000, and a possible loss of a still larger sum; and that, not many months ago, one hundred and eighteen members of the House of Commons were ready to vote sixteen millions sterling for the prosecution of a railway project which, at best, could only be expected to improve the condition of the people by preparing the way for measures calculated to benefit them more directly. Besides, the expenditure on the waste lands is not to be regarded as money irrecoverably sunk, but rather as a loan to the settlers, who should be required to pay interest upon it. Five percent, upon fourteen millions sterling, payable by 1,600,000 acres, would be something less than nine shillings an acre — a very moderate rent to be paid by the perpetual lessee of a farm, with a substantial dwelling upon it.

These anticipations of profit may certainly be not unreasonably pronounced somewhat premature, inasmuch as they take for granted the complete success of an experiment of which many persons would as confidently predict the total failure. The fact of land having been suffered to lie waste up to this time has been cited as a proof of its being unworthy of improvement; if it had promised a fair return for the application of capital, capitalists, it is said, would not have delayed so long to avail themselves of it. To this it may be replied, that most of the resources of Ireland are acknowledged to have been as yet only very imperfectly developed, in consequence either of the poverty or of the apathy of the people; to these causes are owing the neglect of mines and fisheries, and the backward state of agriculture; and it would be only reasonable to account for the neglect of the wastes in the same manner, instead of ascribing it to their inherent worthlessness. Besides, the classification of the wastes adopted in the preceding pages is not founded upon doubtful estimates, but is the result of careful investigation by an engineer of the highest eminence, Mr. Griffith,[34] the General Valuation Commissioner. This gentleman is so little disposed to an extravagant appraisement, that he condemns considerably more than three-fourths of all the wastes, as either unimprovable, or as only improvable for pasture; yet, even after this large deduction, there remains of superior quality nearly enough for the home colonization proposed above. The land of this superior description is represented as capable of being prepared for tillage at an expense which its increased value would fully repay, and the opin-

---

[34] [Sir Richard John Griffith (1784-1878), First Baronet, Irish geologist, mining engineer and chairman of the Board of Works of Ireland. He was the author of the valuation of Ireland, published between 1853 and 1865, and known as "Griffith's Valuation."]

ion coming from an authority of so cautious a character, might, even if otherwise unsupported, be accepted without much hesitation.[35] An attempt will presently be made to prove that it is correct, but let it in the meantime be supposed to be erroneous. Let it be supposed that even the best of the waste lands would never yield any rent, and that it would be necessary for the settlers to be placed in possession of their farms, not as lessees, but as absolute proprietors. Even in that case, the money expended in preparing the land for their occupation, in drainage and sub-soiling, and in buildings, would have been most advantageously laid out, provided only the settlers should thenceforward be enabled to provide for their own subsistence. Even this partial success would be a sufficient recommendation of the scheme. There would be little cause to regret the outlay, even though it should do no more than raise two hundred thousand families from destitution to independence; should relieve the rest of the peasantry from the ruinous competition which now depresses them; and should, at the same time, absolve the public from the necessity of an annual payment of more than one-third its own amount.

Whatever doubts may be entertained of the realization of these results must be of one of two kinds. It must be supposed either that the land after every preliminary improvement would still not repay even the current expenses of cultivation, or that the cultivators would not properly avail themselves of their advantages. Now, when land is said to be not worth cultivating, the meaning is, that the produce would not afford to the capital and labor employed so large a return as they might obtain, if other-

---

[35] Upon *mountain* wastes, as all wastes in Ireland, that are not bog, are called, "is to be practiced," says Young, "the most profitable husbandry in the king's dominions, for so I am persuaded the improvement of mountain land to be." (*Tour*, vol. ii. App. p. 69.) And again, "no meadows are equal to those gained by improving a bog; they are of a value which scarcely any other lands give rise to. In Ireland I should suppose it would not fall short of forty shillings an acre, and rise in many cases to three pounds." (*Ibid.* p. 74.)

wise applied. It is not necessary to inquire whether the Irish wastes are of this character, for the only capital of the colonists whom it is proposed to transfer to them, is labor, and that labor for which there is no demand, and which, consequently, has no market value whatever. Unless employed upon the waste lands it cannot be employed at all — there are no other means whatever of turning it to account; how small soever may be its produce, that produce is all clear gain, which could not have been acquired in any other manner. The question is not whether, if otherwise employed, the colonists might not have obtained a larger remuneration, but whether, in the only occupation open to them, they are able to maintain themselves; — whether the returns from the lands given to them to cultivate will be sufficient for their subsistence.

Now, there is no land so poor that it may not be rendered fertile by artificial means. Its barrenness commonly arises from the deficiency of certain substances, which need only to be supplied in order completely to change its character. To procure the requisite ingredients might perhaps be a work of much time and labor, to pay for which might cost so much as to make the business anything but a profitable employment of money. But no such objection could apply if none but spare and superabundant labor were used; the work, however tedious and toilsome, would then cost absolutely nothing. However great the expenditure of labor, none of it would be wasted, for the labor would only have acquired value by being so expended. No ground is so worthless that an English laborer will not eagerly accept an allotment of it for the occupation of his leisure, and that he will not speedily convert it into a productive garden, benefiting himself proportionably at the same time. Nor is it only unmarketable labor that may be profitably employed in this manner. In long occupied and well-peopled territories, where wages are not extraordinarily high, and where good land is not easily procurable, it would seem that no soil can be so bad that a laborer, to whom it is granted in full property, will not find it for his interest to cultivate it, even though by so doing he should be obliged to neglect other employment. No soil can be imagined more unsuitable for vegetation than the sand with which the maritime provinces of Belgium were once overspread, and with which extensive tracts are still covered. It can be likened to nothing but the sand on the sea shore, which it no doubt originally was, and it offers about the same attraction for the investment of capital; but, although the rash speculator, employing hired labor, who should have undertaken the improvement of such land, would probably have been ruined, the attempt was made with the most complete success by moneyless boors, who, working on their own account, contrived to enrich both themselves and the soil, and, indeed, to make the latter the richest on this side the Alps. The conversion of sand into mould is not yet complete in Belgium, and the process may still be witnessed at every stage. In the first place, broom seed is sown, which will grow anywhere, and the plants from which are fit to be cut in three years, and are then sold for firewood to bakers and brick-makers. The ground has acquired some compactness from the fibers of the roots, and has been enriched by the leaves which have fallen, and by the manure purchased with the price of the faggots. It is now in a fit state to be plowed and to be sown with buckwheat, or even with rye; and, by the time this is reaped, a sufficiency of manure may be collected to allow of a regular course of cropping. As soon as clover and potatoes enable the farmer to keep cows, improvement goes on rapidly. In a few years the soil undergoes a complete change; it becomes mellow and retentive of moisture, and enriched by the vegetable matter afforded by the decomposition of the roots of the clover and other plants. The Flemings seem to want nothing but a space to work upon; whatever be the quality or texture of the soil, they will, in time, make it productive. It is deserving of remark, that their improvements when once begun are seldom abandoned, unless undertaken on too large a scale, in which case the land is soon divided into smaller portions, and improvements proceed from a greater number of centers, and with more certainty.[36]

These examples may serve to show that there is no land, not absolutely incapable of cultivation, of which the produce, though it may not yield profit enough to satisfy a capitalist, will yet not yield some profit — some little over and above the expenses of cultivation. In the expenses of cultivation is included the cultivator's subsistence; there is therefore no land from which the cultivator may not obtain a livelihood. It is true that the Flemish process just described is somewhat tedious, and would be but ill adapted to cultivators who were entirely dependent for subsistence on the land they were reclaiming. It would by no means suit our Irish colonists, for instance, who might perish with hunger while their farms were producing only crops of brushwood. But neither would the adoption of so slow a process be requisite on the better sort of Irish waste land, which bears no sort of resemblance to the sands of Belgium. Much of it, even in its present state, is used as pasture, and the rest, consisting of heathy bog, though at present valueless, has a surface of vegetable matter one or two feet thick, resting generally on a bed of clay or gravel. The intermixture of the upper and lower soils would supply to each what the other principally wants, and this operation, as well as drainage, would be performed before the settlers were placed in possession of their farms. The latter, therefore, from their first occupation, would possess as high a degree of fertility as the primitive soil of Belgium acquires after several years of incessant labor. Indeed, with the addition of lime, (or where lime were not procurable, of seaweed or sea-sand,) they would immediately bear tolerable crops of roots. Of this experience affords abundant proof. The reclamation of waste land has been undertaken of late years, in several parts of Ireland, by private persons, and, as it would seem, with invariable success. Several instances are on record of land naturally worth not a shilling of rent per acre, which, by draining, sub-soiling, and liming, has in

---

[36] *Flemish Husbandry,* pp. 11-13.

the first year been made to produce five tons of potatoes per acre, or corresponding crops of turnips, and in three years' time has been fitted for an ordinary five years' rotation, being then estimated to be worth a rent of 30s or 35s per acre. It is easy to show how a farmer, with a wife and three young children, might obtain a livelihood from eight acres of such land. Two acres, in the first year, would yield 300 bushels of potatoes, (and two hundred would suffice for the consumption of the family,) and the turnips or other produce of the rest of the farm would be much more than enough for the keep of a cow and a pig. By the end of the year, there would be a considerable accumulation of manure, and it would be the farmer's own fault if the quantity did not annually increase, until every portion of his land had been brought into the highest state of productiveness of which it was capable. With abundance of manure at his disposal, all his difficulties would vanish. In the second year, he might substitute oats for potatoes, and in every subsequent year he might sow part of his land with some sort of grain. But even although he should make corn his principal article of diet, he would not, when his land was thoroughly fertilized, require more than two acres to produce food for the direct consumption of his family, so that six acres would remain under grass or green crops for his cattle. A Fleming in such a situation would be able to keep three or four cows, stall fed; and, as we are now considering what the land is capable of, we may assume that an Irishman could do the same. The milk and butter of one cow he might use at home, but the rest of the dairy produce might be sent to market; and no elaborate calculation can be needed to prove that the proceeds would enable him to defray all the expenses incidental to his station in life, and to save a good deal of money besides, even though he should not be absolute owner of his farm, but should be subject to an annual rent of nine shillings an acre.

It will have been observed, that potatoes form as it were the basis of the farming just referred to. They seem to be thought the only crop on which man can subsist, that in this climate can be obtained from newly reclaimed land without the assistance of manure,[37] and to be, consequently, the only provisions which pauper cultivators could raise during the first year. But after failing in two successive seasons, this crop can no longer be safely depended upon; and should the disease, by which it has been twice destroyed, be still continuing its ravages when the waste lands are prepared for tillage, a considerable alteration of plan will be necessary. The change will be a subject for regret, inasmuch as it will occasion a considerable increase of expenditure; but, on the other hand, its effect will be to hasten by a year or two the progress of improvement. One object of every scheme for the benefit of Ireland, and one sign of its success, must be the adoption of better kinds of food by the laboring classes. In attempting to raise the social condition of the people, some higher end should be proposed than that of enabling them to obtain a sufficiency of potatoes. If this only were aimed at, it would be quite unnecessary to allot so much as eight acres of land to a family. Farms of that size were recommended in order that the occupants should be able to make bread their staff of life, and to grow grain enough for their consumption, as in the course of two or three years it was expected they would do. If, however, the potato disease prove permanent, the Irish peasantry must needs be fed on grain at once; and, unless Government prefer to furnish the people with food, instead of enabling them to raise it for themselves, its simplest course will be to supply every settler on the waste lands with manure enough to prepare part of his ground for oats. His first harvest will then supply him with bread instead of potatoes, and this will be the principal difference, so far as he is concerned. His subsequent operations will be nearly the same as in the case previously supposed.

It may here be proper to show, that the management of eight acres of land will not be too severe a task for those on whom it is to be imposed, *viz.*, for a family of five per-

---

[37] Young, however, from land which had been merely pared, burned, and limed, took crops of wheat, rye, and bere [barley], the first year. (*Tour*, vol. ii. App. p. 70.)

sons, including only one male adult, and possessing, besides their land and their industry, no other capital than the small advance made to them for the purchase of indispensable implements and stock. The head of such a family might not be able to procure either a horse or a plow, and might be obliged to use a spade; but this, as every one may see, by comparing a field and a garden, is by far the more efficient instrument when time will allow of its being used; and the only question is, therefore, whether one man could spare time for the spade work annually required on a farm of eight acres. A more than ordinary quantity would be required on waste land, during the first year or two after its reclamation, but still not more than could be easily performed. "A good laborer can trench four perches (each perch being a square of five and a half yards) in a day, or dig eight perches. It will take him thirty days to trench an acre, and sixteen to dig it well."[38] If placed in possession of his farm in October, therefore, he could easily dig six acres before the season arrived for planting potatoes and sowing turnips; and when a regular rotation of crops was established his labors would be greatly abridged. Suppose him to appropriate three acres to corn, one to potatoes, one to clover, and one to turnips, and to keep two under grass. Between harvest and spring he must trench one acre twenty inches deep, and manure it for potatoes, and dig three acres; one acre being under clover, sown with the corn of the previous season, will not require digging, and another will have been sufficiently prepared for wheat by the taking up of a former crop of potatoes. His spade work will occupy him only seventy-eight days, and he will have the rest of the year for wheeling manure, harrowing, sowing, planting, mowing, and reaping, while his wife and children weed the crops, tend the cows and pigs, and perform other light offices.

The whole amount of labor would be but a moderate burden for the united strength of the family, whose own fault alone it would be if they did not prosper. But it is not

---

[38] *Flemish Husbandry*, p. 75.

sufficient to have shown what a mine of wealth lies hidden in the waste land, if there be reason to believe that it would not be properly wrought by the settlers whom it is proposed to place there. A colony of Flemings in such a situation would speedily bring the soil to the highest pitch of fertility, and enrich themselves with the abundant tribute they would extort from it; but Irishmen, it will be said, are not Flemings.[39] The former would, indeed, have the same motives for industry. In their proprietary character, they would possess that strongest of all incentives to exertion, the knowledge that they were working for themselves; they would feel the influence of that affection for their little domains, which, according to Adam Smith, makes small proprietors "the most industrious, the most intelligent, and the most successful of improvers" — of that "magic of property," which, as Arthur Young says, "turns sand to gold." Such impulses might be irresistible by ordinary mortals; but Irishmen are apparently considered exempt from the rules by which mankind in general are governed. It seems to be thought that, with them, self-interest is less powerful than habit; that, having hitherto always lived in constrained inactivity, they now value no privilege so highly as idleness; that, having never possessed anything but the merest necessaries of life, they have little desire for its comforts, or, at any rate, think them not worth the price of steady labor. What little employment is at present offered to them, either in their own potato grounds, or by larger occupiers, is often either neglected, or listlessly performed; and it may be suspected that they would exhibit the same apathy, even if consti-

---

[39] Young has some remarks so singularly apposite that it would be unpardonable not to insert them here. "A few considerable landlords," he says, "many years ago, made the experiment of fixing, at great expense, colonies of Palatines on their estates. They had houses built for them, plots of land assigned to each, at a rent of favor, assisted in stock, and all of them with leases for lives from the head landlord. The poor Irish are very rarely treated in this manner, but when they are, they work much greater improvements than are common among these Germans." (*Tour in Ireland*, vol. ii. App. pp. 24, 25.)

tuted owners of farms large enough to furnish them with constant occupation, more especially when those farms, consisting of land recently reclaimed, demanded more than ordinary assiduity for the development of their resources. In reply to this, reference might be made to the notorious fact, that Irish laborers, when removed to situations in which industry is liberally rewarded, exert themselves as strenuously as those of any other nation; and, even in Ireland, examples are not wanting of peasants not only working hard, but applying themselves with ardor and success to the very occupation their fitness for which we are now considering. Young observed, long ago, that "little occupiers who can get leases of a mountain side, make exertions in improvement, which, though far enough from being complete, show clearly what great effects encouragement would have amongst them;"[40] and he adds, "that the idleness seen among them, when working for those who oppress them, is a very contrast to the vigor and activity with which the same people work when themselves alone reap the benefit of their labor."[41] Among the grounds for this estimate of the Irish character, was an experiment tried by Young himself. On Lord Kingsborough's[42] estate he marked a road, and assigned portions of the waste on each side to such as were willing to form the fences in the manner prescribed, and to cultivate and inhabit the land; allowing each a guinea towards his cabin, and promising the best land rent free for three years, and the worst for five. The eagerness with which the poor people came into the scheme convinced him that they wanted nothing but a little encouragement to enter with all their

---

[40] *Tour*, vol. ii. App. p. 22.

[41] *Ibid.* p. 72

[42] [Edward King, Viscount Kingsborough (1795-1837), Irish antiquarian who attempted to prove that the native inhabitants of the Americas were descended from the Ten Lost Tribes of Israel. As a result of his efforts, a large number of facsimile pre-Columbian codices and accounts by early European explorers were collected and published. The expense of publication of the lavishly illustrated volumes bankrupted him, and he was sentenced to debtor's prison, where he died of typhus.]

might and spirit into the work of improvement. They trusted to his assurance to go to work upon the ditches, and actually made a considerable progress. "In all undertakings of this kind in Ireland," he continues, "it is the poor cottiers and the very little farmers who are the best tools to employ, and the best tenants to let the land to;"[43] and this is confirmed by Mr. Nicholls, who says that "most of the recently reclaimed land which he saw in the western counties was reclaimed by the small occupiers, who drained and enclosed an acre or two at a time."[44] But the evidence taken by the Land Commission,[45] being the latest, may also be considered the most valuable. A practice, we are told, not uncommonly adopted by Irish farmers, is that of "giving a small piece of waste land to a poor cottier or herdsman, for the first three crops, after which the improved portion is returned to the farmer, and a fresh portion is taken on the same terms by the cottier. Here are persons of the very poorest class obtaining a livelihood by the cultivation of waste land, under the most discouraging and least remunerative circumstances that can well be imagined." Where more favorable terms are conceded to the tenants, the progress of improvement is proportionate. On the Lough Ash estate, in Tyrone, about four hundred acres of waste land have been distributed among thirty tenants, most of whom have leases for twenty-one years, and obtained the land rent free for the first part of the term, on condition of paying a gradually increasing rent during the remainder. These tenants took possession of

---

[43] *Tour*, vol. ii. App. p. 72.

[44] Nicholl's *Reports on Irish Poor Laws*, p. 18.

[45] [Thornton refers to the Land Commission established under the Landlord & Tenant (Ireland) Act of 1870. This is considered to have been largely ineffectual, even counterproductive, but of great symbolic importance in Gladstone's efforts to secure Home Rule for Ireland (see Appendix IV). Policymakers made great use of *Griffith's Valuation*. In general, "Irish Land Commission" refers to the commission established under the Land Law (Ireland) Act of 1881, and which under the Ashbourne Act of 1885 and in response to the "Land War" (see Appendix VI), developed into a tenant purchasing commission that assisted in the agreed transfer of freehold farmland from landlord to tenant.]

their respective allotments at different periods, between the years 1829 and 1840. They belonged originally to the "poorest class of cottiers;" but, when visited by the Land Commissioners, "had raised themselves into a comfortable body of farmers."[46]

Examples of this kind may not, however, be numerous enough to establish a national reputation for industry, and it would, no doubt, be safer to assume that the energies of the Irish peasantry would require to be artificially stimulated. Without adopting the theory of the incorrigible laziness of the Celtic race, with which some writers perversely choose to stultify all their own suggestions for the benefit of Ireland, we may acknowledge it to be doubtful whether people who had been dawdling about all their lives, would, when regular occupation was offered to them" spontaneously apply themselves to it. There is certainly some reason to apprehend that if settlers of this description were merely translated to their respective allotments, and there abandoned to their own devices, many of them might prefer sloth and poverty to toil and comfort; and, at any rate, no appeal to their hopes or fears, that might help to rouse them to activity, should be rejected as superfluous. Some direct attempts might be made to imbue them with new and improved tastes, and they should certainly be made acquainted with the advantages of their position, taught how to avail themselves of them, and threatened with their withdrawal in the event of their neglecting to make use of them. One advantage of having the houses on the reclaimed lands built under the superintendence of public officers, would be, that their occupants would receive at once tolerably exalted notions of one sort of comfort of which they might long have remained ignorant, if they had been permitted to build dwellings according to their own fancy, and had taken for their models the vile sties with which they had previously been satisfied. In general, however, it is sufficient, in order to create new wants, that the means of gratifying them be provided. If the colonists could be made to under-

---

[46] *Digest of Evidence on Occupation of Land*, p. 570.

stand, that by taking a little pains they could procure good clothes and good food, they would quickly discover that a whole coat is better than rags, and that a dinner of potatoes is immensely improved by the addition of bread and cheese and bacon. In order to convey to them the needful preliminary information, the whole number of colonies might be arranged in districts, to each of which should be appointed a scientific agriculturist, whose duty it would be to visit periodically every farm placed under his superintendence, and to instruct the owner in the principles of husbandry. Such agricultural teachers are already employed by several landlords, and have in general done much good. When their advice has not been neutralized by superciliousness on their part, it has commonly been very well received. They have easily overcome the prejudices against new practices, entertained by the peasantry, and have persuaded them to adopt improved modes of drainage, better rotations, artificial grasses and other green crops.[47] Equal success might be expected with the settlers on the waste lands, and the more surely, as with regard to them, a little compulsion might be used in case of need. The permanence of their tenure might be declared contingent on their behavior, and they might be threatened with the resumption of their grants unless their farms were brought into cultivation within a specified time.

Such measures, however, would be necessary only with the original colonists, whose vicious habits, inherited from a long line of ancestors, might frustrate any scheme that depended for success on their eradication. But the second and all succeeding generations might be trained betimes in the way in which they should walk. The influence of education might be brought to bear upon them by machinery to be provided in the following manner. The home colonies would either be annexed to villages previously existing, or would constitute distinct communities; and, on account of the situation of the waste lands, the latter arrangement would probably be by far the most general.

---

[47] *Digest of Evidence, ut supra*, p. 28.

To each of the separate colonies might be appointed a schoolmaster, who, besides the usual qualifications for the post, should be required to have studied at an agricultural seminary, and thus to have become competent to impart to the children of farmers the special instruction which such pupils require. Every householder should be required by the conditions of his tenure to send his children, between certain ages, to attend the lessons of this master, whose remuneration might consist partly of a fee for every pupil, partly of a rent-free house and ground, and partly of a rent-charge on the land. In a community consisting at first of 200 families, and occupying consequently 1,600 acres, a contribution of eighteen pence an acre would amount to £120 a year, which, added to the other emoluments of the office, would procure the services of a properly qualified person. The spiritual instruction of the community might be provided for in a similar manner, by the appointment of a priest, who, besides a manse and glebe and the usual ecclesiastical fees, should be allowed a stipend of the same amount as the schoolmaster, and arising from the same source. The rate which it would be necessary to levy for the payment of both religious and secular teachers, and for the satisfaction of the government claim, would not exceed twelve shillings an acre, or only one-third of the rent that might readily be obtained for the land.

With these precautions, it may be sanguinely hoped that the experiment would succeed. The wastes recommended for reclamation are such as would deserve the attention even of a speculator, seeking not a mere livelihood, but a profitable investment for his money; for experience has shown that an outlay of five or six pounds per acre would add twenty or thirty shillings to the rentable value. Six acres of such land, held at the full rent, enable the Belgian tenant-farmer, not only to live in comfort, but to save money. Eight acres, therefore, held in perpetuity at a rent of only one-third the original yearly value, could not be an inadequate provision even for Irishmen, if only the latter could be induced to work; and it is proposed to urge them to exertion by every motive that can stimulate industry. Perhaps, then, we may be permitted to assume that the original grantees would rise from their present indigence to comparative affluence. It remains to be considered whether their prosperity would be permanent, or whether it would be frittered away by the gradual subdivision of the original tenements. The question of the inherent tendency of small properties to continual diminution has already been fully discussed, and it is hoped that sufficient cause has been shown for answering it in the negative. The partition of land, it appears, is seldom carried too far except where the various claimants have, by constant companionship with privation, accustomed themselves to expect nothing more than a bare subsistence, and have no means of obtaining even that, except from the occupation of a piece of ground; and it is probable that even Irishmen, when relieved from the necessity which now leaves them no alternative but to divide the holdings of their parents, would refrain from a course of which they could not fail to perceive the ruinous consequences. With all their Irishism they are not altogether void of reason, but would probably act in much the same manner as other rational beings in similar circumstances. If brought up in the enjoyment of competence they would not content themselves with a miserable pittance, merely because they could derive it from land of their own. If their patrimony were insufficient to maintain them in the style to which they had been accustomed, they would rather dispose of it and seek a livelihood elsewhere. Such are natural inferences from observation of what happens among peasant proprietors in other countries. Still, if attention be confined to Ireland, it cannot be denied that subdivision has long been the universal practice there not indeed among peasant proprietors, for there are none such in the island but among the miserable cottiers, from whom it is proposed to select the future proprietors. It is possible that with these men, notwithstanding the change in their situation, habit might be more powerful that prudence, and that the continual subdivision of farms might in two or three generations plunge the descendants of the colonists into the destitution from which their forefathers had been raised. Such a result, although very unlikely to occur, is nevertheless possible, and in a matter of so much moment it would be unwise to leave anything to chance. All ground for apprehension might however be removed, assurance might be made doubly sure, the possibility of excessive subdivision might be prevented, by the adoption of regulations respecting the succession to the farms to be formed on the waste lands. The construction of such rules would doubtless be a work of great delicacy. In legislating for small estates two opposite evils are to be guarded against their too frequent consolidation not less than their excessive partition. The former is, indeed, by far the most difficult to prevent, for contiguous properties have so much chemical affinity for each other that very strong opposing forces are necessary to prevent their combination. Small properties have scarcely anywhere stood their ground permanently, unless gavelkind, or some similar custom of inheritance, has prevailed; and if the law of primogeniture were to be enforced among the colonists of the Irish waste lands, the class of small proprietors would probably sooner or later disappear. But, on the other hand, to establish gavelkind would be to give a legal warrant for the very partition, against which extraordinary precautions are supposed to be necessary in Ireland; and gavelkind, besides, by ensuring to every child a portion of the family estate, would unduly weaken parental authority. In this dilemma a middle course would perhaps be the most advisable.

When it was proposed to divide the reclaimed wastes into allotments of eight acres, it was not intended to attach any special importance to that size, or to recommend that it should be protected against subsequent alteration. There is, however, a minimum size which properties must possess in order to deserve the name of farms, and a maximum size which they cannot exceed without ceasing to be peasant properties. These limits cannot be defined, for they differ in different situations with the productiveness of the soil and the skill and industry of the cultivator; but we will suppose that in Ireland, under good management, five acres would furnish a family with full occupation and adequate subsistence, and that fifty acres would elevate the owner above the condition of a mere husbandman. If it should be thought desirable to prescribe these as the most usual boundaries for the possessions of the settlers and their descendants, without, however, absolutely prohibiting the future formation of any of larger or smaller size the end might be attained by some such rules as the following. An owner of more than five acres might be allowed the power of alienation during his lifetime, provided that he did not dispose of a smaller portion than five acres. A person whose estate did not reach that limit should not be permitted to diminish it, but if desirous of alienating, should be required to alienate the whole. Every landowner having children might be allowed to select from amongst them one or more to be his heirs, provided that he bequeathed to no one more than fifty acres, without making the same provision for as many of his other children as his estate would permit; and provided also, that he bequeathed to none a portion of less than five acres, unless, after division into portions of five acres, one portion of inferior extent should remain, of which he might then be permitted to make a separate bequest. In the case of persons dying intestate, the eldest son might, if the estate were under five acres, be entitled to the whole, and if it exceeded that limit, might take the principal dwelling-house and five acres adjoining. The remainder of the land might be distributed among the other children, or among as many of them, in order of seniority, as could be put in possession of five acres each. If any land then remained, it might, if less than five acres, be given to the eldest of the children previously unprovided for; and if it exceeded five acres, it might be divided equally among all the children, care being taken in such partition that every inheritance should be compact, and not composed of scattered fragments. It will no doubt be perceived that a law of succession like this, though professedly designed to prevent the size from falling below five acres, would not only permit, but would favor, the formation of some properties of smaller size. It must also be remarked, however, that it would limit the number of such properties; and would moreover prevent a property of less than five acres, when once formed, from being again subdivided. With these precautions, the existence of such properties, instead of being an evil, would be attended with the best consequences. If there were no farms too large to be cultivated exclusively by the occupiers, pieces of land too small to furnish their owners with adequate employment and subsistence might be productive of idleness and poverty, for the deficiency of their resources could not be supplied. But in Ireland there are, and no doubt always will be, a considerable number of farms extensive enough to require the assistance of hired labor, and upon those farms, petty proprietors, insufficiently employed at home, might obtain supplementary occupation. Their pieces of ground would not constitute their principal means of livelihood, but would merely answer the same purpose as the allotments occasionally granted to English laborers, and this the more efficaciously as they would be held on much more favorable terms. Now, the occupation of a little land for cultivation in their intervals of leisure is not only advantageous to agricultural day laborers, but seems to be almost indispensable to enable them to live in comfort and security. This they can seldom do when they are entirely dependent upon wages. It seems impossible so to accommodate the supply of agricultural labor to the demand as that the latter shall be fully satisfied, and yet that labor shall be adequately rewarded. And for this reason. Agriculture requires different quantities of labor at different seasons. If, then, the number of laborers be equal to the demand in the busy season, it must exceed the demand in the slack season. But as even during the first period, competition will have been keen enough to prevent wages from rising above the sum required for the maintenance of a family, at other times it must depress them below that amount, so that the laborer who has no resource but his hire, must be reduced to distress during part of every year. Where day laborers enjoy competence, it will be found almost invariably either that they are artisans or manufacturers as well as husbandmen, or that they hold a little land in their own possession. In many parts of the Continent they have both these additional resources. In England they have neither. In England, accordingly, when their employers have no immediate occasion for their services, they must apply for eleemosynary aid, and, in many rural parishes, half the laborers are every winter entered on the list of pauper pensioners. In the settlements to be formed on the Irish wastes, such of the laborers as inherited small plots of ground, would be raised above this degrading necessity.

Colonization of the waste lands thus offers a means of speedily raising the most destitute portion of the Irish people to independence and comfort, and of permanently securing those blessings to their descendants. But the advantages of the scheme would not be confined to those most directly affected by it, but would be shared largely by the remainder of the peasantry, and more or less by every section of the nation. By the removal of nearly 200,000 families from the lands already cultivated, an end would be put to the present ruinous competition in the land and labor markets; labor would command, and land be obtainable at, reasonable prices; rent would fall to the amount which the farmer could pay without impoverishing himself, and wages would rise, in consequence both of the decrease in the number of laborers, and of the increase of the means of the farmers. Improvement to this extent would take place naturally and as a necessary consequence of the reclamation of the waste lands, and legislative interference would be requisite only to promote and confirm it. With these views, two suggestions may be offered; one, the enactment of a law rendering the grant of leases obligatory, a measure which, though no longer recommended by the same urgent necessity, would, when tenants were able to negotiate with landlords on more equal terms, be no longer open to the same objection as at present; and the other, the allotment to the laborers remaining on the present cultivated area of plots of common land, of half an acre or an acre in extent, on the same conditions as the grants made to the settlers on the wastes. The whole body of peasantry — laborers, cottiers, and farmers — would then, for the first time, be placed in situations in which their subsequent lot would depend upon their own exertions. Specific instruction might still be necessary to teach them the value of the means at their command, but were this afforded, it cannot be doubted that industry would require no other stimulus than self-interest. Industry would introduce plenty, and plenty be accompanied by content. Tranquility would succeed to desperation and violence, and capital would no longer be deterred from flowing wherever a suitable field were offered for its employment. Canals and railways would at once mark and facilitate the progress of enterprise, mines would be worked, fisheries and such manufactures as were adapted to the country established, the conveniences of civilized life would be multiplied and brought within the reach of every class of the community. The advance of national prosperity would correspond with that of individual happiness. The whole empire would receive a vast accession of vigor when its most exhausting drain was converted into an abundant source of wealth, and when the festering wound in one of its principal members was at length healed.

A scheme so simple, yet promising such brilliant results, may perhaps, on that account alone, be summarily rejected as visionary. Large professions are generally received with distrust, the stronger and more natural, in proportion as they are declared to be easy of fulfillment. The condition of Ireland is commonly regarded as almost hopeless; ingenuity has long perplexed itself in attempts to investigate the nature of her disorder; every remedy hitherto applied has failed to afford even partial or temporary relief. It will not, then, be readily believed that the means of effecting a perfect cure were always at hand, open to view, but unnoticed or unappreciated. Yet, when every other prescription has been tried in vain, a new proposal is at least entitled to examination; and the one offered in the foregoing pages has stronger recommendations than that of mere novelty. Its adoption would procure for the peasantry an extension of territory, which, even if it were not, as argued, the only practicable means, would certainly be an infallible means of procuring for them that additional employment without which they can never emerge from their present debasement. They themselves, with an instinctive perception of what their situation requires, are resolute in their demands for land, and are even now engaged with its actual proprietors in a fearful struggle, of which it is impossible to foresee the end. Yet, to pacify them by assigning additional tracts for their occupation is not even pretended to be an object of any scheme hitherto propounded, save of this for the reclamation of the waste lands, and of another, already alluded to — for emigration to British America.[48] The latter, beset as it is with difficulties, apparently insuperable, has nevertheless attracted a considerable share of attention; the very simplicity and practicability of the former are perhaps the cause of its having been treated with comparative neglect. Great statesmen will scarcely deign to listen unless some complicated project — some "great thing" — be submitted for their consideration. They disdain to use plain and obvious methods for the cure of national leprosy, even as Naaman, the Syrian, hesitated to wash in Jordan, and be clean, while there were Abana and Pharpar, rivers of Damascus, better than all the waters of Israel.

---

[48] [Canada.]

7. Ireland, Forecast from 1873

Neglect of Suggestions offered in preceding Chapter — Failure of similar plans wherever tried — Causes of such failure — Precautions which might have prevented it in Ireland — Remedial and pacifying Expedients actually adopted in Ireland —Continuance, nevertheless, of Irish Disaffection — Governmental interposition for factitious creation of a Peasant Proprietary no longer desirable — Removal of Legal Obstacles to natural growth of such a Proprietary the only legislative aid required — Interest of existing Landowners in fostering such natural growth

In respect of sentiment not less than of statement of fact, the preceding chapter, has, by lapse of time, become in portions obsolete; yet it is left very nearly as originally written five and twenty years ago, in hopes, as I frankly own, that the courteous reader may judge how good on the whole the advice then given was, and how different, if it had been forthwith followed, might now be the condition of Ireland. True, plans very similar to the one recommended, have occasionally been tried on the Continent, and have in every instance utterly failed, one example, fairly typical of the rest, being thus described by Col. Mure;

"In 1852, when, owing to the potato blight, which since 1846 had more or less devastated the country, together with the absorption of hand weaving by steam power, the greatest distress prevailed among the dense population of Flanders, the Government was induced to purchase certain lands in the Commune of Lommel, in the wildest parts of the Campine, in order there to establish a colony of impoverished Flemish peasants, the object being partly to relieve Flanders of its superabundant population, and partly to introduce that skill and industry which for fifty generations have distinguished the Flemish cultivator, and thereby advance the reclamation of hitherto almost useless lands.

"Two hundred and forty acres were purchased and divided into twenty small farms. Of each farm five acres were reclaimed, sown, and fenced; excellent steadings were built, and irrigation supplied from the canals *gratis*; good roads were made; even trees were planted for firewood — everything, in fact, that a reasonable being could desire; a church and school were erected.

"These farms were let to twenty Flemish families on a redemption lease of thirty years. For the first five years no rent was exacted, the annual rent for the remaining twenty-five years graduating on a small increasing scale until the full purchase-money of £120 per farm was paid off; there were various modes, however, by which the tenant was enabled to redeem, which I need not enter into. There were also certain conditions, but all of the most advantageous kinds; sub-letting was forbidden.

"The result was that, before ten years had elapsed, the tenants, apparently considering that the Government was indebted to them, gradually neglected to fulfill any conditions whatever; became idle, insolent, and indifferent; and, instead of being an example of skill and industry to the neighborhood, soon became remarkable for every vice which follows in the train of irresponsibility and dependence. Finally, the property, which had cost the State £10,400, was sold for £1,600 by auction, to my informant himself, who, on entering, evicted the vagabond Government pensioners. The lands are now let on the usual conditions, are tolerably cultivated, and in course of time will be valuable property."[1]

Really, it does look as if private energy were unable to survive the torpedo-like touch of governmental support. Certainly, from Indian railways downwards, every private enterprise languishes which government guarantees. In the worst parts of the Campine, a region comprising within its limits the greater part of the provinces of Antwerp and of Belgian Limburg, the tourist may see what almost the whole of Flanders once was — a waste, as far as eye can reach, of intermingling moor and marsh. Thirty years ago, few and far between were the oases that diversified the Campine wilderness; but, to the present writer,

---

[1] Letter to the *Times*, Jan. 24, 1870.

while traversing it last autumn from end to end, in more than one direction, there was a species of disappointment in remarking how much and how fast the progress of reclamation is interfering with the picturesque effects which some clever landscapes of the modern Belgian school of painting had led him to look for. It has now become difficult to get absolutely out of sight of fields under crop, or of fir plantations in process of clearance for conversion into arable land, or at any rate of land which is being trenched, in order to be planted with firs, with a view to the same eventual conversion. These improvements are the work of volunteers without other prompting than that of self-interest, and there are few Flemish peasants without land of their own who would not gladly undertake, and gladly pay for permission to undertake similar improvements. Yet, when some of these very peasants were conveyed carriage-free to the Campine, and set down on allotments already reclaimed to their hand, the receipt of so much preliminary help seems to have disabled them from helping themselves. They contrived to persuade themselves that all the solicitude bestowed on them must somehow have been no more than their due, which it was rather indeed a favor on their part to accept, and that to do anything for themselves would be a wanton surrender of dignity, and of the right to have everything done for them. Without disparagement of the Irish character, it may be suspected that Irishmen, similarly circumstanced, would not have effectually resisted the demoralizing influences to which even Flemings succumbed. They too, no doubt, if subjected to the coaxing and petting by which children are spoiled, might have responded by behaving like spoiled children. This danger was not, however, overlooked in the recommendations offered above for the colonization of Irish wastes, and resort to a little wholesome compulsion was suggested as a suitable precaution against it. Somewhat stern supervision would no doubt have been indispensable to prevent the colonists from idling, and much judgment would have been required for selection of good disciplinarian superintendents. This however would have been the chief preliminary difficulty. If there be no British regiment of which, whatever be the preponderance in its composition of the Irish element, we do not feel justly confident that, well led; it will go anywhere and do anything, what room can there be for apprehension that agricultural trainbands, albeit composed exclusively of the same element, would, under suitable leadership, have proved themselves fully equal to the subjugation of Irish waste lands? The enterprise might, indeed, have occupied many tedious campaigns, checkered by not a few disheartening reverses, but success in the end would have been certain, if only the patience of the commanders and of the on-looking and cash-advancing public had held out long enough.

No such peaceful warfare was however attempted; but in its stead, those several alternative expedients examined a while ago in connection with it, have, one after the other, been resorted to. Railways have been extensively made, and although, as a matter of course, not less extensively jobbed,[2] present themselves in numerous directions as smoothened tracts along which progress of every sort may speed with materially accelerated strides. Some millions sterling of public money have been laid out on other public works, either directly by the State or through the medium of loans to private individuals, and the result in arterial drainage and the like, if not quite full money's worth, is at any rate a conspicuous return for the money. Emigration has taken place spontaneously, on a scale on which the boldest fancy would have deemed it incapable of being artificially urged on a scale without historical parallel save in Israel's Exodus from Egypt. That standing reproach to England, that standing insult to Ireland, the Church of a small minority, rich with the spoils of the Church of a majority,[3] no longer stands to gall to madness the sensitive pride of a generous people, although the one single principle — that of restoration to the rightful owners — that could fully justify the disendowment, was unluckily lost sight of. By the operation of the Encumbered and Landed Estates Courts, an eighth of the surface of

---

[2] [Subjected to "political pork."]
[3] [The established Episcopal Church of Ireland.]

Ireland has been relieved from the dead weight of a pauper proprietary, whose superincumbent pressure served only to squeeze periodically out of the soil some few drops more of its remaining fertility. Finally, by the Landlord and Tenant Act of 1870, a powerful stimulus has been applied to the grant of leases, and some imperfect security of an inferior kind provided where that of leases is withheld. Measures these, or half measures as the case may be — they, each and all, may claim to be regarded as healing processes. How far, then, has their combination resulted in re-establishment of the national health? The reply given by Fenian[4] riot and Home Rule[5] rant is not encouraging. "Never," says Judge Longfield, "were Irish farmers more prosperous than at the present moment; never were they more discontented."[6] Even so slight, as yet, are the symptoms of abatement in that national agitation which, if only by frightening away capital, prevents the sowing of the first seeds of social regeneration. Neither, indeed, to ensure the indispensable calm, will any merely soothing measures suffice, unaccompanied by monitory manifestations of self-conscious strength on the part of the ministering agency; and, unhappily, all the legislative energy recently exhibited in regard to Ireland has been neutralized by pitiable executive weakness. No amount of beneficence can gain credit for benevolence for an administration which systematically accepts treason as an apology for murder, and suffers policemen to be knocked on the head unavenged, provided political motives are urged for the assault. Its utmost liberality will then be construed into timidity, from which, by further bullying, any amount of further concessions may be extorted. No government need hope to be respected that dares not, in self-defense, meet force by force, putting down sedition with a strong hand, and putting down even trial by jury where juries ally themselves with sedition. That any British statesman, of whatever complexion, should venture on a policy of such Cromwellian decision is, however, in these

---

[4] [See Appendix V.]
[5] [See Appendix IV.]
[6] *Cobden Club Essays.* First Series, p. 7.

days out of the question. Is it not one of our national glories that ours is a government by party, carried on by an unremitting "strife of Freedom," wherein, as has been said, "everyone may get a share of what is going;" Whig and Tory, Conservative and Destructive, all alike, ranking party zeal first among the virtues, and patriotism at best but second, and, by motions and counter-motions in their struggle for place and power, keeping up an edifying show of administrative activity, and reducing administrative action as nearly as possible to zero?[7] There is the respect that makes the Irish difficulty of so long life, and threatens to render it immortal unless, in the absence of any extrinsic impulse towards the repression of disorder, the growth of a native party of order naturally take place or be artificially fostered. Now, might not the couple of hundred thousand peasant proprietors, whose settlement on the waste lands was hypothetically provided for in the last chapter, have constituted a nucleus of such a party? "As a matter of fact," says Lord Dufferin,[8] "few of the actual occupiers of land are tainted with Fenianism. Scarcely any farmers have been implicated in that conspiracy, though, perhaps, some of their relatives (in other words, persons with a much more modified interest in land than themselves) may have been entrapped. The tenant of a piece of land, even under the alleged disadvantageous condition of his existence, has much more to lose than to gain by the overthrow of the existing order of things."[9] But, if it be thus with mere occupiers, mere tenants-at-will, with an interest in the land modified down to almost vanishing point, how would it have been with our supposed peasant owners, with an interest altogether unmodified in keeping what they had got? Might not these in case of emergency have been relied upon for enrolling themselves as "Defenders" or "United Irishmen"

---

[7] [Constitutional scholar Albert Venn Dicey (1835-1922), believed party politics to be one of the greatest dangers to democracy in both the United Kingdom and the United States.]
[8] [Frederick Hamilton-Temple-Blackwood, First Marquess of Dufferin and Ava (1826-1902), British (Scots-Irish) diplomat.]
[9] *Irish Emigration*, p. 201.

with views the very opposite of those of the bands so designated in 1798.[10] The time for creating a numerous peasant proprietary in the summary mode suggested has, however, long gone by, and is not now to be recovered.[11] How seldom, alas, does England, in respect of Irish reforms, take time by the forelock![12]

Still, indeed, there remains in Ireland enough and more than enough both of waste lands convertible into peasant freeholds, and of peasants whose labor could not be better utilized than in so converting them — themselves experiencing simultaneously a corresponding conversion. Moreover, thanks to emigration, there would now be comparatively ample breathing time within which to perform all subsidiary operations with needful forethought and deliberation. Yet, prepossessed as I naturally am in favor of a plan which, although frequently fathered upon Mr. Mill and others, has by Mr. Mill himself been distinctly declared to be originally mine,[13] I would not now advocate its adoption even on a limited scale, partly because I feel that the advocacy would be as ineffectual as ever, but partly, also, because there is no longer the same pretext or occasion for it. The tenure of land, when not artificially warped, but left free to take whatever shape circum-

---

[10] [The reference is to the "Wexford Rebellion" of 1798, which set the tone for Irish/English relations throughout the 19th century.]

[11] [This is true only if ownership is restricted to the limited amount of landed capital. If extended to other forms of capital, e.g., industrial and commercial capital to be formed in the future, the amount available is, to all intents and purposes, unlimited. See Appendix XI.]

[12] [That is, show respect for the fact that nothing stays the same over time.]

[13] Alluding to proposals for the colonization of Irish wastes by Irish peasants, Mr. Mill says; "This plan has been strongly pressed upon the public by several writers, but the first to bring it prominently forward in England was Mr. W. Thornton, in a work (Overpopulation and its Remedy) honorably distinguished," etc. Principles of Political Economy, first edition, 1848, p. 392. I may mention that the first edition of my Peasant Proprietors was published some weeks before the first edition of Mr. Mill's Political Economy appeared.

stances are calculated to give, generally adapts itself to the social requirements of time and place; and the condition of a country must be very peculiar, and scarcely less critical than that of Ireland five and twenty years ago, to warrant a legislature in attempting to accelerate the assumption of any particular shape. But the condition of Ireland has within the last twenty-five years changed very materially; slight as may have been the progress made towards a solution of her social problem, the problem itself has become greatly simplified; her epidemic misery has diminished greatly both in extent and intensity, and what remains of the disease is not too desperate to be expected to yield to none but desperate remedies. Fully persuaded, as I continue to be, that a peasant proprietary is one of Ireland's foremost needs, I nevertheless believe that it may now be left to grow up spontaneously, without other legislative aid than would consist in removal of the obstacles which past legislation has heaped in its way. Of some of these, the Encumbered and Landed Estates Courts have already made, and are making short work; and cessation of the factitious encouragement given by law to primogeniture and entails, together with the substitution of some cheap and simple machinery for verifying titles to land, for the labyrinthine tissue of legal complexities through which search has now to be made for them, would go far to dispose of the rest. If all estates with which it was for the interest of the owners to part could be brought to market without more let or hindrance, and be sold there without payment of higher market tolls or other fees than those to which mercantile goods and chattels are liable, they would, it may be presumed, equally with miscellaneous merchandise, pass into the possession of the customers best fitted to utilize them. They would be offered for sale in portions of all sizes, large and small, and partly, no doubt, in portions small enough to come within the means of the most numerous class of customers — of the petty farmers, to wit, who, beggarly looking as they and all their environments are, often have, tied up in an old stocking, a good store of sovereigns lying idle until called forth to furnish a daughter's dower.[14] To judge from what happens elsewhere in analogous circumstances, the owners of these petty hoards would be rather too eager than the reverse to avail themselves of the opportunities offered for territorial investment; and, over and above the numerous petty freeholders coming consequently into being, there would be a much greater number of freeholders in prospect, who, in the five, ten, and fifteen acre farms scattered around them, would see ladders by which they might hope to mount from the grade of journeymen to that, first of tenant farmers, and then of farmers of their own acres. To insist upon the immense benefit to the entire peasantry of these transformations, immediate and prospective, would be but to repeat once again what has already been repeatedly urged throughout this volume. What rather I feel to be incumbent upon me is to admit that completest realization of the benefit anticipated would still fall far short of what I conceive would result from a really perfect land system. According to my ideal on that subject, there should be no property in land save that of the whole nation in its corporate capacity; and those Asiatic countries in which the State, as trustee for the nation, is sole landed proprietor, would, in my opinion, be infinitely to be congratulated, were there but adequate security that the rights involved in the trust would be duly appreciated and judiciously exercised by those who have to administer it.[15] In countries, however, in which such national ownership has either never existed or has been inconsiderately relinquished, its establishment or restoration by fair means is not to be expected on this side [of the] millennium[16] — nor yet by foul means, without a deluge of revolutionary bloodshed such as has not been paralleled, even aqueously, on this side [of] the Flood, and such as, on its sub-

---

[14] "Moreover, we know from bank returns that Irish farmers have actually £17,000,000 lying idle in banks." Cliffe Leslie's *Land Systems*, p. 111.
[15] [See Appendix XII]
[16] ["The Coming of the Kingdom."]

sidence, would leave surviving but a small remnant of the nation to avail itself of the eventually emergent national right. With reference to which hopelessness of theoretical perfection in the matter, it were not perhaps amiss for the most advanced of land reformers to aim at something lower and more practicable than their present *summum bonum* — the "nationalization" of the soil — and to content themselves with striving to reduce the evils of private proprietorship to a minimum. Having so brought their aspirations within practicable limits, they would probably recognize the spontaneous intermixture of peasant proprietors among the present monopolists of land as an important move in the right direction; nor are there wanting considerations, though of an opposite character, calculated to commend the same movement equally to the most obstinately prejudiced of anti-reformers. Already in the murmurs, passing ever and anon into growls, of a landless multitude — who, as soon as they awake to full appreciation of their recently conceded political powers, will perceive themselves to be absolute masters of every domestic situation — whoso lists, may distinguish sounds ominously resembling "the surly laughter of ocean preluding a storm." But, to prevent storms from breaking upon land, what more effectual than a breakwater? — what appearance more welcome, to the dwellers on a menaced shore, than that of such a barrier forming itself naturally? and what sort of toleration would there in such case be for port rules, ballast regulations, or the like, calculated to obstruct the deposition of suitable materials?

To the whole existing order of landlords, scarcely more to Irish than to English and Scottish, the parable is spoken. All alike may profit by pondering over its moral, on condition, however, of not lingering too long in meditation. In every quarter of the United Kingdom a storm against landlordism is audibly brewing, which, if allowed to break, will shake the edifice to its foundations, not, assuredly, leaving undislocated the superstructure. Yet landlordism, even if a hundred times more unpopular than it has, so far, become amongst ourselves, might be rendered one of the most popular of institutions, by simply having its privileges, now so invidiously concentrated, made freely accessible to all — the meanest farm laborer included; and to this change in its character the only remaining impediments are legal ones, of which landlords and their legal advisers are the chief upholders. On the legal counsel concerned in the case, the most presumptuous of unprofessional outsiders would shrink from obtruding advice; but it ought not to be hopeless to invite landlords to consider whether the immunity of periodical bankruptcy which entails confer, is a really valuable privilege; and whether the dignity involved in the tedious formalities now hampering the sale of land is adequate compensation for the depreciation, by a third or more, of the market value of land thereon consequent; whether at any rate it is wise, for the sake of retaining these minor outposts, to impede the formation of a breakwater which, by conversion from landless into landed, of a good proportion of the sea of men foaming in the front, may prevent their main position from being swept away.[17] It rests with themselves to have, or not to have, in a seemingly inevitable and not distant controversy as to their continued existence as a class, the whole rural population as decidedly for them, as, in Ireland at least, the main bulk thereof is at present decidedly against them. But in order to resolve wisely on the course to be taken they must be wise betimes; for much longer to defer will be discovered too late to have been little short of madness.

---

[17] In the Appendix [II] will be found some striking remarks of M. de Laveleye, which no one who has aught to fear from agrarian convulsion should omit to read.

Appendices

I. Letter to the Author from Mr. Le Beir

Letter to the Author from Mr. Le Beir, Secretary of the Royal Agricultural Society of Guernsey, on the Produce of Wheat in that Island

Guernsey, Grand Moulin
13 January 1848

My Dear Sir,

I am glad that our humble islet draws your notice on account of its great productiveness in wheat, and that it has kept a hold on your memory. There is no mistake in the report unless on the part of the grower, and a mistake might certainly sooner occur in grain than in roots, of which a fair average perch out of a *vergée* is chosen, and seen dug, and weighed by a sub-committee of the general Agricultural Committee. In corn, hitherto, the prizes have been awarded to the best marketable qualities, the extended attention required from the committee, from the cutting to the winnowing of the corn, having deterred them from a further examination; so that it has been more out of curiosity than otherwise, that an account of the produce and a sheaf of the same corn have been required to accompany the bushel sample at the winter show. The largest produce in the last three years has been 9½, 10, and 9 English quarters to the English acre, as declared solemnly by the growers, men of the highest respectability, in the following manner. Suppose ten quarters to the acre; 500 sheaves per *vergée*, (I have seen 530), yielding 8 bushels of 44 lbs. Guernsey per 100 sheaves, give 10 quarters of 4 bushels Guernsey. Now, as the Guernsey quarter and *vergée* bear the same proportion to the English quarter and acre, namely, two-fifths, the calculation is easy. In this case it would be 1,250 sheaves to the acre, at 253 lbs. Guernsey, the 100 sheaves, giving 4,400 lbs., which, reduced by 55 lbs. Guernsey (about the weight of the English bushel), produces 80 English bushels, or 10 quarters. Pure seaweed ashes, as the rate of 100

- 215 -

bushels an acre, are the best manure. It gives strong straw and heavy grain. The ashes are five-pence a bushel.

Yours most sincerely,

N. Le Beir.

II. Remarks by M. de Laveleye

Remarks by M. de Laveleye on the Anti-Revolutionary Influence of Peasant Proprietorship

It may be thought a matter for surprise that, in Flanders, feelings hostile to social order nevertheless do not manifest themselves, and that agrarian outrages are never perpetrated as in Ireland, although I think it certain that, in consequence of excessive competition, the Flemish farmer is much more ground down by his landlord than the Irish tenant. The fact that in Flanders, as in all countries in which landed property is distributed among a large number of owners, the ideas called socialist in the bad sense of the word do not obtain, is to be accounted for as follows:[1] —

"The Flemish tenant, although ground down by the constant rise of rents, lives among his equals, peasants like himself, who have tenants whom they use just as the large landowner does his. His father, his brother, perhaps the man himself, possesses something like an acre of land, which he lets at as high a rent as he can get. In the public house, peasant proprietors will boast of the high rents they get for their lands, just as they might boast of having sold their pigs or potatoes very dear. Letting at as high a rent as possible comes thus to seem to him to be quite a matter of course, and he never dreams of finding fault with either the landowners as a class, or with property in land. His mind is not likely to dwell on the notion of a caste of domineering landlords, of "bloodthirsty tyrants," fattening on the sweat of impoverished tenants, and doing no work themselves; for those who drive the hardest bargains are not the great landowners, but his own fellows. Thus the distribution of a number of small properties among the peasantry forms a kind of rampart and safeguard for the holders of large estates; and peasant prop-

---

[1] *Cobden Club Essays, First Series*, pp. 273 and 274.

erty may, without exaggeration, be called the lightning conductor that averts from society dangers which might otherwise lead to violent catastrophes.

"The concentration of land in large estates among a small number of families is a sort of provocation of leveling legislative measures. The position of England, so enviable in many respects, seems to me to be in this respect full of danger for the future."

III. The Great Hunger

The astonishing thing about the Irish Great Famine of 1846 to 1852 as well as the global situation today is that what seems to be an obvious solution to the problem was and continues to be set aside or ignored. What is even more astonishing about proposals for a lasting solution to the Famine, at least from the Irish point of view, is that it was an English economist who developed the most viable plan for relief and for finally achieving a stable political and economic order in Ireland. Perhaps most astonishing of all is that the British government failed to take notice of the plan, thereby losing an opportunity that could never be regained. At least today there still remains hope that some global political or financial leader, or the community of economic scholars, will wake up to see the potential in Thornton's solution, as refined and applied in the binary economics of Louis Kelso and Mortimer Adler, and current proposals for Capital Homesteading that could be applied throughout the world.

That English economist was William Thomas Thornton, author of *A Plea for Peasant Proprietors*, first published in 1848 and revised in 1874. The year before the Famine began, Thornton wrote *Over-Population and Its Remedy* (1846). This was a refutation of Malthusian economics, similar in many respects to the "post scarcity" thought of Kelso and Adler — particularly the expanded capital ownership aspect and what Professor Robert Ashford has called, the "principal of binary growth."[1] Two years later Thornton applied the principles he had detailed in the earlier volume in *A Plea for Peasant Proprietors* as a financially feasible and politically sound solution to the

---

[1] Dr. Robert H. A. Ashford, "The Binary Economics of Louis Kelso: A Democratic Private Property System for Growth and Justice," John H. Miller, ed., *Curing World Poverty: The New Role of Property*. St. Louis, MO: Social Justice Review, 1994, 99-132.

Famine. The question is, given the basic soundness of Thornton's proposal, why wasn't it implemented?

The Context of Thornton's Proposal

The labyrinthine complications of 19th century Irish political economy offer a possible explanation why Thornton's "plea" went unheard. A complete understanding of the subject is clearly beyond the scope of this analysis, but we can grasp enough to appreciate the significance of Thornton's work.

To oversimplify grossly, two events shaped Ireland and its relations with Great Britain in the 19th century. Politically, the "Act of Union" that took effect January 1, 1801 brought together intellectuals and the politically active in a common cause: repeal of the Act and reestablishment of "Home Rule" in some form. Out of the repeal effort of the 1830s came the "Young Ireland" movement of the 1840s, the "Irish Republican Brotherhood" of the 1850s, the "Fenian" uprising of 1867, the Home Rule agitation of the 1870s, the "Land War" of the 1880s, the combination of agrarian and nationalist interests in the 1890s, and, ultimately, the Easter Rising of 1916, the Civil War of the 1920s, partition, and the continuing tensions of today.

Economically, the Great Famine was the pivotal event in recent Irish history. It had a disastrous effect on the ordinary people of Ireland, generating popular support for land reform. This manifested in the political activity of the Irish National Land League and its successors, and, eventually, a joining of nationalist and agrarian interests into an uneasy alliance that turned on itself almost as often as it confronted what leading activists considered the eternal British misrule of Ireland.

The False Problem of Scarcity

It is impossible to understand Ireland in the 19th century — or today — without knowing something about "The Great Hunger," *An Gorta Mór*, as it is known in Irish. The Famine is the defining event in modern Irish history. This is evident in the belief, valid or not, that the Famine was deliberate genocide. Modern explanations that appear to excuse government inaction serve only to confirm the belief that the English were to blame. As Thomas Gallagher described it in his book, *Paddy's Lament* (1982), the Famine has been a "prelude to hatred."

A review of the events surrounding the Famine reveals that, in all likelihood, it was not a fixed policy of genocide, nor even indifference, but a general feeling of helplessness in the face of an unprecedented disaster, and economic institutions that, even today, people do not fully understand, that led to the ineffectiveness of relief efforts.[2] This, in turn, appears to have been caused by reliance on discredited economic theories, notably those of Thomas Malthus. Beneath it all was an unquestioning reliance on assumptions of insufficiency and the fixed (and disproved[3]) belief that it is impossible to finance new capital formation without first cutting consumption and accumulating money savings.[4]

Bound by these assumptions, the general consensus was that the Great Hunger was graphic, if regrettable proof of Malthus's theories. These were first published in Malthus's 1798 *Essay on Population*, and discredited many

---

[2] Cf. "It happens all too frequently, however, under the salary system, that individual employers are helpless to ensure justice unless, with a view to its practice, they organize institutions the object of which is to prevent competition incompatible with fair treatment for the workers. Where this is true, it is the duty of contractors and employers to support and promote such necessary organizations as normal instruments enabling them to fulfill their obligations of justice. But the laborers too must be mindful of their duty to love and deal fairly with their employers, and persuade themselves that there is no better means of safeguarding their own interests." Pope Pius XI, *Divini Redemptoris* ("On Atheistic Communism"), 1937, § 53.

[3] See Harold G. Moulton, "Commercial Banks and the Supply of Funds," *The Formation of Capital*. Washington, DC: The Brookings Institution, 1935, 75-90.

[4] "So far as I know, everyone is agreed that *saving* means the excess of income over expenditure on consumption." John Maynard Keynes, *The General Theory of Employment, Interest, and Money* (1936), II.6.ii.

times since, as Joseph Schumpeter reported in his *History of Economic Analysis*:

> The teaching of Malthus' *Essay* became firmly entrenched in the system of the economic orthodoxy of the time in spite of the fact that it should have been, and in a sense was, recognized as fundamentally untenable or worthless by 1803 and that further reasons for so considering it were speedily forthcoming. It became the "right" view on population, just as free trade had become the "right" policy, which only ignorance or obliquity could possibly fail to accept — part and parcel of the set of eternal truth that had been observed once for all. Objectors might be lectured, if they were worthy of the effort, but they could not be taken seriously. No wonder that some people, utterly disgusted at this intolerable presumption which had so little to back it began to loathe this "science of economics" quite independently of class or party considerations — a feeling that has been an important factor in that science's fate ever after.[5]

In common with other critics of Malthus, Thornton noted in *Over-Population and Its Remedy* that while poor people seem to reproduce beyond their ability to support themselves, the population of middle class small proprietors grows more slowly, and is frequently stable, matched to the productive capacity of the local economy.

John Weyland had noted the same thing in 1816 in *The Principles of Population and Production*,[6] his devastating refutation of Malthus's theories. Weyland observed that poor people tended to reproduce at great rates, the middle class tended to reproduce at replacement rates, and the rich below replacement. Weyland concluded, as did R. Buckminster Fuller[7] a century and a half later, along with

---

[5] Joseph A. Schumpeter, *History of Economic Analysis*. New York: Oxford University Press, 1954, 581-582.

[6] John Weyland, *The Principles of Population and Production*. London: Baldwin, Cradock & Joy, 1816.

[7] R. Buckminster Fuller, *Utopia or Oblivion: The Prospects for Humanity*. New York: Bantam Books, 1969, 200-201.

Jane Jacobs[8] that the level of economic development and standard of living determines the rate of population growth. This is a cornerstone of Kelso's "post-scarcity" economic paradigm. It is not the other way around, as Malthus asserted, and as many people still believe.

Thus, the solution to the "population problem" is to develop economically. To raise living standards and slow population growth, encourage widespread participation in economic development through direct ownership of capital. Do not reduce population and hope that standards of living will rise.[9]

The Effect of Malthusian Assumptions

A significant barrier to understanding Thornton's solution was the near worship of what was termed "the free market." The market, however, was anything but a free market to and in which everyone had equal access and opportunity.[10] While one of the essential components in Kelso's binary theory of economics is the free market, free markets are undermined when universal access to capital ownership is concentrated or corrupted politically by those seeking monopoly powers or special protections against open and just competitive market forces.

Reliance on past savings to finance economic development guaranteed that the few with economic power were able to manipulate the horror of the Famine and turn it to their own purposes. These were the members of the tiny elite eulogized as a *"chosen* people"[11] — emphasis in the

---

[8] Jane Jacobs, *The Economy of Cities.* New York: Vintage Books, 1970, 117-121.

[9] William Thomas Thornton, *Over-Population and Its Remedy.* London: Longman, Brown, Green, and Longmans, 1846, 118-120.

[10] See Norman G. Kurland, "A New Look at Prices and Money: The Kelsonian Binary Model for Achieving Rapid Growth Without Inflation," *The Journal of Socio-Economics,* 30 (2001) 495-515.

[11] "The principle of popular government is that the supreme power, the determining efficacy in matters political, resides in the people — not necessarily or commonly in the whole people,

original — a generation later by Walter Bagehot in *The English Constitution*, 1867, and applied in *Lombard Street*, 1873, his analysis of the London money market. The ordinary English man or woman, to say nothing of the government, was appalled by what was happening. At the same time, the economic elite and the financial "experts" — those who, according to Bagehot, were the *real* rulers of the British Empire — persuaded the public and the government that, given Malthusian assumptions, the Famine was inevitable. Worse, any interference with the so-called "free market" (so it was claimed) would result in a greater catastrophe.

The economic elite and the financial experts were, however, not the real problem. As today, the problem was rooted in flawed ideas spread by intellectuals. Chief among these ideas were those about money and credit rooted in the economics of David Ricardo (1772-1823), but translated into public policy — and entrenched in the public mind — by John Ramsay Macculloch (1789-1864). Macculloch was the economic mentor of Samuel Jones-Loyd, First Baron Overstone (1796-1883), framer of the British Bank Charter Act of 1844. The Act embedded Malthusian concepts of insufficiency into law and the financial system, even into the culture itself. These were the very concepts countered by Kelso and Adler in their two collaborations, but most especially in the second, *The New Capitalists*, with the provocative and yet profound subtitle, "A Proposal to Free Economic Growth from the Slavery of [Past] Savings."[12]

More than anything else, the Great Famine persuaded subsequent generations that economics is "the dismal science," offering no hope, only despair. In this view of eco-

---

in the numerical majority, but in a *chosen* people, a picked and selected people." [Emphasis in original.] Walter Bagehot, *The English Constitution*. Portland, Oregon: Sussex Academic Press, 1997, 17.

[12] Louis Kelso and Mortimer Adler, *The New Capitalists: A Proposal to Free Economic Growth from the Slavery of Savings*. New York: Random House, 1961.

nomics, common sense as well as common humanity had to give way in the face of economic or political necessity.

David Christy used similar arguments in 1855 in his apology for slavery, *Cotton is King*. More than Harriet Beecher Stowe's *Uncle Tom's Cabin*, Christy's book polarized attitudes that made the American Civil War seemingly inevitable. *Cotton is King* convinced Southern slave owners that their economic survival, as well as the economic wellbeing of the entire United States and the British Empire, depended on the deplorable yet allegedly necessary institution of chattel slavery to produce cotton to supply the mills of Manchester. Today the same arguments are advanced to justify welfare systems, State control of the economy, and the institution of "wage slavery" — the condition, first described by Aristotle, of nominally free but propertyless workers, utterly dependent on an employer.[13]

A horrifyingly "logical" conclusion was thus forced on Ireland and England by the presumably iron dictates of Malthusian doctrine. As a result, it appeared that economic necessity demanded that there be no interference with the presumably natural course of events in Ireland.

Even relief efforts had to be carefully selected to yield no real benefit — for that would interfere with the "free market." As Thomas Gallagher described the official relief efforts,

[T]he British government insisted upon substituting useless for useful labor, with the inevitable result that Irish industry was paralyzed, the land allowed to go unheeded, and, most important, the natural inclination of the people to help themselves undermined. This British system of relief led neither to an increase of food nor to the production of goods that could be exchanged for food. It did what it was intended to do: diminish the capital of Ireland, increase by a proportionate amount

---

[13] Aristotle, *The Politics.*, I.viii.

the poverty of her already starving people, and coerce them to leave their own country.[14]

We can dispute Gallagher's conclusion that the *intent* of the inadequate relief efforts was to induce the Irish to emigrate (although Thornton mentioned a proposal to ship a "colony" of two million Irish to Canada at government expense), but it is clear that such was the *effect*. Consistent with what would be congealed in Keynesian economics a century later,[15] the only purpose of these projects was to provide people with a bare subsistence out of redistributed existing wealth, sufficient only to keep them alive. This not only wasted resources that could have been put to productive use, they diverted the people employed on them from gainful activity.[16] It is to the eternal credit of the Society of Friends — the Quakers — that for the most part they ignored the "logic" of these bad ideas and worked selflessly in famine relief without regard to differences in religion or culture.

The Great Hunger

What was *An Gorta Mór* — "The Great Hunger"? Most simply put, the Irish Famine can be described as the inevitable result of a system designed to fail, just as today's global economy is built on the same unsustainable assumptions, as Kelso and Adler explained in *The Capitalist Manifesto*.[17]

From the initial partial English conquest of Ireland in the 12th century down to the 1840s, the effects of government policy, though not necessarily the intent, had been to deprive the ordinary people of the country of ownership of capital, whether in the form of livestock, land, or technology. By the mid-19th century, the vast majority of the people of Ireland subsisted on what would otherwise be sub-economic plots as a result of the prevalence of "rack-

---

[14] Thomas Gallagher, *Paddy's Lament, Ireland 1846-1847: Prelude to Hatred*. New York: Harcourt Brace Jovanovich, Publishers, 1982, 92.

[15] Keynes, *General Theory, op. cit.*, III.10.vi.

[16] Gallagher, *Paddy's Lament, loc. cit.*

[17] Kelso and Adler, *The Capitalist Manifesto, op. cit.*, 10-11.

renting." Rack-renting was a system of raising rents as high as possible. In Ireland, this resulted from a seemingly endless process of subletting that ensured plots would be as small as possible, and rents as high as possible.[18]

Only the potato made it possible for people to survive even marginally on such small plots of land as tenants-at-will with no rights, instead of owners with property rights or leaseholders with the "tenant-right." Consequently, not only was poverty widespread, the country was subject to all the dangers of a one-crop subsistence economy. In the 1820s Dominic Corrigan, a Dublin physician and pioneer in diagnosing heart disease (for whom "Corrigan's pulse," an aortic valve insufficiency, is named), warned the government of the problem. He predicted that "a pestilence and disease of unprecedented magnitude will befall us" unless some means was found to diversify crops and provide new sources of food.[19]

In September 1845 disaster struck. A blight — phytophthora infestans — that had affected the potato crop all across Europe reached Ireland. Where the failure of the crop had caused hardship in Europe, in Ireland it caused almost instant catastrophe. Hundreds of thousands of people died from starvation and starvation-related disease.[20]

---

[18] See Maria Edgeworth's biting satire, Castle Rackrent (1800).

[19] Dominic Corrigan, "On the Epidemic Fever of Dublin, Part I," Lancet, 1829, 2:569-575; "On the Epidemic Fever of Dublin, Part II," Lancet, 1829, 2:600-605.

[20] In her book, The Great Hunger (New York: Harper & Row, Publishers, 1962), Cecil Woodham-Smith stated, "How many people died in the famine will never precisely be known. It is almost certain that, owing to geographical difficulties and the unwillingness of the people to be registered, the census of 1841 gave a total smaller than the population in fact was." (411) She then followed with the observation that, "Officers engaged in relief work put the population as much as 25 per cent. higher; landlords distributing relief were horrified when providing, as they imagined, for 60 persons, to find more than 400 'start from the ground'." (Ibid.) Thus, landlords, who should have had a

Ironically, there was more than enough food grown in Ireland to stave off the famine, just as in other parts of Europe where other crops were able to take up the slack when the potato crop failed.[21] Similarly, Kelso and Adler pointed out that in today's global, high-tech economy, capital produces marketable goods and services in almost unbelievable abundance, yet workers and their families typically live paycheck to paycheck — if they have jobs.

Unfortunately, in common with today's worker who, as Kelso and Adler observed, owns little or nothing in the way of the commercial and industrial capital that produces the bulk of marketable goods and services in a modern developed economy, most of the Irish did not own the land on which these other crops were grown. Unlike the case with industrial and commercial capital — effectively unlimited (or, at least, limited only by the physical potential of society to produce more to satisfy human wants and needs) — this was not a problem that could be solved by creating new land. Most of the food was shipped out of the country to generate cash income for the largely absentee landlords, and feed other people.[22] Conse-

---

generally good idea of the number of people from their rent rolls — a much better source than official census statistics for the size of the population — and who were probably the primary source of data for the 1841 census, were underestimating by more than 400%. The presumed exaggerations of Irish nationalists that more than 4 million died as a result of the Great Famine become, if not believable, at least understandable.

[21] Christine Kinealy, *This Great Calamity: The Irish Famine, 1845-1852.* Dublin: Gill and Macmillan, 1995, 354.

[22] "For it must be remembered that Ireland was one of those rare countries — the only one in Europe, in fact — where there was a surplus of both population and food. Since the surplus food was earmarked for consumption not by the 'surplus' Irish but, rather, by the industrialized British, who did not produce even enough, much less surplus, food and who as a result did not want an industrialized Ireland, something had to be done to get rid of the 'surplus' Irish. In Parliament, no mention was ever made of the 'surplus' British, whose food had to be imported, who would have starved had they not been supplied with the very surplus Irish food that the Irish were denied even during

quently, the obvious step in any famine — prohibiting the export of food — was not taken. Ostensibly this was for fear of interfering with the myth of a "free market," even though closing the ports to food exports had been one of the first steps taken in the 1780s when crops failed.

The Great Famine thereby became the defining event of the 19th century for Ireland, and dictated relations between Ireland and Great Britain down to the present day. As John Mitchel (1815-1875) of the "Young Ireland" movement commented, "The Almighty, indeed, sent the potato blight, but the English created the Famine."[23]

Whether or not the Famine was engineered as Mitchel and many others claimed and continue to claim down to the present day, the fact is that the so-called "free market" that allegedly justified the lack of effective government measures was far from free. As is the case today, as Kelso and Adler explained, when the vast majority of the population is not free to own capital or lacks the means to do so through access to capital credit and collateral, whether in the form of limited land or effectively unlimited technology, and the bulk of the marketable goods and services do nothing to increase the wealth or wellbeing of the country in which they are produced, non-owning workers can only be described as subsisting within a system in which they are burdened with "a yoke little better than that of slavery itself."[24]

The evils of agricultural and, later, industrial capitalism kept the Irish in a state of complete economic and political subjugation. Ordinary propertyless people were powerless before the economic and political power of the financial elite, Bagehot's "chosen" people. Consequently,

---

the famine years when the potato, their food, turned up rotten in every field and garden." Gallagher, *Paddy's Lament, op. cit.*, 93-94.

[23] John Mitchel, *The Last Conquest of Ireland (Perhaps)* (1861), quoted in Peter Duffy, *The Killing of Major Denis Mahon.* New York: HarperCollins, 2007, 312.

[24] Pope Leo XIII, *Rerum Novarum* ("On Capital and Labor"), 1891, § 3.

in Ireland the "free market" and capitalism — even private property — became the enemy. It is no wonder that the cause of Irish nationalism and socialism came to be so intertwined.

Prelude to Homesteading

As a remedy to the widespread poverty that afflicted Ireland, Thornton proposed that the vast tracts of idle "waste land" in Ireland be purchased by the government and allotted in economic plots to Irish families, who would be supported by an allowance until they could grow their own food and produce a surplus for market.

After bringing the land into full production, the families would either hold the land by perpetual lease with a nominal rent sufficient to cover the interest on the government bonds used to finance the project, backed by the purchase value of the land itself,[25] or start making payments on the land out of profits, and within a relatively short time would own it freehold in fee simple.

The scheme relied on purchasing undeveloped landed capital at a low price — its current value as waste land. The new money created by the bonds would first be used to finance the purchase and development of the land, and then be cancelled or retired as the payments for the land were received — assuming that the bonds did not result in a permanent (if asset-backed) floating debt.

Thus, even if Thornton did not explicitly realize the financial operation of his proposal,[26] the money could be

---

[25] This method of finance, an application of the "Banking Principle," is similar to the "Rentenmark" system implemented by Hjalmar Schacht (1877-1970) to stabilize the hyperinflation in Germany in the 1920s, and which succeeded in providing the basis for a sound currency until the Reichsmark was demonetized by the Allies in 1948. See Hjalmar Horace Greeley Schacht, *Confessions of "The Old Wizard": The Autobiography of Hjalmar Schacht.* Boston, Massachusetts: Houghton Mifflin Company, 1956; John Weitz, *Hitler's Banker: Hjalmar Horace Greeley Schacht.* New York: Little, Brown and Company, 1997.

[26] See Kelso and Adler, *The New Capitalists, op. cit.*, for the application of advanced techniques of corporate finance to broad-

created as needed, as long as what the money was spent on provided the "future savings," that is, sufficient income in the future from the production of marketable goods and services, to pay back the money. There would thus be no problem with either inflation or deflation.

There was, of course, the question of maintenance during the period it took for the land to become fully productive. Thornton estimated this at three to five years, judging from the rate of improvement on land of lesser quality in Flanders and other areas in Europe. He noted, however, that the government was spending millions of pounds sterling on relief efforts and on infrastructure for which there was currently no demand. Using the same funds to maintain families relocated on to unproved land would result in an estimated immediate savings of £5 million a year for two years until the land became productive.

We can view Thornton's "plea" as a precursor to Abraham Lincoln's Homestead Act and Emancipation Proclamation in the United States a decade and a half later. In place of the presumably essential past savings, Thornton used undeveloped waste land. This still tied the proposal to the availability of a limited form of capital. This would not have been a factor had industrial and commercial capital been included. These are effectively limited only by human ingenuity, where land and many natural resources are limited by their very nature.

What made the proposal feasible, however, was the beneficial effect that capital ownership has on economic growth. Thornton stated — and provided evidence to back up his claim — that widespread capital ownership increases the rate of economic growth.

In *Binary Economics*, Dr. Robert H. A. Ashford, professor of law at Syracuse University, substantiates this claim. Ashford explains that the concept of "binary growth" holds that economies grow steadily larger as private capital acquisition is distributed more broadly among

---

ened capital ownership; also, Harold G. Moulton, *The Formation of Capital, op. cit.*

the population on market principles. This concept also focuses on the importance of unleashing the unutilized or underutilized capacity of all economic systems to produce in greater abundance.[27]

Although Thornton's examples were limited to landed capital, the same principle applies to all other forms of capital, commercial and industrial. The technology "frontier" is effectively unlimited. Nevertheless, as a corollary to the principle of binary growth, Thornton noted that, in areas where people owned the land they tilled, they never ceased to improve the productiveness of their capital. The same or even larger size plots of better land in other areas, when farmed by tenants or hirelings, even with better technology, invariably produced at a lower level.[28]

Thornton strengthened his case in a revised edition of his *Plea*, published in 1874. The rewritten first chapter emphasized historical examples of countries and empires that had grown strong and wealthy when ownership of capital was well-divided, and which fell into decay once ownership of capital became concentrated.

This can be explained very easily. As Kelso and Adler pointed out and is the case today, sustainable economic and social development relies on opening up opportunities for people without capital to acquire and own capital. In this way ordinary people can participate in the production of marketable goods and services with both their human (labor) and their non-human (capital) inputs. As technology advances and displaces human labor from the production process, it becomes essential that people without direct ownership of capital become owners of capital.

---

[27] Robert H. A. Ashford and Rodney Shakespeare, *Binary Economics: The New Paradigm*. Lanham, Maryland: University Press of America, 1999, 37-41, 273-306, 320-325.

[28] This is consistent with the findings of the National Center for Employee Ownership in Oakland, California, that worker-owned companies with profit sharing and participatory management outperform otherwise comparable firms.

Why Was Thornton Ignored?

The question then becomes why such a reasonable proposal, and one that promised so much, wasn't implemented at the earliest possible date. Our analysis suggests the following.

Thornton's proposal may have been ignored because of two factors. One, landowners simply refused to sell the unused land, and the government refused to condemn the land and force a sale under eminent domain for the common good. This is a weakness when dealing with a form of capital in fixed amount, such as land, and does not apply to the effectively unlimited forms of capital provided by advancing technology. A program based on equal access to ownership of future, as-yet unformed industrial and commercial capital, without any redistribution except for redistribution of opportunity, would have had a better chance of success.

Two, as noted, and although he might not have realized it, Thornton's method of finance was an application of "the Banking Principle," based on Say's Law of Markets, the real bills doctrine, and the "Quantity Theory of Money."[29] Unfortunately, parliament had just enacted the Bank Charter Act of 1844[30] that, after decades of debate, repudiated the Banking Principle of Adam Smith, Henry Thornton (no relation) and Jean-Baptiste Say. The Banking Principle would have allowed for an "elastic" banknote currency backed with private sector hard assets to supplement private sector bills of exchange, and itself supplemented with gold and silver coin, that expands and contracts with the needs of commerce, industry and agriculture, and is thus neither inflationary nor deflationary. The new Act went with the Malthusian-Ricardian Currency Principle that imposed an "inelastic" banknote cur-

---

[29] See Norman G. Kurland, "A New Look at Prices and Money: The Kelsonian Binary Model for Achieving Rapid Growth Without Inflation," *The Journal of Socio-Economics*, 30 (2001) 495-515.
[30] 7 & 8 Vict. c. 32.

rency in fixed amount, backed with government debt and supplemented with gold and silver coin.

Parliament was not going to nullify its own act barely four years after it had passed it, regardless how bad the situation was for Ireland or the common people of England. Of course, when private business interests of the City of London demanded an increase in the money supply in 1847, 1857, and 1866 (the financial crisis brought on by the Overend, Gurney and Company bank failure[31]) to meet a continuing series of currency crises brought on by the flawed system implemented by the 1844 Act, the Bank of England was instructed to inflate the currency, backing the increase with more government debt rather than the present value of existing and future private sector marketable goods and services.

In the 1874 edition of *A Plea for Peasant Proprietors*, Thornton explained why he reiterated his proposal, even though he thought it impracticable under then-current conditions. One, the government had completely ignored the "plea" a quarter of a century before when it would have been to the great benefit not only of Ireland, but the entire United Kingdom.

Two, Thornton wanted the reader to compare what the situation could have been like in the 1870s had the proposal been adopted. In all likelihood, for instance, there never would have been a Fenian uprising, and the increased agitation for "Home Rule" in the 1870s would have received little or no impetus. Thornton noted that, while many small landowners were sympathetic to the Fenians, few of them actually took part in the rising, or gave more than "moral support," while a large measure of support for Home Rule advocates resulted — indirectly — from lack of ownership.

Three, the proper institutional framework was not in place, and there was no sign that the British government had any intention of taking advantage of an obvious op-

---

[31] See *Overend Gurney & Co., Ltd. v. Oriental Financial Corp., Ltd.* (1874-75) LR 7 HL 348.

portunity. If carried out without institutional reforms supporting private enterprise, Thornton's proposal would have failed. The situation would simply have duplicated the same pattern into which Ireland had been locked for centuries. This is similar to the importance of the support of the late Senator Russell Long of Louisiana, whose leadership was critical to the effort to institutionalize the Employee Stock Ownership Plan (ESOP) and embody it in law.[32]

What Thornton did suggest in light of changed conditions, however, was corporate ownership by the State, with rights secured to leaseholders almost as if they were freeholders. This would have the advantage of dealing with the problem of a limited form of capital. There are, however, at least three problems.

One, Thornton's proposal relied not just on the State permitting the program, but on carrying it out. As Thornton himself admitted, the State is usually the worst choice to do anything that the private sector can do.

Two, State ownership is almost certain to be administered politically, rather than economically or in accordance with free market principles.

Three, State ownership does nothing to address the problem of limited land realistically, or open up access to the means of acquiring and possessing other, effectively unlimited forms of capital.

There is a problem with giving the State a broader role than it really should have. It is a basic principle of democracy that the economic role of the State must be strictly limited.[33] Government is a very powerful and very specialized tool essential to a well-run social order. That does not mean, however, that the government can do anything and everything better than the private sector. As Thornton himself commented, "Really, it does look as if private en-

---

[32] See Norman G. Kurland, "Dinner at the Madison: Louis Kelso Meets Russell Long," *Owners at Work, Ohio,* Winter 1997/1998.
[33] Alexis de Tocqueville, *Democracy in America*, Volume I. New York: Alfred A. Knoph, 1994, 57-58.

ergy were unable to survive the torpedo-like touch of governmental support. Certainly, from Indian railways downwards, every private enterprise languishes which government guarantees."[34] As he stated later in another book, "Since the fall of the Roman Empire, there has never been a Government whose strong side has been Public Works."[35]

The State's proper role should be limited to ensuring that everyone has equal opportunity (not results), and that abuses are corrected and the malefactors punished. The solution to a limited asset is that, instead of vesting corporate ownership of the land, natural resources, and infrastructure in the State, vest corporate ownership of such capital in a private, for-profit corporation. If owned by every citizen as a right of citizenship by granting each citizen a single lifetime, no-cost, non-transferable, voting, fully participating share in the corporation, we could achieve Thornton's "corporate ownership" of land without vesting it in the State.

It should be noted that private ownership through a corporation, unlike corporate ownership by the State, does not change the nature of private property. Even universal ownership through a corporation held through shares conveying the full rights of private property (*e.g.*, voting and receipt of the full stream of income) does not abolish private property. All that is changed is how the principle is applied in a specific situation. As Dr. Heinrich Rommen explained,

The positive institutions of property do not have the character of something holy. On the contrary, the common good requires of the lawmaker that he prudently introduce changes into the system of property and adapt it to new economic conditions. A complex commercial and industrial economy obviously calls for a different

---

[34] William T. Thornton, *A Plea for Peasant Proprietors*. London: Macmillan and Company, 1874, 255.
[35] William T. Thornton, *Indian Public Works and Cognate Indian Topics*. London: Macmillan and Co., 1875, 1.

system of property than is required by a simple natural economy.[36]

To clarify, "property" is not the thing owned; the *res*, as lawyers say. Rather, property is, one, the right every human being has by nature itself to be an owner, especially of whatever is required to provide him- or herself and his or her dependents with a material sufficiency. Two, property is the socially determined bundle of rights that define how an owner may use what he or she owns. In general, no one may use what he or she owns in any way to harm him- or herself, other individuals, or the common good as a whole.[37]

Universal ownership of a limited form of capital such as land through a private corporation, then, is not a negation of private property, as corporate ownership by the State would necessarily be. It is simply an application of the principle of private property in a new form. As Rommen explained,

"Thou shalt not steal" presupposes the institution of private property as pertaining to the natural law; but not, for example, the feudal property arrangements of the Middle Ages or the modern capitalist system. Since the natural law lays down general norms only, it is the function of the positive law to undertake the concrete, detailed regulation of real and personal property and to prescribe the formalities for conveyance of ownership.[38]

Does this invalidate either Thornton's basic proposal or its applicability for today? Far from it. The essential proposal remains sound and firmly rooted in common sense principles of economics and finance as explained by Kelso and Adler — and of moral philosophy, as Thornton, perhaps, realized when he published *Old-Fashioned Ethics and Commonsense Metaphysics* the year before he revised

---

[36] Heinrich A. Rommen, *The Natural Law: A Study in Legal and Social History and Philosophy.* Indianapolis, Indiana: Liberty Fund, Inc., 1998, 228.
[37] Kelso and Adler, *The Capitalist Manifesto, op. cit.,* 66.
[38] *Ibid.,* 59.

A Plea for Peasant Proprietors. Updated applications of the principle of "peasant proprietorship" hold great promise as a possible solution for our current economic troubles.

Thornton's Continued Relevance

Given the speed with which modern capital can be put into production[39] — note should be taken of the rapidity with which the United States got into full production and experienced full employment in World War II — implementation of a program of expanded capital ownership in the United States or any other developed country could reasonably be expected to begin turning things around within three to six months. As effective demand grows in response to the release of hoarded cash paid out in dividends instead of being diverted to reinvestment or sterile savings, and new capital is formed to satisfy previously unmet domestic wants and needs,[40] full employment of both labor and capital should be reached in 18 to 24 months.

The key to reform is to realize that existing institutions and ways of doing things, especially how new capital is financed, must be reformed to meet the needs of all people, not just an elite. The elite should not be made to suffer for supposed crimes, however, or be singled out for punitive treatment. That would simply be to substitute one injustice for another. Instead, by eliminating the use of existing accumulations of savings as the presumed sole source of financing for new capital, humanity can be emancipated from the slavery of past savings, and univer-

---

[39] The principle that levels of production cannot be increased in the short run, a belief held by all three mainstream schools of economics (Keynesian, Monetarist/Chicago, and Austrian), is predicated on the disproved assumption that there is a lag time between when the decision is made to finance new capital formation, and the presumably essential accumulation of money savings to finance the expansion.

[40] See Harold G. Moulton, *The New Philosophy of Public Debt.* Washington, DC: The Brookings Institution, 1943, 27-29.

sal capital ownership achieved without redistribution, additional taxes, or increased government debt.

Without fundamental systemic change, especially in tax law, central banking and how new capital formation is financed, nothing but superficialities will change.[41] Reliance on existing accumulations of savings as the source of financing for new capital leads inevitably to either capitalism or socialism, or an unworkable admixture of the two in response to the increasingly violent pendulum swings between the two allegedly mutually exclusive alternatives as each one fails in turn.

If the Famine and its aftermath teach us nothing else, it teaches us that. As Cecil Woodham-Smith acknowledged in the conclusion of her monumental study of the Great Hunger, "The famine was never 'over', in the sense that an epidemic occurs and is over. The poverty of the Irish people continued, dependence on the potato continued, failures of the potato, to a greater or lesser extent, continued, and hunger continued."[42]

The time to act is now. The only question is whether our leaders have the courage to act, and the vision to see the possibilities of a future in which the economy operates for the benefit of everyone, not just a presumably elect or *chosen* few.

---

[41] See Norman Kurland, Dawn Brohawn and Michael D. Greaney, *Capital Homesteading for Every Citizen.* Arlington, Virginia: Economic Justice Media, 2004; Norman Kurland, "Beyond ESOP: Steps Toward Tax Justice," *The Tax Executive*, April and July 1976.

[42] Woodham-Smith, *The Great Hunger.* New York: Harper & Row, Publishers, 1962, 406-407.

IV. Home Rule

In Chapter 7 of his 1874 revision of *A Plea for Peasant Proprietors*, William Thornton made a reference to "Home Rule rant," implying that an adoption of his proposal in 1848 would have rendered the "rant" either ineffectual or non-existent. Naturally, this raises the question for readers outside of Ireland and the United Kingdom just what this "Home Rule rant" might be, and why Thornton considered it significant.

Following the Irish Rising of 1798 — "the Wexford Rebellion" — the British parliament decided to impose direct rule on the Kingdom of Ireland as a way of securing a stable and lasting peace. This would unify the former Plantagenet Lordship with the kingdoms of England and Scotland, and the Principality of Wales. England and Wales had been amalgamated under an act of union in 1536, while England and Scotland had been joined in 1707.

A discrete Kingdom of Ireland dated from June of 1541 when, at the urging of the Anglo-Irish Parliament, Henry VIII Tudor declared that he was now "King of Ireland" in his own right, instead of temporal "Lord of Ireland" under the pope. The move is not free from the suspicion that it was an effort on the part of the Anglo-Irish parliament to curry favor with a king whose absolutist tendencies had by then become notorious. Since the 12th century the justification for English rule of Ireland had been the "Papal Bull" *Laudabilitur*, a document of questionable authenticity. With Henry's repudiation of the pope's spiritual authority, such a declaration of independence from any temporal authority the pope might have was an obvious move.

Politically, the 1800 Act of Union joining Ireland with Great Britain on January 1, 1801 meant that the Catholic majority in Ireland would now become a minority in the United Kingdom. While the Catholics in Ireland and Great Britain had no civil rights, as long as the Irish were ruled from Dublin, the parliament had to take them into consideration. Ruled from Westminster, they were no more a factor in politics than the Catholics of England, Scotland and Wales.

Catholics were debarred from most public jobs and could not vote. This latter was not much of a disability for the Irish peasantry. The ordinary Irishman lacked the property qualification that also prevented most Englishmen from voting. It did, however, ensure that there would be no Catholic voice at all in the government from among those who would otherwise have qualified for the franchise and to hold office.

The Act of Union was passed partly on the strength of a promise that Catholics would be emancipated, that is, granted civil rights. This promise was not kept for thirty years. An abortive rebellion led by Robert Emmet, a Protestant, was used to justify the failure to extend civil rights to Catholics on the grounds of their presumed inherent disloyalty. It was only after Daniel O'Connell forced the government's hand by winning a parliamentary election for which, legally, he was not eligible to stand, that the Prime Minister, the Duke of Wellington, decided to compromise and get the necessary laws passed for emancipation.

Parliament was able to impose a financial gerrymander by raising the property qualification to vote from 40 shillings (£2) to £10. This reduced the number of potential Irish Catholic voters by nearly 95 percent. At the very least, however, there would be some representation for Catholics in Westminster, and Catholics could now legally enter professions previously barred to them.

Attaining emancipation made repeal of the Act of Union and restoration of Home Rule the central "Irish Question" for the next century. After the 1870s, Home Rule was the single most important factor in Irish politics, and a major factor in the politics of the Empire itself. William Gladstone, the British Prime Minister, and the Liberal Party saw Home Rule as a way of reconciling the growing spirit of Irish nationalism with membership in the Empire, while Conservatives and Unionists saw it as the biggest threat to political integrity. To pacify the "Home Rulers," the Conservatives and Unionists passed a number of acts beneficial to Ireland during this period, to which Thornton alluded in the 1874 revision as removing the justification of the "ranting" for Home Rule.

From the 1830s until his death in 1847, O'Connell and his "Repeal Association" made nullification of the Act of Union and the reestablishment of a separate kingdom under the British Crown the focus of their efforts. The idea was to institute something similar to the "dual monarchy" of Austria-Hungary under the Hapsburgs.

The term "Home Rule" dates from the 1860s. During the decade that saw the Fenian Rising, the object was to reestablish a parliament in Dublin that would handle domestic affairs, and leave foreign relations to the Imperial Parliament in London. While the goal of the Fenians and the Irish Republican Brotherhood was complete independence from Great Britain, they were willing to cooperate — for a time — with the Home Rule movement. Charles Stewart Parnell later worked toward a parliament in Dublin with limited powers as an interim measure.

In the 1870s, the goal was the establishment of a federal system for the United Kingdom. Isaac Butt, a barrister who had previously been a member of the Conservative Party, forged links between the Constitutional and Revolutionary branches of the nationalist movement by defending members of the Fenian Society in court during the trials that followed the 1867 rising. Butt established the Irish Home Government Association. Under William Shaw, the Association became the Home Rule League in November 1873, the idea being to remain part of the United Kingdom, but with limited self-government.

After Shaw's death, Parnell, a Protestant, brought the Home Rule movement together as the Irish Parliamentary Party. By the 1885 general election, the party's strength had grown to the extent that it won 85 out of 103 seats in Ireland, and one seat, Liverpool, in England. This showing impressed Gladstone, and the Prime Minister sponsored the Irish Government Bill of 1886, arguing in a famous three-hour speech that it would be better to grant Home Rule now in honor, than later in humiliation.

The Bill failed to pass the House of Commons by a mere 30 votes. The ensuing riots in Belfast caused a split in the Liberal Party. The Liberal Unionist Association joined with the Conservative Party on the issue of Home Rule until 1914. Gladstone lost his position as Prime Minister.

On his return to power in 1892, Gladstone again sponsored a Home Rule bill, the Irish Government Bill of 1893. This time the Bill passed the House of Commons by 30 votes, but was defeated in the House of Lords. The nationalist movement again divided on this second failure of the political process, infusing new life into groups convinced that they could achieve their ends only by violence.

The Home Rule Act of 1914 was never implemented on the grounds that the First World War constituted an emergency that superceded the Irish Question. The Easter Rising of 1916 and the declaration of Irish independence also changed the situation materially. Consequently, when the Government of Ireland Act of 1920 passed, replacing the 1914 Act, Home Rule was established only for parts of Ulster, and the country was partitioned.

V. The Fenian Rising

In addition to his mildly pejorative reference to Home Rule agitation in his 1874 revision of *A Plea for Peasant Proprietors*, William Thornton noted that widespread ownership of landed capital was a factor that undermined active support for something called "Fenianism." Taken from the name of a mythical Irish hero, Fionn mac Cumhaill ("Finn McCool") and his band of followers, the Fianna, the 19th century Fenian movement sought to make Ireland an independent republic. The movement culminated in an abortive rising in 1867. While the failure of the rising effectively ended the movement, Fenianism as an ideology remained an important factor in Irish politics.

The Fenian Rising of 1867 had its direct roots in the establishment of the Irish Republican Brotherhood in the late 1850s. The failure of the "Young Ireland" rebellion of the 1840s, born out of Daniel O'Connell's repeal movement, was due in large measure to the Great Famine. After this, political reaction set in. The Irish nationalist movement shifted its emphasis from independence and Home Rule, to agrarian reform, a move that may have inspired William Thornton's *A Plea for Peasant Proprietors*. This was a more popular and sustainable cause than rebellion in light of the horrors of the Great Hunger, and responded directly to the increasing agitation over longstanding grievances of the farmers.

The Tenant Right League was established, calling for "fair rent, fixity of tenure, and free sale." Many of the leaders of the nationalist movement moderated their stand. The Catholic Defense Association joined in a united front with the Tenant Right League, and a number of nationalist leaders accepted places in the government.

This was widely interpreted as infidelity to the cause. This construction was strengthened when the two most prominent Catholic Defense leaders, John Sadleir and William Keogh, were held to have betrayed the cause by accepting political office.

- 245 -

Sadleir became Junior Lord of the Treasury in Lord Aberdeen's coalition government. He was later found to have engaged in financial fraud on a massive scale. He ruined thousands of his Irish and English supporters by embezzling more than £1.5 million. He committed suicide in 1856 to avoid prosecution. His brother James was also implicated, but fled to Switzerland. James was murdered in Geneva in 1881 in the course of a robbery when a thief tried to take his watch.

Keogh became Solicitor-General for Ireland and Attorney General for Ireland in the Aberdeen government. He was known as "So-Help-Me-God Keogh" from the number of times he had sworn publicly never to accept a bribe or preferment from the British government. Keogh became infamous for the severity, even savagery of the punishments inflicted on the Irish nationalists he sentenced. Keogh's friends claimed that he did exercise some leniency in the case of Charles Kickham, the celebrated journalist, novelist and poet. Keogh expressed sympathy for Kickham before sentencing him to fourteen years penal servitude, or temporary slavery. Some authorities believe Keogh became insane in his later years, and may have committed suicide after trying to kill his own valet.

In consequence, the nationalist movement reoriented itself once again toward independence and Home Rule. James Stephens, a tutor who had been involved in the Young Ireland movement, founded the Irish Republican Brotherhood in Dublin on St. Patrick's Day in 1858. Stephens traveled to the United States, and, with John O'Mahoney and Michael Doheny, both formerly affiliated with the Young Ireland movement, established Fenianism in America under the headship of O'Mahoney. Stephens collected $3,000 in donations and returned to Ireland.

Few other members of Young Ireland became involved in the Fenian movement, and new people had to be enlisted in both Ireland and America. With the funds he collected in the United States, Stephens financed a speaking tour throughout Ireland, in the process putting together a new organization. Thousands of recruits signed up.

The movement received its greatest impetus, however, with the funeral of Terence Bellew MacManus, a Young Ireland leader who died in San Francisco, California in 1861. MacManus had been sentenced to penal servitude in Australia, but escaped to America.

The American Fenians decided that MacManus's body should be shipped home to Ireland for burial. There were demonstrations as it made its way across the country. In New York City there was a massive turnout, and Archbishop John Joseph Hughes blessed the coffin.

Possibly mindful of the violent anti-Catholic demonstrations that had accompanied Nicholas Wiseman's appointment as Cardinal-Archbishop of Westminster when the Catholic hierarchy had been reestablished in England in 1850, as well as the need to maintain order, Archbishop Cullen of Dublin decided to forbid MacManus to be buried from any church in his diocese. This was probably intended to reassure the British government that Catholics were as good citizens and loyal as anyone else, but it had the opposite effect. Hundreds of thousands of spectators watched as fifty thousand men marched in procession behind the coffin, while the interment itself was the occasion of a nationalist speech by one Captain Smith. The Irish episcopate and most of the clergy followed the lead of Archbishop Cullen and condemned Fenianism.

In 1863 John O'Leary, Charles Kickham and Thomas Clark Luby founded *The Irish People*, the official Fenian journal, as a weekly. It rapidly gained a large circulation. In 1865, the government shut down the paper and arrested Jeremiah O'Donovan Rossa, O'Leary, Kickham, Luby, and Stephens. Rossa was given a life sentence, as it was his second offense, he having been convicted of treasonous conspiracy in 1858.

According to some authorities, the severity of Rossa's sentence was due in part to his conducting his own defense. When the Crown read selected portions of some articles from *The Irish People* as evidence against Rossa, Rossa insisted that, to give proper context, every word of every issue be read into the record. When the prosecution protested, Rossa relented to the extent that he did not insist on reading the advertisements.

Stephens's subsequent escape from a maximum security facility baffled the government for years before it was revealed that it had been arranged with the help of secret Fenians among the prison guards. In 1866 the government suspended *habeas corpus* in Ireland and arrested hundreds of known Fenians.

Organizing and drilling continued, however. The novelist Reverend Patrick Augustine "Canon" Sheehan of Doneraile recalled that as a boy he would see the men secretly marching and drilling in the woods near his home. He always retained admiration for the Fenians and support for their cause. As he wrote shortly before his death in 1913 in *The Graves at Kilmorna*, the Fenians were "strong silent men into whose character some stern and terrible energy seemed to have been infused. There were no braggarts among them. Their passion was too deep for words and that passion was all consuming, fierce unswerving love for Ireland."

The Fenians in America were able to purchase large quantities of surplus weapons, ammunition, and other military supplies left over from the American Civil War. This was evidently with the connivance of friends in the government. The U.S. government also later turned a blind official eye to the crossing of a large body of Fenians into Canada near Buffalo, New York. This force under General John O'Neill, captured Fort Erie on May 31, 1866. Little else was accomplished.

American munitions were also shipped to Ireland, where Stephens's successor, Thomas J. Kelly, tried to organize a rising in County Kerry in February 1867. The idea was to initiate a guerilla campaign throughout Ireland and make the country ungovernable. At the same time, elements in Dublin would join with Irish soldiers in the British Army that were expected to mutiny in support of the rising.

On March 5, 1867 there was another attempt that was thwarted in part by informers and the unexpected occurrence of a twelve-day blizzard. The effort dissolved in a series of minor skirmishes. When it became obvious that the coordinated rebellion had failed, most of the Fenians simply went home.

Later that year Kelly went to England to attend a meeting of English "Centers," as organizers were called, in Manchester. He and Thomas Deasy were arrested. Edward O'Meaher Condon organized a rescue effort that failed, during which a police sergeant was killed. Kelly, Deasy and Condon were executed, becoming known as "the Manchester Martyrs."

The Fenians declared a Provisional Government. This was a move of little practical use, but of enormous symbolic importance. Declaring that they had resorted to violence only because they saw no other option, they proclaimed,

We aim at founding a Republic based on universal suffrage, which shall secure to all the intrinsic value of their labor. The soil of Ireland, at present in possession of an oligarchy, belongs to us, the Irish people and to us it must be restored. We declare also in favor of absolute liberty of conscience and the separation of Church and State. We intend no war against the people of England; our war is against the aristocratic locusts, whether English or Irish, who have eaten the verdure of our fields.

Intentional or not, the phrasing gave a socialist twist to the aims of the Fenians and the Irish Republican Brotherhood. It found its echo in one interpretation of a provision in the Easter Proclamation of 1916, and remains a plank in the Sinn Féin platform.

VI. The Irish National Land League

In his 1874 revision of *A Plea for Peasant Proprietors*, William Thornton expressed a hope that the recent land reform legislation would bring about a peaceful resolution to the increased agitation for agrarian reform in Ireland. As the legislation was largely ineffectual, Thornton's hope was not realized. All that was accomplished was to fuel increased agitation, and drive nationalist and agrarian interests into the same camp and the formation of an uneasy alliance.

Dashing Thornton's expectations, a fall in agricultural prices hit Europe and the United States in 1874, hard on the heels of the publication of his revision. This was followed by a series of bad harvests due to wet weather throughout Europe that led to widespread distress in Ireland. Unlike the case in most of Europe, however, land rents in Ireland were not abated in the event of a bad harvest. The province of Connaught was particularly hard hit. A regional famine in 1879 made matters even worse.

In October 1878, the Mayo Tenants Defense Association was formed in Castlebar. In April 1879 the first in a series of mass meetings was held, consciously reminiscent of those organized by Daniel O'Connell to protest the 1800 Act of Union. A number of local land leagues were organized to protest the exorbitant rents being charged, especially in Connaught. The various organizations and initiatives were brought together under one umbrella with the founding of the Irish National Land League — *Conradh na Talún* — by Michael Davitt on October 21, 1879, with Charles Stewart Parnell as president.

Parnell, Davitt, and a number of others went to America on a fundraising tour. The response was phenomenal. Branches of the League were established in Scotland. The "Crofters Party" adopted the program and secured a Reform Act in 1886.

Realizing that something had to be done about the inequities pervasive in Ireland, the government had passed an ineffectual land reform act in 1870. Probably in response to the formation and activities of the League, additional — and equally ineffective — acts were passed in 1880 and 1881. Some rents were abated, but the attempt was regarded as a token. Parnell and other League leaders harshly criticized the efforts of the government.

Parnell and the others were imprisoned in Kilmainham Jail in October 1881 under the Irish Coercion Act for allegedly "sabotaging" the Land Act. This backfired on the government by causing widespread resentment against what was viewed as arbitrary action. Parnell took advantage of his increased prestige and issued the "No-Rent Manifesto," calling for a "rent strike" until he and the others were released. This added impetus to the "Land War" that began in 1880, and revived "the three Fs" of the Tenant Right League: Fair Rent, Fixity of Tenure, and Free Sale.

The No-Rent Manifesto was only partially implemented, but it was enough to disrupt society seriously. A "rent strike" would typically be followed by evictions, but when the case was brought to court, witnesses frequently changed their stories, invalidating earlier testimony. This made the legal system virtually unworkable. The community would boycott tenants who paid rent. The League officially discouraged violence, although crimes against persons and property increased, resulting in additional coercion acts.

Parnell's goal was for tenant farmers to become owners — freeholders of the land they farmed. He was opposed to ownership through the State on behalf of "the people." Davitt, on the other hand, pushed for nationalization and State ownership, publicizing his views with the slogan, "The land of Ireland for the people of Ireland."

Evictions continued until "Ashbourne's Act" in 1885 made it unprofitable in most cases. Agricultural prices had recovered to some extent, and landlords were losing money for failing to come to terms with their tenants. Despite some amelioration, the Land War entered a second phase in 1886 and continued until 1892. During this phase the movement changed its "Plan of Campaign" from an outright rent strike, to having tenants offer the landlord what the National League (the successor to the National Land League) considered a fair rent. If this was refused, the tenant paid the rent to the League, which withheld payment until the landlord accepted the reduced rent.

The National Land League was suppressed in October 1881. Soon afterwards Lord Cavendish was murdered in Phœnix Park, Dublin, by a secret society calling itself "the Invincibles." Discouraged, Parnell announced his retirement from public life. Instead of retiring, however, he allowed himself to be persuaded to form a new organization, the National League, in 1882. This was, to all intents and purposes, a continuation of the outlawed organization, which added Home Rule to its platform, and pursued a "constitutional strategy" of parliamentary action.

Following the Phœnix Park murder the government introduced a "Crimes Bill" and abolished trial by jury in certain cases. Search and seizure without warrant was instituted, and secret courts of enquiry were established. In selected cases newspapers could be suppressed, and public meetings banned. The violence only increased.

An attempt was made to implicate Parnell in the Phœnix Park murder, but failed. He was effectively untouchable until December 1890 when his involvement with a married woman, Katherine O'Shea, became known. Details are unclear to this day, but it was enough to split the movement and end Parnell's career. The majority "anti-Parnellite" League members formed the Irish National Federation, headed by John Dillon. John Redmond assumed leadership of the minority that remained. Paradoxically, the two factions came together in the general election of 1892 and retained all 81 of their seats in parliament.

In 1900 the remnants of the National League joined with the United Irish League and the Irish National Federation and reformed the Irish Parliamentary Party under Redmond's leadership.

VII. William Thornton and Distributism

At first glance, William Thornton's proposal for vesting the people of Ireland with direct ownership of at least a part of the arable land of the country seems to be a virtual blueprint for an arrangement of society that in the early 20th century G. K. Chesterton and Hilaire Belloc would call "distributist." As described by Chesterton, the chief spokesman for the duo that George Bernard Shaw ruefully termed the two-headed "Chesterbelloc" beast, distributism is the economic arrangement of society into a system in which a sufficiently large number of people directly own the means of production. This approach posits ownership of capital as the primary means of generating income. There is a preference, socially and legally, for the small, family-owned enterprise. As Chesterton put it, distributism is "a policy of small distributed property."[1]

Given this definition, Thornton's *A Plea for Peasant Proprietors* and his later *On Labour* (1869, 1870) read like distributist manifestoes put together by someone with practical experience in the "real world." This addresses a serious problem with distributism.

One of the flaws of distributism (admitted by its founders), is that it is rather vague both as to specifics and on how to achieve the desired results. Reading one of Chesterton's romantic fantasies or clever essays, we are struck with the unreality of his realism. There are a number of profound insights into human nature, but very little about the "grunt work" that occupies most of the time of the happy villagers and carefree cottiers who will presumably inhabit the distributist idyll once (by some unspecified miracle) it is established.

It becomes obvious that, for all the similarity of language and goals, Thornton's homely practicality is in

---

[1]G. K. Chesterton, "The Beginning of the Quarrel," *The Outline of Sanity*. Collected Works, Volume V (San Francisco, California: Ignatius Press, 1987), 45.

sharp contrast to Chesterton's idealistic flights. Where Chesterton has suppositions and reasonable-sounding if unproved hypotheses, Thornton has statistics and hard data to back up a careful analysis. Chesterton matches wits with ideologues and ridicules the practicality of the worldly; Thornton matches the experts fact for fact, meeting them on their own ground and beating them on it.

For all his talk about commons and cows, there is very little in Chesterton about such mundane subjects as drainage and that inevitable, unpleasant, but extraordinarily necessary and valuable byproduct of livestock: manure . . . which Thornton mentions more than thirty times in this single work, and at great length in the article on "Agriculture" he contributed to the 1875 *Encyclopedia Britannica*. Thornton might give in to the temptation to use a little overblown language once in a while. This was, after all, expected when writing of the Irish, those masters of the English language, as Carlos Fuentes reminded us. Thornton might, for example, refer to the contents of the farm urine tank as "libations to the Sterculine Saturn." This cleverness, however, seems to be presented as a bit of comic relief while making an important point. It is never itself the point of a passage as it so often seems to have been with Chesterton.

Chesterton rambles on about how it should be possible to lead the simple life and enjoy one's self on a small bit of land. Thornton explains exactly how much land there should be, how long it should take to develop and get into full production, what crops to plant, and how to maintain fertility of the soil — and even the amount of backbreaking toil to be expected and how many hours of it per day could be expected. Where Chesterton hints that simple technology is to be preferred, Thornton states precisely why the spade is often preferred to the plow on small plots of ground, and duly acknowledges the beneficial effects of advanced machinery, even railroads — when appropriate. Chesterton might rhapsodize over a pint and a pipe. Thornton would tell you how to grow and cure tobacco and brew beer. It is difficult to imagine Thornton sending a telegram from a distant town to his wife asking where he was supposed to be.

With respect to the "small is beautiful" ideology that has attached itself to distributism, Thornton would have had as little sympathy as Chesterton for the idea that "big business" or anything beyond a vague "human scale" or not produced on a small farm or in the village workshop is *automatically* anti-human. As he made clear in his comprehensive article in the *Encyclopedia Britannica*,

> The extended use of iron and steel in the construction of agricultural implements is materially adding to their durability, and generally to their efficiency, and is thus a source of considerable savings. While great improvement has taken place in this department, it too commonly happens that the village mechanics, by whom a large portion of this class of implements is made and repaired, are exceedingly unskilled, and lamentably ignorant of the principles of their art. They usually furnished good materials and substantial workmanship, but by their unconscious violation of mechanical laws, enormous waste of motive power is continually incurred and poor results are attained. This can probably be remedied only by the construction of the more costly and complex machines being carried on in extensive factories, where, under the combined operation of scientific superintendence, ample capital, and skilled labor, aided by steam power, the work can be so performed as to combine the maximum of excellence with the minimum of cost.[2]

Given all this, there still seems to be a strong affinity between Thornton's goal and that of distributism. That makes it all the more baffling as to why neither Chesterton nor Belloc, nor any of their latter day followers have done any serious investigation of Thornton's proposal or, especially in light of the current economic problems and the general failure to advance the goal of establishing "the

---

[2] William Thomas Thornton, "Agriculture," *Encyclopedia Britannica*, 7th Edition (1875).

Distributist State," of the Just Third Way as applied in Capital Homesteading.

One possibility presents itself. It appears that Chesterton and Belloc accepted without question the disproved dogma that you can't finance new capital formation without first cutting consumption. Under that assumption, most people are permanently cut off from ownership if they rely on existing financial tools and institutions that depend on past savings.

To their credit, Chesterton and Belloc refused to consider the Keynesian expedient of "re-editing the dictionary,"[3] that is, changing the definition of natural rights such as life, liberty, and property, and thus their "substantial nature," thereby abolishing them. Consequently they may have felt they had no choice but to retreat into a romantic Never-Could-Be Land and hope things would get better after the inevitable crash.

Chesterton, Belloc and their followers could — and do — assuage their frustrations by poking feathers at the obvious fallacies on which the Powers-that-Be rely. The most obvious of which, of course, is the belief in the necessity of concentrated ownership of capital. The latter day distributist, however, continues to ignore the most obvious fallacy of all that makes concentrated ownership seemingly inevitable: the slavery of past savings. This renders even their most salutary admonitions ineffectual.

The presumed necessity of past savings to finance new capital formation can — if accepted — excuse the lack of action and general ineffectiveness of the distributist movement. Failure of the rich to open their purses for the benefit of others can be blamed on the personal greed and lack of virtue on the part of the capitalist or politician. The necessity of organizing in social justice for the common good and restructuring such basic institutions as money and credit can then be ignored, trivialized, or set

---

[3] John Maynard Keynes, *A Treatise on Money, Volume I: The Pure Theory of Money.* New York: Harcourt, Brace and Company, 1930, 4.

aside as impracticable in light of the presumed lack of virtue on the part of the people in power.

Another possibility is that the very specificity of Thornton's proposal and Capital Homesteading might strike the modern distributist as just a little too close to unpleasant and odorous reality. Thornton's continual references to manure might strike the modern distributist, essentially playing at returning to the soil while supported by the surrounding high tech civilization, as a trifle too close to the grim and grimy reality of true subsistence farming.

As for Capital Homesteading, the talk about natural rights and duties and what comes across as rigid insistence on the right definition and what it means tends to get dismissed as being judgmental. The Just Third Way emphasis on gaining a true understanding of money and credit that doesn't rely on conspiracy theory or blaming the greed and selfishness of the wealthy elite grates on the nerves of anyone committed to a simplistic solution. The complicated financial transactions and institutions explained come across very much like a way of explaining away and apologizing for the crimes of the wealthy against the poor. People should just share what they have, right? and everyone would have enough, right?

As a matter of fact, that *is* right — but what people should be sharing are not goods and wealth belonging to others, but viable ideas like Thornton's proposal and Capital Homesteading that have the promise of turning things around.

VIII. The Principle of Binary Growth

A theme that runs through both editions of William Thornton's *A Plea for Peasant Proprietors* is that, contrary to the views expressed by the leading economists of the 19th century (and, consequently, the 20th and the 21st), concentrated ownership of capital — land in this case — is not essential to optimize the rate of economic development. Thornton's observation and analysis correlates with what Dr. Robert H. A. Ashford of the University of Syracuse School of Law calls the principle of "binary growth."

Binary growth holds that economies grow steadily larger as private capital acquisition is distributed more broadly among a population on market principles. This principle also focuses on the importance of unleashing the unutilized or underutilized capacity of all economic systems to produce in greater abundance.[1] The principle of binary growth derives from Say's Law of Markets and its application in the real bills doctrine.

In plain language, the principle of binary growth is based on the fact that if all new capital is financed using "pure credit," that is, financing that is not based or dependent on existing accumulations of savings, and the ownership of all new capital is broadly distributed throughout the economy, the new owners will first use the income generated by capital to pay for the capital itself, then to meet consumption wants and needs. This is the essence of Say's Law: absent redistribution or almsgiving, the only way for people to purchase and consume the marketable goods and services that others produce, is to produce some marketable good or service for which others are willing to trade.

Freed from what Louis Kelso and Mortimer Adler called the slavery of past savings, income that previously would

---

[1] Robert H. A. Ashford and Rodney Shakespeare, *Binary Economics: The New Paradigm*. Lanham, Maryland: University Press of America, 1999, 37-41, 273-306, 320-325.

have been saved and diverted into reinvestment in new capital instead of consumption would now be available for consumption. As Dr. Harold G. Moulton[2] pointed out, the demand for capital is derived from consumer demand. Diverting income from consumption to reinvestment makes it less likely that new capital will be "feasible," that is, pay for itself out of future profits. Moulton called this "the economic dilemma." He described the "dilemma" in *The Formation of Capital* (1935).

The situation is actually worse than Moulton's analysis would suggest. The fact is that, even where there are high rates of savings, little if any of the savings go into capital investment. If the savings did go into new capital investment, consumption would remain at adequate levels. This is because, as far as the producer of capital goods is concerned, new capital formation is included in consumption, as Moulton pointed out in his critique of Friedrich von Hayek's analysis.[3] This still reduces demand for what the new capital will produce in some degree, but does not appear to be a significant factor in the drop in consumer demand observed when savings increase.

Nor are government borrowings of existing savings a drag on the economy. The practice of deficit spending financed by emitting bills of credit instead of existing savings obscures this point, at which Moulton hinted in *The New Philosophy of Public Debt* (1943). Government borrowing from existing savings simply shifts consumption patterns. It does not increase or decrease aggregate consumption. As long as government borrowing is confined to existing pools of savings, it can (in a sense) be viewed as shifting the tax burden around from one period to another. The wealth exists; it is only a question of whether the government spends it before or after taxing the citi-

---

[2] President of the Brookings Institution of Washington, DC, from 1916 to 1952.

[3] Harold G. Moulton, *The Formation of Capital*. Washington, DC: The Brookings Institution, 1935, 164-166.

zens.[4] (Interest payments on government debt can be viewed in the same way, as long as the discussion is confined to borrowings from existing savings.)

The most serious problem with restricting consumption under the belief that this is the only way in which new capital formation can be financed is much less obvious — and much more damaging — than would otherwise appear. Savings that are neither reinvested into new capital nor borrowed and spent by government constitute "hoarding," that is, sterile accumulations of unconsumed cash withheld from any form of consumption.

Traditionally, the bulk of hoarded or sterile cash has gone into time deposits of various types, and reserves of commercial banks. Consistent with the logic and operation of fractional reserve banking, these savings provide the "anchor" for an increase in loans for new capital investment.[5] Since the current economic downturn began, however, American companies have accumulated massive amounts of sterile cash. Some commentators estimate that, as of this writing, these accumulations are in excess of $2 trillion — the total annual "growth increment" of new capital in the United States a decade ago.

This cash is neither paid out to shareholders in the form of dividends, who could then use it for consumption, nor used to finance new capital formation, which would also, as Moulton explained, increase consumption. Nor, as

---

[4] The difference between government borrowing out of existing savings, and "borrowing" by emitting bills of credit is that in the former case it is simply a question of when the government taxes wealth that already exists. In the latter, the government is spending the present value of future taxes, based on the assumed present value of marketable goods and services that *might* be produced in the future. The former is constrained by the amount of wealth that actually exists. The latter is constrained only by the imagination of the politician.

[5] Moulton reaffirmed the validity of Say's Law of Markets and its application in the real bills doctrine, and demonstrated the falsity of the Keynesian "multiplier theory" in *The Formation of Capital, op. cit.*, 77-84.

commercial banks have reduced lending, are the savings being used to increase the number of loans. Instead, in a graphic demonstration of the proof of the principle of binary growth, the cash is simply hoarded.

The volatility of the global stock markets since the downturn began suggests the possibility that the cash is being channeled into the secondary market for debt and equity. Combined with money creation for speculation, and increased government spending financed by emitting bills of credit, such stock market transactions may have artificially inflated GDP, giving the illusion that the economy is experiencing a recovery when, in fact, no such thing is taking place.

As Moulton explained in *The Recovery Problem in the United States* (1936), a work in which he accurately predicted the "Depression within the Depression" of 1937-1938, genuine and sustainable economic recovery can only be achieved by focusing on two critical factors: *production* and *employment*.[6] Nor can it be production of goods and services for which no market exists, or "employment" in "created jobs" that serve no purpose other than to provide people with income.

The principle of binary growth is therefore critical in any viable program of economic recovery. Given that, consistent with Say's Law, no one can purchase what others produce unless he or she produces marketable goods and services for which others are willing to trade, ownership of capital as well as labor becomes essential if an economy is to be able to meet the wants and needs of people. This is because, as Jean-Baptiste Say and countless others have pointed out, the effect of advancing technology is to replace labor in the production process: "A new machine supplants a portion of human labor, but does not diminish the amount of the product; if it did, it would be absurd to adopt it."[7] At the point where the productiveness of capi-

---

[6] Harold G. Moulton, *The Recovery Problem in the United States.* Washington, DC: The Brookings Institution, 1936, 114.

[7] Jean-Baptiste Say, *A Treatise on Political Economy* (1803), I.vii.

tal exceeds that of labor, the worker must either suffer continuing decreases in income as the value of his or her labor decreases relative to the value of capital, or him- or herself become an owner of the capital that is replacing human labor.[8]

Nor are the principle of binary growth alone or the declining value of labor relative to capital the only reasons for expanding capital ownership among as many people as possible — although as Pope Leo XIII observed, "We have seen that this great labor question cannot be solved save by assuming as a principle that private ownership must be held sacred and inviolable. The law, therefore, should favor ownership, and its policy should be to induce as many as possible of the people to become owners."[9]

Thornton's analysis in *A Plea for Peasant Proprietors* suggests a corollary to the principle of binary growth. Thornton noted that small holdings of land tend to be worked more profitably than large holdings, a circumstance he attributed to the effects of ownership. Although Thornton's examples were limited to landed capital, the same principle applies to all other forms of capital.

Thornton observed that, in areas where people owned the land they tilled, they never ceased to improve the productiveness of their capital. The same or even larger size plots of better land in other areas, when farmed by tenants or hirelings, even, at times, with better technology, almost always produced at a lower level.

Thornton went on at some length about conditions he had observed in the Channel Islands, Guernsey, Jersey, and Alderney.[10] These islands were characterized by large numbers of small farms owned by those who worked them, were invariably prosperous, and were afflicted with

---

[8] See Charles Morrison, *An Essay on the Relations Between Labour and Capital*. London: Longman, Brown, Green, and Longmans, 1854, 111-132.

[9] Pope Leo XIII, *Rerum Novarum* ("On Capital and Labor"), 1891, § 46.

[10] See Chapter I in this volume.

few extremes of wealth or poverty. For the 1874 revision of the *Plea*, Thornton added several pages of historical examples of countries and empires that had grown strong and wealthy when ownership of capital was well-divided, and which fell into decay once ownership of capital became concentrated.

With respect to the economies of scale realized by aggregating capital, this is a valid point against small capital — but not small capital ownership. When ownership of capital as well as the capital itself is aggregated, there are at least two adverse effects.

One, of course, the principle of binary growth is negated. Income from capital flows by right to the owner of the capital. As technology advances and takes over more and more of the burden of production from human labor, increasing amounts of income go to owners of capital instead of owners of labor. The capital owner cannot consume all the income that his or her capital produces, and is "forced" either to reinvest the excess, or hoard it. Since, as we have observed, the latter results in a reduction of consumption (both of consumption goods *per se* and of capital goods), the rate of economic growth slows. Depending on the rate at which "sterile" wealth is accumulated, the economy can not only stop growing, but start to implode on itself.

Two, those who do the work of production are separated from those who own the means of production. This gives those doing the productive work less of an incentive to maximize or optimize production. Hirelings, however loyal or dedicated, rarely put forth the same effort as an owner, nor have the same "eye" for seeing every opportunity and taking advantage of it.

Modern management theory that aims at making workers "feel like owners" neglects to take into account the fact that, however successful initial efforts may be at making people feel like owners, eventually the workers realize that they are not, in fact, owners. They do not have the rights that necessarily accompany ownership. A backlash of resentment is inevitable as workers feel that they have been deprived of rights they never really had in the first place.

As Kelso and Adler explained, aggregating capital does not mean that *ownership* of the capital is necessarily aggregated, that is, concentrated in the hands of a few. The ideal situation to strive for is one in which the worker-owners of a company "feel like owners" because they have the rights of ownership, and this is reflected in the profitability of the company. According to the National Center for Employee Ownership in Oakland, California, worker-owned companies in which ownership is combined with the rights of ownership — *e.g.*, profit sharing and participatory management — outperform otherwise comparable companies by a factor of 1.5.

Combining economies of scale realized by aggregating capital, with the increased productivity observed when owners work with their own capital appears to be the optimal arrangement. The apparent paradox of concentrating capital while at the same time deconcentrating ownership of capital seems to give us the best of both worlds.

IX. The Guernsey Case

In both editions of *A Plea for Peasant Proprietors*, William Thornton held out the "Channel Islands" of Guernsey, Jersey, Alderney, and the others in the group, as exemplars of what peasant proprietorship could accomplish. Unfortunately, a number of groups that have inadequate or partial understandings of money, credit, banking, finance — and, above all, private property in capital — attribute the prosperity of the islands in the 19th century to another cause.

Specifically, monetary theorists advancing a distorted Keynesian system often cite the case of the Guernsey Market House in the early 19th century as proof of their contentions. The theory is that all that is necessary for an adequate and stable currency and general prosperity is for the government to use its alleged money creation power and issue money to circulate as a non-repayable debt the government owes to itself.[1]

As often related, the story is that, to finance various public works, the States of Guernsey, the governing body of the "Balliwick of Guernsey," as the British Crown dependency is called,[2] issued debt-free and interest-free money that it spent on infrastructure and public works. This allegedly eliminated taxation and inflation, and brought universal prosperity to Guernsey.[3]

---

[1] See Harold G. Moulton, *The New Philosophy of Public Debt*. Washington, DC: The Brookings Institution, 1943, 51-52, 53-71..
[2] The "Channel Islands" consisting of the Balliwick of Guernsey and the Balliwick of Jersey off the coast of Normandy are not part of the United Kingdom, but the last remnant of the Duchy of Normandy belonging to the British Crown. The third Crown dependency, the Isle of Man, is in the Irish Sea, almost equidistant from Ireland and Great Britain.
[3] Olive and Jan Grubiak, *The Guernsey Experiment: A Study of the Well-Known 19th Century Essay in Monetary Reform*. Hawthorn, California: Omni Publications, 1960.

As we have seen in his lengthy discussions on the lack of poverty in the Channel Islands compared to the level in Ireland of his day, however, Thornton attributed the prosperity he observed in Guernsey to well-divided property, not to manipulation of the currency by the government. This suggests that the actual facts may be somewhat different than reported by the monetary theorists. On investigation, this turns out to be the case.[4]

In 1815, the governing body of the Channel Island of Guernsey, *les Estats du Guernesey* ("the States of Guernsey"), proposed to issue £3,000 of State notes to purchase supplies and pay workmen for the construction of a market house. The market house was expected to produce rental revenues of £150 *per annum*.

It was not until 1820, however, that the notes were actually authorized and issued, in the amount of £4,000, and the market house constructed. Subsequent issues of paper notes were made for other capital projects, infrastructure improvements and for replacing worn notes in circulation. Virtually all notes were eventually redeemed out of revenues generated by the various projects, as demonstrated by their extreme rarity for collectors of paper money.[5] What traditional economists found completely unaccountable in this "experiment" by the States of Guernsey was that the introduction of a paper currency did not cause an inflationary rise in prices.

There are four assumptions implicit in the analysis of conventional economists, any one of which makes understanding what Guernsey accomplished virtually impossible. 1) Paper money is, at best, a second-rate substitute for gold. 2) The total amount of wealth in an economy is fixed. 3) Issues of paper money are automatically inflationary, but 4) this inflation can be kept to a manageable

---

[4] Norman Angell, *The Story of Money*. New York: Frederick A. Stokes Company, 1929, 266-271.

[5] Albert Pick, *Standard Catalog of World Paper Money, Fifth Edition—Volume Two, General Issues*. Iola, Wisconsin: Krause Publications, Inc., 1986, p. 544.

level by limiting the issues to the present value of existing savings.

The real explanation is far simpler.

Financing the construction of a market house, roads, and schools with State notes of paper was not inflationary in the island of Guernsey because the currency was asset-backed. The value of the notes was determined by the present value of the anticipated future marketable goods and services to be provided, or the taxes to be collected. Use of the market house, roads, bridges and other infrastructure was not free of charge. The government of Guernsey charged rent for the market stalls, tolls for the roads and bridges, and taxes and port fees for sea walls and similar structures. This revenue was used to retire the debt incurred in the form of banknotes — promissory notes — floated to finance the construction of the capital.

The fact is that the amount of wealth in an economy is not static. The actual amount of paper money printed was not important. Nor did it matter whether it exceeded the amount of existing wealth, *i.e.*, productive capacity currently in use and past accumulations of savings.[6]

What is important is that, 1) the amount of money in the economy multiplied by the "velocity" of money (*i.e.*, the average number of times a unit of currency is spent in a year) does not exceed the price level times the number of transactions, and 2) all money, whatever form it takes, is directly backed by the issuer's private property stake or other enforceable claim in the present value of the capital that will produce the marketable goods and services that will be used to redeem the money in the future, or existing inventories of such goods by means of which the money can be redeemed on demand.

What the States of Guernsey did was "monetize" a portion of the present value of the future revenue to be realized from the construction of infrastructure sufficient to

---

[6] See Norman G. Kurland, "A New Look at Prices and Money," *op. cit.*

pay for the construction of the infrastructure. When the revenues were received by the government, the funds were used to retire the debt, and thereafter provided a stream of income which the government was able to use for State expenditures, thereby lowering — but not eliminating — taxes.

What was important was that the printing press money paid for the creation of actual productive wealth. Each paper note was backed by the ability of the new wealth to generate revenue; in the instance of the market house, a rental income of £150 *per annum*. The State, of course, remained the owner of the infrastructure, even though it was not uncommon at that time for such infrastructure to be financed as profit-making enterprises by private individuals and corporations.

In short, the States of Guernsey created an asset-backed currency that, because it brought about an increase in wealth and productivity, was non-inflationary. The amount of money in circulation was increased, but so was the present value of real wealth in the economy — the revenue-generating physical plant of the market house — and in the same degree. Had it turned out that the new wealth created was not productive, inflation would indeed have resulted. On the other hand, had productivity of the new wealth exceeded the amount of money created to finance its construction, currency appreciation (as opposed to deflation) would have resulted. The paper notes would actually have increased in value, along with all the other currency in circulation.

The only "trick" involved in the issuance of a paper currency is how it is used, not how much or how little is issued. Had the States of Guernsey issued their notes to erect a statue to some politician, carry out a war, or make welfare payments to people on the dole, as the proponents of "let the government print and spend its money into circulation" and maintain it as a non-repayable debt that the nation owes to itself suggest, the issues would have been purely inflationary. The phantom inflation that economists and monetary theorists looked so hard to find would have been immediately apparent. The currency in that case would have been backed by the debts incurred to carry out the projects. Because the paper was used to pay for the creation of productive capital assets, however, the currency was backed by the present value of the productive power of the wealth that it financed.

The rule for any currency is that it is backed by whatever the issuer creates with it. If the currency is used to finance debt, the currency will be backed by debt and be purely inflationary. If the currency is used to finance productive assets, the currency will be backed by assets and be non-inflationary. That is the rule for *any* currency — paper, gold, tobacco, wood, or leather. The intrinsic value of any currency is completely incidental to the function, meaning and use of that currency. In that sense, it is better to have a circulating medium of no intrinsic value at all. This is because then the issuers and users of the currency will not be blinded by the glister of the material itself. They will be able to see the medium of exchange for what it is — a symbol, as was noted by Louis Kelso:

Money is not a part of the visible sector of the economy; people do not consume money. Money is not a physical factor of production, but rather a yardstick for measuring economic input, economic outtake and the relative values of the real goods and services of the economic world. Money provides a method of measuring obligations, rights, powers and privileges. It provides a means whereby certain individuals can accumulate claims against others, or against the economy as a whole, or against many economies. It is a system of symbols that many economists substitute for the visible sector and its productive enterprises, goods and services, thereby losing sight of the fact that a monetary system is a part only of the invisible sector of the economy, and that its adequacy can *only* be measured by its effect upon the visible sector.[7]

---

[7] Louis Kelso and Patricia Hetter, *Two-Factor Theory: The Economics of Reality*. New York: Random House, 1967, 54.

X. Pure Credit

Looking at the common sense of William Thornton's proposal for a compensated redistribution of "waste" land in Ireland, we have a hard time trying to understand why the British government completely ignored it. The only possibility that makes even marginal sense is that, as with many otherwise feasible plans, it came to grief over the financing — which, in turn, was dictated by bad economic ideas and concepts, such as the fixed belief in the necessity for cutting consumption to accumulate savings in order to finance new capital formation.

The fact is that if private individuals or, especially, the government, have inadequate or flawed ideas about money, credit, banking and finance, serious economic problems are going to crop up, as they have in our day. Money, like the State itself, is a very powerful social tool. A well-regulated and sound financial system is invaluable, possibly even essential for a just social order.

Unfortunately, when the financial system is not well-regulated, or the principles on which the system is based are not sound, then disaster is never but a short step away. Fortunately, getting a grasp of sound principle isn't too difficult, if we don't allow ourselves to be blinded by the mistakes and preconceptions of the past.

Even more fortunately, anyone who can understand the convolutions of 19th century Irish politics that provided the context of Thornton's proposal should have little or no trouble with the theory of "pure credit." This is not surprising. The modern struggle between economic development based on what Louis Kelso and Mortimer Adler called the slavery of past savings,[1] and that based on pure credit and "future savings," is the direct result of something related to the event that set the tone for relations

---

[1] See Louis Kelso and Mortimer Adler, *The New Capitalists: A Proposal to Free Economic Growth from the Slavery of Savings.* New York: Random House, 1961.

between Great Britain and Ireland for the whole of the 19th century.

The story is almost comic. In 1797 the news swept through England that the French had landed an invasion force in Wales in support of a planned uprising in Ireland. This was an event that came to be known as "the last invasion of England."

As invasions go, it wasn't much. Four French warships carrying 1,400 men landed at Carregwastad Head near Fishguard on February 22. This was supposed to be coordinated with Theobald Wolfe Tone's efforts in Ireland.

Originally intended as a diversion, on February 23 the French force got drunk on some looted casks of wine, fought a few engagements with local militia and one of the local housewives — "Jemima the Great" as she is known tongue-in-cheek in local legend — got drunker, and surrendered on February 24. The British captured two of the French vessels, a frigate and a corvette (a vessel smaller than a frigate), and the other two French warships returned home. After waiting for additional French aid, the Irish rose in 1798, the "Wexford Rebellion."

Despite the comic opera aspect of the event, word of the "invasion" spread through Wales and England, panic hard on its heels. People rushed to their banks to withdraw all their funds in gold. Reserves got so low that Sir William Pitt's government permitted (or ordered, depending on your source) the Bank of England temporarily to suspend convertibility of its banknotes into gold. This temporary measure lasted for more than two decades. Convertibility of the paper pound into gold was not restored until 1821.

Trying to figure out why England didn't immediately go into a financial meltdown when the paper currency wasn't convertible into gold was productive of a knockdown, drag-out political and economic fight for the next half century. This was between people who thought that money consists of coin and State-issued banknotes, and people who thought that money is anything that you can use to settle a debt. What we need to understand the situation — and William Thornton's financing proposal — is the theory of pure credit, and some economic history.

The Theory of Pure Credit

The basic theory of pure credit is simple. First, however, we need to define what we mean by "pure credit": money created by extending credit based not on the present value of existing accumulations of savings, but on the present value of marketable goods and services to be produced in the future. The credit is "pure," that is, not dependent on what has been done in the past, only what can be done in the future. This is, in fact, how most money has been created throughout human history.

For thousands of years before the invention of currency, that is, "current money" of a uniform and standard value that circulates within an economy, money contracts existed. "Money contract" is, in fact, redundant. In a sense, *all* contracts are money, and all money is a contract, a promise to deliver something of value, a marketable good or service, thereby settling a debt.

A money contract is, technically, a "bill of exchange." Bills of exchange are further divided into mortgages and bills of exchange proper. A mortgage differs from a bill of exchange proper (which we shall refer to from here on simply as a "bill of exchange") in that a mortgage is backed by or represents the present value of an existing marketable good or service, while a bill of exchange is backed by the general creditworthiness of the issuer.

Usually the issuer's creditworthiness is a measure of other people's faith that the issuer will deliver the stated value in marketable goods or services, or their equivalent, at some future date or on the occurrence of some event. Most simply put, a bill of exchange is backed by the present value of the future marketable goods and services that the issuer of the bill promises to deliver to the holder in due course of the contract.

Here we have to insert a complication. What we've just described is the way *private sector* bills of exchange work.

Governments also issue bills of exchange, except that they call it "emitting" instead of "issuing" or "drawing," and a "bill of credit" instead of a "bill of exchange."

There's one more difference between a private sector-issued bill of exchange and a government-emitted bill of credit. As we said, a bill of exchange is backed by the issuer's creditworthiness, measured by the opinion that others have of the issuer's ability to deliver the promised marketable goods or services or the value thereof on maturity: the present value of the issuer's future stream of income or production out of which the issuer will make good on the promise conveyed by the bill of exchange.

A bill of credit is also backed by the issuer's creditworthiness. In the case of a bill of credit, however, the issuing government's creditworthiness is measured by the opinion that others have of the government's ability to collect taxes in the future in order to be able to make good on the promise conveyed by the bill of credit.

In other words, the issuer of a bill of exchange has to make good on it him- or herself. The issuer of a bill of credit — always a government; "bill of credit" is a specialized "constitutional" term — on the other hand, has to be able to tax what *other* people produce in order to make good on the promise. The emitter of a bill of credit is, in effect, making promises for other people to keep, and relying on its power to tax them to make good on those promises. If a government loses its power to tax, or if there is nothing to tax, then the bills of credit — and the currency backed by the bills of credit — become worthless.

A bill that is issued or emitted for no more than the present value of the expected future stream of revenue to result from production or taxation is called a "real bill," that is, it has real value. A bill that is issued for *more* than the present value of the expected future stream of revenue to result from production or taxation, or that has no present value behind it at all, is called a "fictitious bill," that is, a fake or a phony bill. Real bills are non-inflationary. Fictitious bills are inflationary to the extent they exceed the present value that the issuer reasonably expects to produce or collect.

The issuer of a bill can use the bill as money in one of two ways. The first, and most common, is to use the bill as money directly. An issuer or "drawer" of a bill can pay for marketable goods and services produced by others with the issuer's promise to pay in the future. Because a bill only becomes money when accepted in payment of a debt, a bill used directly as money is called a "merchant's" or "trade acceptance."

Since a bill will typically be accepted by a holder in due course at less than its face value as a result of the time value of money and the risk associated with the issuer's creditworthiness, an initial transaction involving a bill is called "discounting." Subsequent transactions are called "rediscounting" until the bill is presented by the holder in due course to the issuer on maturity for redemption.

Despite the fact that the greater part of the money supply in any economy has always consisted of various forms of bills of exchange used in transactions between individuals and businesses, it is sometimes more convenient to have an individual or institution of recognized creditworthiness substitute his, her or its name for that of a possibly unknown or untrustworthy issuer. This institution is called a bank — specifically, a "bank of issue" or "bank of circulation." A bill discounted or rediscounted at a bank of issue is called a "banker's acceptance."

A bank of issue is a specialized financial institution that takes deposits, makes loans, and issues promissory notes. A promissory note is a special type of bill of exchange that a bank of issue trades for a private issuer's bill of exchange. A bank's promissory note can be used to back smaller denomination promissory notes called "banknotes," or a demand deposit (checking account) created in the name of the original issuer of the bill of exchange for which the bank of issue traded its promissory note. The most common type of bank of issue today is the commercial or mercantile bank.

Another type of bank is the "bank of deposit." A bank of deposit is more limited than a bank of issue, because a bank of deposit cannot create money by accepting bills. A bank of deposit is limited to taking deposits and making loans. It cannot issue promissory notes to trade for bills of exchange, and thus cannot deal in pure credit. Common types of banks of deposit are savings and loans, credit unions, and investment banks.[2]

A "central bank" is a "bank of issue for banks of issue." Its special function is to rediscount bills of exchange originally discounted by commercial banks and coordinate the activities of its member banks to ensure a uniform, stable, asset-backed "elastic" currency so that there is always enough liquidity in the system to keep it running. "Open market operations" are a means whereby a central bank purchases paper issued by non-member banks, businesses, and individuals. In the modern world, open market operations have generally been diverted away from the private sector and used to finance non-productive government spending.

That's an extremely condensed version of the theory. To try and explain practice would take several volumes, and isn't relevant to our goal. All we need to understand is how a financial system can be run without relying on existing accumulations of savings — "pure credit," that is, credit that is not tied down by whatever has been accumulated in the past, but instead is tied to what can be produced in the future.

Back to Our Story

Following the suspension of convertibility of Bank of England banknotes into gold in 1797, the economists began debating how it was possible to have avoided disaster when gold was no longer the basis for the currency. Based

---

[2] Adding to the problem of concentrated ownership of capital is the way virtually all investment banks function to make the rich richer, and erect barriers to capital ownership by ordinary people without savings or collateral. This "recycles" the savings of the rich, instead of opening up opportunities for capital ownership by everyone.

on the work of Adam Smith in *The Wealth of Nations* a quarter century before, bankers like Henry Thornton (no relation to William) and economists like Jean-Baptiste Say worked out the basic theory presented above. This was summarized in "Say's Law of Markets," the "real bills doctrine," and (later) the "Quantity Theory of Money."

Very briefly, Say's Law (he didn't develop it, just gave what is probably the clearest explanation of it) is that we don't really purchase what others produce with this thing we call "money." Rather, money is just a symbol of what we produce with our labor and capital. Money is the "medium of exchange." By means of money, we can trade our surplus goods and services for the surplus goods and services others produce.

The real bills doctrine (again, briefly) is that, as long as the money we create by issuing bills of exchange and having them accepted does not exceed the present value of existing and future marketable goods and services in the economy, there will be no inflation. Together, Say's Law and the real bills doctrine sum up the essence of the "Banking Principle." The Quantity Theory of Money, M x V = P x Q, describes the mathematical relationship between how much money there is, how often it is spent, the amount of production, and the price level.

The trouble was that you also had the "Currency Principle." In contrast to the Banking Principle, the Currency Principle is simplicity itself. The idea is that "money" consists exclusively of coin and State-issued or authorized banknotes backed by gold or government debt. The only way to have money, and thus finance new capital ventures such as land acquisition by peasants, is to cut consumption and accumulate savings in the form of money.

Obviously, this means that the only people who can own *future* capital are, in general, those who already own *present* capital. Nobody else — especially people who were going through one of the most horrific famines in history and who couldn't possibly cut consumption — has the ability to save enough to purchase capital, particularly as technology advances and capital becomes increasingly expensive.

The common sense of the Banking Principle shows up the flaws in the Currency Principle immediately. That didn't matter, however, in early 19th century England and Ireland. The people who backed the Banking Principle had sound theory and practice on their side. The people who backed the Currency Principle had the self-interest of the already wealthy and the desire of politicians to spend money without raising taxes on theirs. It comes as no surprise that the Currency Principle carried the day.

David Ricardo (1772-1823) set out to correct the theories of Adam Smith. The theory that we're interested in, of course, is the Banking Principle found in Book II of *The Wealth of Nations*. Smith adhered to the real bills doctrine, although he didn't call it that. The term wasn't current until Henry Thornton, a banker, wrote a book in 1802 with the ponderous title, *An Enquiry into the Nature and Effects of the Paper Credit of Great Britain*. Thornton, too, set out, in part, to correct a few mistakes he believed Smith had made.

Thornton, however, thought that Smith had a good grasp of the basic theory. As a practicing banker, though, Thornton realized that Smith had gotten some technical details wrong. Consequently, Thornton's corrections of Smith took up, at most, a couple of paragraphs in *The Paper Credit of Great Britain*.

Ricardo, on the other hand, decided that Smith didn't know what he was talking about in several critical areas. This was not just a matter of correcting a few technical details. Ricardo believed that Smith was mistaken in his basic theory in many areas, such as the labor theory of value, the theory of rent, and so on.

The theory that concerns us, however, is Ricardo's understanding of money and credit. Ricardo believed that it is impossible to finance new capital formation until and unless consumption is reduced and money savings accumulated. Further, "money" is not anything that can be used to settle a debt, as Smith held, but coin and banknotes. (The dispute within the Currency School whether demand deposits — "checking accounts" — are part of the money supply would wait another century, and is not completely resolved to this day.)

The crux of the issue is that, where Smith maintained that the purpose of production is consumption, Ricardo had to include "and reinvestment to finance new capital" as an increasingly important purpose of production. This created a paradox that in the 1930s Dr. Harold G. Moulton of the Brookings Institution would call "the economic dilemma." That is, if new capital can only be financed by cutting consumption, no sane businessman will ever finance new capital because the demand will no longer exist to make the new capital financially feasible.

Resolving this paradox requires that we realize that we shouldn't rely on *past* savings for financing, but on pure credit *future* savings. Ricardo, however, couldn't make that leap because he was locked into a flawed definition of money.

Ricardo passed this flawed understanding of money on to John Ramsay Macculloch (1789-1864), a Scottish economist, author and editor whom William Thornton referenced approximately a dozen times in his *Plea* — and not in a very complimentary way.

This makes sense. Thornton was all in favor of widespread ownership of both landed and industrial capital. Macculloch, as the inheritor of Ricardo's mantle (Macculloch was considered the head of the "Ricardian" school of classical economics), believed that concentrated ownership of capital, whether land or machinery, is essential to financing new capital. This was so the rich could afford to save and buy more capital in order to create jobs for people who have only their labor to sell.

Thornton appears to have had a better understanding of money than is generally acknowledged. Schumpeter revealed this unconsciously in his *History of Economic Analysis* when, in commenting on Thornton's critique of the "wage-fund doctrine" (of which Macculloch, unsurprisingly, was considered the premier exponent) he stated,

Both Longe and Thornton blur the issue — and incidentally betray inadequate grasp of the "classic" analysis — by speaking of "money" without making sure that this money stands for physical goods.[3]

The problem with Schumpeter's comment is that money does *not* stand for physical goods. This implies (among other things) that the amount of money is limited to the value of *existing* inventories of marketable goods and services. On the contrary, as anything that can be used to settle a debt, money stands not for the goods themselves, but for the *present value* of existing *and future* marketable goods and services, the *value* of which, or its equivalent, is deliverable either on demand or on maturity to the holder in due course of the money. The whole theory of pure credit rests on this understanding of money.

A proposal such as Thornton made would have sounded like rank socialism to Macculloch. Macculloch necessarily believed that the rich are a special breed to be nurtured and protected with privileges and benefits to ensure that they will be ready, willing and able to finance new capital to create jobs. Macculloch's theories also justified backing banknotes with a limited amount of debt-backed State-issued bills of credit, and rejected private sector asset-backed bills of exchange as the backing for the currency.

Macculloch was thus able to tell the wealthy and political elite of early-19th century Great Britain exactly what they wanted to hear. Being rich and powerful was not only God's Will, but the way a sound economy and financial system *had* to run if the sun was never to set on the British Empire, predestined for all time to rule the world. The fact that, as Walter Bagehot maintained in mid-century in *The English Constitution* (1867), the *real* rulers of the Empire were members of the wealthy commercial class, not the Widow of Windsor or her unemployed son, simply corroborated this belief.

---

[3] Schumpeter, *History of Economic Analysis, op. cit.*, 670n.

Consequently, Macculloch's views had enormous influence on the financial and political elite of the British Empire. Even after his death in 1864, as with Keynes in the 20th and 21st centuries, Macculloch bound the intellectual elite and politicians as "the slaves of some defunct economist."[4] Macculloch's influence was of critical importance when the charter of the Bank of England came up for renewal in 1844, and ensured that bad ideas about money and credit would be embedded into public policy down to the present day. Lord Overstone, a banker in real life, was a fervent believer in Ricardo's — and thus Macculloch's — theories.[5] It didn't help any that Lord Overstone inherited Macculloch's library on the latter's death.

Further, as the owner of an investment bank and not a commercial or mercantile establishment, Lord Overstone did not appreciate the difference between the kind of bank he ran, and the special function of commercial banks and the Bank of England, generally considered the first true central bank. Lord Overstone understood *deposit* banking, not *issue* banking, and was thus the worst choice to frame the legislation for the British Bank Charter Act of 1844. Nevertheless, with the assistance of Sir Robert Peel, Lord Overstone got the Act passed, and locked the British Empire into unsound principles of money, credit, banking and finance that have persisted — and continued to spread — down to the present day.

Thus, it is no wonder that, even if the British government had been in any way inclined to adopt Thornton's proposal to build ownership of Ireland at least partly into the people of Ireland, it would have deemed the idea impossible. They would have tossed it aside without further consideration.

---

[4] Keynes, *General Theory, op. cit.*, VI.24.v.
[5] See Lord Overstone, *The Evidence Given By Lord Overstone on the Bank Acts.* London: Longman, Brown, & Co., 1858.

XI. Capital Homesteading

While William Thornton's proposal for building capital ownership into the people of Ireland was visionary, there was a built-in flaw. As he pointed out in his 1874 revision of *A Plea for Peasant Proprietors*, in many circumstances even in his day — and even more so in ours — there simply wasn't enough land to go around to satisfy the demand for productive assets and make everyone a capital owner.

This is rooted in the limited nature of land itself. Restricting the capital that can be owned by ordinary people to land instead of including the effectively unlimited technological frontier severely constrains opportunities for capital ownership. As Thornton observed, this has a serious effect on people's social, political, moral and, especially, economic development. "Power," as Daniel Webster observed, "naturally and necessarily follows property." Without property in capital, people become, effectively or in fact, the property of others. As the Center for Economic and Social Justice puts it, it is a case of "own or be owned." In the generation following Thornton, in America in the 1890s Frederick Jackson Turner stated his conviction that the end of "free" land available under Abraham Lincoln's Homestead Act meant the end of democracy.

Time appears to have validated Turner's hypothesis and Thornton's observations. In the 1830s Alexis de Tocqueville commented that in America, the government — especially the federal government — seemed hardly to rule at all. Americans had the habit of forming associations to carry out tasks that today many people automatically assume are the function of government, from directing traffic, to building the roads that carried the traffic.

We can use the proportion of the money supply created by the private sector through the issuance of bills of exchange as a measure of the increasing State control over the economy — and thus people's lives. In the 1830s Congressman George Tucker estimated that between 95-99%

of the money supply in the United States consisted of privately issued bills of exchange, not coin, or banknotes backed by government debt.[1] A century ago, it was estimated that 75-80% of GDP consisted of this "private sector money."[2] A rough calculation for 2008 reveals that approximately 60% of the transactions that constituted GDP consisted of private sector bills of exchange. Clearly, as opportunities for capital ownership by ordinary people have disappeared, the State has stepped in and exercised increasing control over the economy in a futile effort to make up for the lack of widespread capital ownership.

Government control seems inevitable, given the lack of capital ownership on the part of most people and the displacement of human labor from the production process by advancing technology. In the United States Abraham Lincoln's 1862 Homestead Act temporarily halted the apparently inescapable State takeover of the economy to ensure the wellbeing of the people — as opposed to the State's proper role of ensuring equality of opportunity for people to take care of themselves.

In many respects, the Homestead Act in the United States was the realization of Thornton's vision, albeit on somewhat different terms than he proposed. For example, where Thornton had to take existing property rights into account, the rights of Native Americans to the land homesteaded were not considered.[3] Further, Thornton had to include in his proposal some means of financing acquisition of land by the State and subsequent transfer to families, to be held either freehold or by "perpetual lease," an arrangement Thornton considered tantamount to freehold

---

[1] George Tucker, *The Theory of Money and Banks Investigated.* Boston, Massachusetts: Charles C. Little and James Brown, 1839, 132.

[2] Harold G. Moulton, *Principles of Money and Banking.* Chicago, Illinois: University of Chicago Press, 1916, II.39.

[3] There is a parallel between the land homesteaded in the United States and the Elizabethan and Jacobean plantations in Ireland. In both cases, any claim to the land by the indigenous peoples was set aside, often by treaties or other agreements of questionable legality.

ownership. In the United States, the land was already considered part of the public domain, and needed only some systematic mechanism to transfer title. The idea, however, was the same. Give people the opportunity to become owners of landed capital, and they will lift themselves out of poverty, to their own benefit and that of the nation at large.

The problem, however, remained the same. Landed capital is limited, and there can never be enough to satisfy everyone who wants or needs capital in order to generate an adequate and secure income. Consequently, consistent with Say's Law of Markets, as ordinary people lose the ability to participate in the production of marketable goods and services, they lose the ability to purchase what they need to satisfy their wants and needs without some form of redistribution. Not surprisingly, this redistribution has resulted in an increasing role for the State. At the same time, the method of financing new capital formation has resulted in greater and greater inequities in capital ownership, and thus in wealth and income.

Fortunately, the solution has also remained the same. We only need to realize, one, that the analysis of Louis Kelso and Mortimer Adler in *The Capitalist Manifesto* remains fundamentally sound. That is, all non-human productive assets — anything that cannot be included under the heading of "labor," the specifically human input to production — can be grouped under the heading of "capital."[4]

Two, just as every human being owns his or her own labor by the natural right of private property, every human being has the natural capacity to own anything else that can be owned, especially capital: productive assets.

Both of these propositions are obvious once we think about them. The traditional classic division of the factors of production into labor, land and capital is done for reasons that have no bearing on this analysis. Land and

---

[4] We reject the term "human capital" as dehumanizing, as it connotes "human thing," an oxymoron.

other capital can be combined in a single classification with little or no effect even on mainstream economics.

Further, given that private property is a natural right, there can be no logical distinction between labor and capital, with the sole exception that, while someone other than the owner of human labor can contract for labor and thus have a legal claim on it, no one can legitimately own another human being as private property as he or she would own capital.[5]

Given that every human being has the natural right to own capital on the same terms and in the same way that he or she owns his or her own labor, and that there is no effective difference between land and other forms of capital, it necessarily follows that, if there is insufficient land available to meet the demand for — and the necessity of — universal capital ownership, then other forms of capital must be substituted for land if everyone is to have the opportunity to become a capital owner. What is needed is a "Capital Homestead Act" to duplicate the success of Lincoln's land-based Homestead Act, but in a way that it can be sustained without reliance on a limited form of capital or redistribution of existing wealth.

In a democratic and just economy everyone should have an equal opportunity and equal access to the means to own shares in companies that use advanced technology. Just as Thornton proposed for the 19th century Irish economy, the U.S. — or Irish — economy, for example, should have programs that eliminate artificial tax and credit barriers to help every citizen become an owner of industrial and commercial capital as well as agricultural. Every family could then earn income from both jobs and capital that every family member would own.

This raises the question of how such capital acquisition can be financed. Thornton relied on State financing.

---

[5] The technical enslavement of convicts does not violate this principle. A convict is "owned" by the State, not private individuals, and has forfeited his or her right to liberty as the result of conviction for a crime.

Given the poor record of State programs of virtually all kinds — which Thornton himself admitted — State financing should be avoided whenever possible. This leads to the need for a fundamental reform in the way in which new capital formation is financed by the private sector.

Today many people, even the poor, can use consumer credit to buy items such as cars, TV sets, clothing, and homes. These purchases, however, are consumer items. They are not income-earning property. Purchasing such things on credit can make the borrower even more economically vulnerable than before.

At the same time, before the current economic downturn, the United States alone added about $2 trillion worth of new productive assets in both the public sector and private sector, or $7,000 for every man, woman, and child in the country. The way in which the bulk of these new assets is financed, however — a better use of credit — creates few new owners and widens the gap between "haves" and "have-nots," seemingly mandating an increasingly level of State control of the economy.

Fortunately, there is an alternative that is neither socialism (concentrated State ownership or control) nor capitalism (concentrated private ownership or control), and does not rely on redistributing existing wealth. This "Just Third Way" would be a free enterprise market economy, generating private sector profits — but with ownership of the new growth systematically flowing to every individual citizen.

With access to capital credit repayable with the full pretax earnings of the capital itself, everyone could gain ownership in the world's expanding technological frontier. We wouldn't have to take away wealth from those who already own capital.

A Capital Homestead Act on these terms would be a modern version of Thornton's proposal and an extension of Lincoln's 1862 Homestead Act to capital in addition to land. Using "pure credit" financing collateralized with capital credit insurance and reinsurance, Capital Homesteading on these terms would take nothing away from present owners. The program would link every citizen (including the poorest of the poor) to the profits from sustainable economic growth made possible by advancing technology. Every worker and citizen could gain a share in power over technological progress and the tools and enterprises of modern society. As Thornton observed was the case in lands where "peasant proprietorship" was the rule, all citizens would participate in a more democratic *economic* process, just as they now participate in the democratic *political* process through access to the ballot.

Based on figures from the U.S. economy a decade ago before the current economic downturn,[6] under Capital Homesteading, a child born today could gain by age 65 an estimated $462,000 in tax-sheltered assets, $61,000 in annual pre-tax income, and $1.8 million in dividends.

A Capital Homestead Act would embody a number of programs so that every child, woman and man could get interest- (but not cost-) free capital credit from a local bank to purchase corporate shares or other capital assets that have the potential to pay for themselves out of future earnings. Dividends tax-deductible at the corporate level would pay off the loans, including bank service fees and premiums to cover capital credit default insurance.

Within a relatively short period of time, the Homesteader would become a full owner of the shares. These would generate a decent and regular lifelong income from the earnings of the capital the Homesteader accumulates over the years. These assets could be passed on to the next generation.

---

[6] Paradoxically, because of the drop in reinvestment, new capital formation, and the decay in infrastructure since the onset of the economic downturn, the amount of potential new capital available to private ownership (including many things traditionally owned by government) is much greater, and should result in much faster rates of growth and capital accumulation should a Capital Homestead Act be passed.

XII. The Citizens Land Bank

In William Thornton's 1874 revision of *A Plea for Peasant Proprietors*, he suggested that an ideal solution to the problem of equal access to capital would be for the State to take corporate ownership of all the land, and offer it on perpetual leases to tenants who would have State-granted and protected rights analogous to that of true ownership. Paradoxically, this followed Thornton's unequivocal statements in the *Plea* and other works that anything in which the State has a hand is almost necessarily doomed to failure.

In the 1848 edition, it was not entirely clear from Thornton's language whether he meant actual freehold proprietorship, or effective proprietorship via a "perpetual lease" (renewable forever at the option of the lessee) conveying almost the same rights as a freehold. In his 1874 revision, however, Thornton made it apparent that, in his opinion (probably for political reasons as well as personal inclination), the perpetual lease was to be preferred over freehold.

Thornton's apparent reversal of his insistence on peasant *proprietorship* is probably rooted in two reasons. One, holding land on a perpetual lease is the same as a freehold for all intents and purposes. With the State as landlord, Thornton — a lifelong bureaucrat — appears to have reasoned that the lease rights would be more secure than under a private sector landlord, and the problem of constant subdividing of estates be avoided.

That Thornton himself had already made a very strong case that freeholding does not result in a constant subdivision seems to have passed him by. Further, the State has, from the early 20th century on, proven a very frail reed on which to lean, especially where private property rights are concerned, whether lease- or freehold.

Under the influence of Keynesian economics in particular, which is predicated in part on a redefinition of private property and the assumption that the State has absolute power to alter any and all contracts at will,[1] a lease held from the State — in common with all other contracts — could easily be subject to alteration or voiding at the whim of the party or individual in power on the grounds of political or economic necessity.

Two, land is limited by its very nature. When land is the only form of capital that ordinary people are permitted to own, an increasing demand for it is inevitable as advancing technology removes human labor from the production process. We see this in the modern "distributist movement" that effectively limits the form of capital to land and small artisan workshops. A global economy characterized exclusively by low-tech subsistence farming and small, individual manufacturing would have been preceded by massive starvation and death on a scale that would dwarf the Great Famine in Ireland.

Thornton's "ideal" that the State be the universal landlord for the new class of peasant proprietors is similar to the proposal of Henry George, the American agrarian socialist. In *Progress and Poverty*, published in 1879, a few years after Thornton's revision — although there is no evidence that George was even aware of Thornton's work — George proposed that the State become the effective owner of all land and natural resources. This could be done, in George's view, by taking all "rent" from land (the classical economic triad is that rent comes from land, interest from capital — in classical economics, the means of production other than land and labor; not to be confused with "financial capital," *i.e.*, money — and wages from labor) as a "single tax," thereby removing all benefit to private ownership of land. As George explained his scheme,

> What I, therefore, propose, as the simple yet sovereign remedy, which will raise wages, increase the earnings of capital, extirpate pauperism, abolish poverty, give re-

---

[1] John Maynard Keynes, *A Treatise on Money, Volume I: The Pure Theory of Money.* New York: Harcourt, Brace, Jovanovich, 1930, 4.

munerative employment to whoever wishes it, afford free scope to human powers, lessen crime, elevate morals, and taste, and intelligence, purify government and carry civilization to yet nobler heights, is — *to appropriate rent by taxation.*

In this way the State may become the universal landlord without calling herself so, and without assuming a single new function. In form, the ownership of land would remain just as now. No owner of land need be dispossessed, and no restriction need be placed upon the amount of land any one could hold. For, rent being taken by the State in taxes, land, no matter in whose name it stood, or in what parcels it was held, would be really common property, and every member of the community would participate in the advantages of its ownership.[2] [Emphasis in the original.]

George — and Thornton — however, forgot one important fact. As Daniel Webster observed in the Massachusetts Constitutional Convention of 1820, "Power naturally and necessarily follows property." Understanding that "property" refers not to the thing owned, but to the natural right each person has to be an owner, and the socially determined bundle of rights that define how an owner may use, that is, *control* what he or she owns — including receipt of the income — this makes sense.[3] We may have something in our possession, but if another can do whatever he or she likes with what we nominally own, we don't really own. As John Locke observed, "For what property have I in that which another may by right take, when he pleases to himself?"[4] Making the State the "universal landlord" is tantamount to a grant of absolute power.

Thus, the State should never own capital, including (or especially) land. This is because production of marketable goods and services is not the State's function. Ownership

---

[2] Henry George, *Progress and Poverty* (1879), 405-406.
[3] "Property in everyday life, is the right of *control*." Louis O. Kelso, "Karl Marx: The Almost-Capitalist," *Journal of the American Bar Association*, March, 1957.
[4] John Locke, *Second Treatise of Government*, § 140.

of capital gives the State control over its citizens, where it should be the citizens who control the State.

It would seem, then, that the logical solution to limited types of capital — in addition to opening up access to other, non-limited forms of capital — is to vest corporate ownership of such capital in a private, for-profit corporation. If owned by every citizen as a right of citizenship by granting each citizen a single lifetime no-cost, non-transferable, voting, fully participating share in a for-profit land planning and development corporation, Thornton's "corporate ownership" of land could be achieved without State ownership. Everyone could become a direct owner of the land.

These principles are embedded in a proposal CESJ calls the "Citizens Land Bank," or "CLB."

The CLB is a proposed social tool designed to encourage a just, free and non-monopolistic market economy. It would apply the democratic principles of equal opportunity and equal access to the means to participate as an owner as well as a worker. It would demonstrate that anything that can be owned by government can and should be owned, individually and jointly, by the citizens of a country.

The CLB is a major feature in a proposed national economic agenda known as "Capital Homesteading." Capital Homesteading is designed to reform existing monetary, credit and tax barriers to provide every person an equal opportunity to share in the governing powers and profits from new entrepreneurial ventures, new technologies, new structures, and new rentable space built upon the land.

A CLB is not socialism or communism. These are systems based on the abolition of private property in the means of production. A CLB would not take away property rights from present owners, nor would it redistribute current accumulations of wealth or income.

It would not be the Wall Street model of capitalism, where ownership of the means of production and ownership power are concentrated in the top 1 percent of society and artificial barriers exclude non-owners from equal ownership opportunities.

It would not be an amateur or unstructured approach to land development or "management by committee." It would not be a vehicle for owning or financing local enterprises competing in the marketplace.

The CLB would provide a private sector means by which homes, enterprises, rentable space and technologies built upon the CLB-owned land could be broadly owned by workers and other local stakeholders. (In this context, the CLB holds great promise for solving the serious problem of financing "brownfield" redevelopment and fostering new industries in cities. The concept of "vertical farming" in urban areas should be more fully investigated, especially when financing sources do not rely on existing accumulations of savings.)

The CLB would generate a new source of taxable incomes from new and expanded private sector jobs and ownership stakes. It would empower each citizen and family with the means to build an adequate and secure income, and with a real voice in the development decisions of the community.

The CLB would provide every citizen with income to contribute to the costs of running an effective local government and providing essential public services, as well as for his or her own wellbeing. It would offer hope of eventually eliminating the dependency of any citizen on welfare or charity of others or fear of technological displacement.

Thornton's proposal to encourage "Peasant Proprietors" was feasible in 1848 even as the Irish nation was suffering from one of the most devastating tragedies of the 19th century. It remained feasible when he revisited the proposal in 1874. Applying advanced concepts of corporate governance and finance, and extending it to other forms of capital, the proposal is even more feasible today.

XIII. The Homeowners Equity Corporation

The "Easter Proclamation" of 1916 asserted a right of ownership of Ireland by the people of Ireland. Logically, this includes dwellings as well as agricultural, industrial and commercial capital. In this Appendix we briefly outline a solution to the housing crisis in Ireland and America. This solution would not force taxpayers to foot the bill for a temporary and extremely ephemeral "stay of execution" in the form of a massive, government-funded bailout of predatory lenders. This puts off foreclosures for a time, but leaves the basic problem untouched. Further, by creating a replicable exemplar in a local community, other communities will have a model for a permanent, financially sound, and politically feasible solution to the subprime mortgage crisis. Such an approach can grow organically, strengthening local communities and their residents, and thus preventing similar crises from developing in the future.

One of the political advantages in William Thornton's *A Plea for Peasant Proprietors* was that it would save the government and the public charities money if the Irish could be made into small landowners instead of tenants-at-will. As tenants, they were subject to all kinds of abuse and mistreatment at the hands of largely absentee landlords and their agents. One problem was where people would get the money.

The answer is, where capital is concerned, money should never be a problem. Capital that pays for itself out of its own future profits is a good investment, and can be self-financing. Consequently, a fundamental principle of finance is to create money by monetizing the present value of future production ("pure credit") *only* for capital that is expected to pay for itself out of the income resulting from the sale of marketable goods and services the capital is intended to produce. This was the principle that, perhaps unconsciously, William Thornton embodied in his *Plea*. Consequently, it is usually better to own than to rent. This principle works well for capital, such as land and machinery, but does not directly address the problem of housing, the single largest expense item for most people today.

The difficulty is that a house falls somewhere between a true capital good and a consumption good. On the one hand, a house used as a primary dwelling is clearly a consumption item. It ranks with food and clothing as one of the most basic of basic necessities. On the other, a house is, in a sense, an income-generating asset, if we use the concept of "imputed rent" and consider that "rent" as capital income. The idea is that an owner, by living in the dwelling, forgoes rental income, and this should be considered the same as actual income. The "Homeowners Equity Corporation," or HEC, is thus designed to turn a house into an actual capital asset at the same time the owner lives in it, thereby qualifying for pure credit financing.

In 2008 the collapse of the Irish housing market triggered its current economic meltdown. Putting political interests ahead of sound financial principles, both Ireland and the U.S. bailed out the financial services industry to support the inflated prices of "toxic" mortgages. Acting counter to the common sense embodied in the laws of supply and demand as well as financial responsibility, when the housing market in Ireland went crumpled, the government bailed out the banks that were trying to keep prices up.

Consequently, the inventories of houses for foreclosure sales started to rise. Rather than let prices drop to meet demand (which ran the risk of forcing the banks into the Irish equivalent of Chapter 11 reorganization), the government imposed a moratorium on new home construction until current inventories dropped to an acceptable level. At the same time, the inflated prices discouraged buyers. Consequently, the banks were forced into reorganization anyway, with the new owner being the government instead of private individuals.

A possible solution to the housing foreclosure crisis that could be implemented along the lines of Thornton's proposal in both Ireland and the United States would be to pass enabling legislation for a Capital Homesteading vehicle called the "Homeowners Equity Corporation," or "HEC." The Homeowners Equity Corporation was developed as a way of allowing former owners of foreclosed homes to become tenants in their homes under a "rent to buy" arrangement. A unique feature of the HEC is that a tenant would be a shareholder of the corporation from which he or she rents the house.

The goal of the HEC is to turn excess inventories of overpriced homes into usable living space at market prices, and generate some cash that can be used to pay down debt. The banks (and thus the government) would take a hit, but it's sound financial and accounting practice as well as good politics to divest a company or a State of non-performing or toxic assets. Keeping prices artificially high so that no sales result benefits no one, and causes more problems than it solves. Sales at real market prices recognize reality, and reduce outstanding obligations by the amounts realized.

That, of course, is only the first step. Divesting the banks of toxic assets and transforming them into productive assets through HECs should kick-start the Irish — and the U.S. — economy, particularly since the building trades are seen as a core industry in Ireland, and a leading economic indicator in the U.S. The key is to ensure that all new private sector investment is financed in ways that creates new owners, rather than continues to concentrate capital ownership in a shrinking wealthy elite.

A HEC — there should be a number of them, even in the same region, to ensure competition — would be a for-profit stock corporation. It would purchase foreclosed residential properties in a local community at their deflated or true market value. Aggregating a number of properties in one (albeit broadly owned) corporation would spread the risk of default of any single home mortgage. A "lease-to-equity" arrangement would enable homeowners facing foreclosure or typical renters to 1) remain in their residence or rent an adequate dwelling, 2) pay off the un-inflated market cost of the residence, and 3) build up equity as shareholders of the HEC. Local real estate developers could manage the renter-owned HEC under a management contract, with provisions for housing inspections and maintenance. Preference for management contracts should be given to companies that are 100% worker owned, and that practice participatory management and profit sharing.

The HEC would allow citizens to escape from the worst forms of credit. These are loans for consumer goods that don't pay for themselves and are often made to people who can't repay the loans. Citizens could then use the better forms of credit. These are loans to purchase capital assets that pay for themselves and that turn non-owners into owners of income-producing assets. The HEC is based on a new monetary and tax approach that promotes the financing of feasible private sector capital formation in ways that create new owners of that growth and thereby spreads purchasing power throughout the economy.

One of the key characteristics of the Homeowners' Equity Corporation is that it would minimize risks of fore-closure for the resident-shareholder by acting as a form of capital credit "insurance" through pooling of risk. There will always be a certain percentage of homes that are un-occupied for a time, and that do not generate revenue, but the "renter's" equity would be based on the amortization of the principal on the mortgage of a particular home. It is obviously much easier to make payments on 100 houses, of which 90 are occupied and generating rent payments, than on a single house with no rent payments coming in.

The HEC would also provide a means for those who cannot afford monthly lease payments on their home, to participate in the lease-to-equity program. Vouchers linked to need (for a specified length of time) could be provided by private charity, or government grants. For example, 25% of a HEC resident-shareholder's income would go to cover housing leases, including HEC management services. The amount of the voucher to supplement this would be the difference between the homeowner's total income and the monthly lease payments. To protect against people playing the system, there would need to be a limit on how much of a voucher someone could receive and for how long they could receive a voucher to remain in a particular residence owned by the HEC.

The right to ownership — property — asserted in the Easter Proclamation of 1916 can today be realized in an efficient and just manner, without harming the rights of anyone, whether through redefinition, outright abolition, or any other unjust measures that mainstream economic thought deems "necessary":

We declare the right of the people of Ireland to the ownership of Ireland, and to the unfettered control of Irish destinies, to be sovereign and indefeasible. The long usurpation of that right by a foreign people and government has not extinguished the right, nor can it ever be extinguished except by the destruction of the Irish people.

XIV. Just Third Way Resources

The Just Third Way resource most immediately relevant to the publication of this Just Third Way edition of William Thornton's *A Plea for Peasant Proprietors* is *Capital Homesteading for Every Citizen: A Just Free Market Solution for Saving Social Security*, by Norman G. Kurland, Dawn K. Brohawn, and Michael D. Greaney, published in 2004 by Economic Justice Media, an imprint of the Center for Economic and Social Justice. *Capital Homesteading* is currently in revision, but this is primarily to update figures and statistics, and does not affect the principles or applications of Capital Homesteading described in the first edition.

Ashford, Robert H. A., and Shakespeare, Rodney, *Binary Economics: The New Paradigm*. Lanham, Maryland: University Press of America, 1999.

Briefs, Goetz A., *The Proletariat: A Challenge to Western Civilization*. New York: McGraw-Hill Book Company, 1937.

Conant, Charles A., *A History of Modern Banks of Issue*. New York: G. P. Putnam's Sons, 1927.

Crosskey, William Winslow, *Politics and the Constitution in the History of the United States. Volumes I and II*. Chicago, Illinois: The University of Chicago Press, 1953.

Ferree, Rev. William J., *The Act of Social Justice*. Washington, DC: The Catholic University of America Press, 1943.

Ferree, Rev. William J., *Introduction to Social Justice*. Arlington, Virginia: Center for Economic and Social Justice, 1997.

Fullarton, John, *On the Regulation of the Currencies of the Bank of England*. London: John Murray, 1845.

Greaney, Michael D., *In Defense of Human Dignity: Essays on the Just Third Way, A Natural Law Perspective*. Arlington, Virginia: Economic Justice Media, 2008.

Greaney, Michael D., *Supporting Life: The Case for a Pro-Life Economic Agenda*. Arlington, Virginia: Economic Justice Media, 2010.

Greaney, Michael D., *The Restoration of Property: A Reexamination of a Natural Right*. Arlington, Virginia: Economic Justice Media, 2011.

Hildreth, Richard, *The History of Banks, To Which is Added a Demonstration of the Advantages and Necessity of Free Competition in the Business of Banking*. Boston, Massachusetts: Hilliard, Gray & Company, 1837.

Kelso, Louis O., and Adler, Mortimer J., *The Capitalist Manifesto*. New York: Random House, 1958.

Kelso, Louis O., and Adler, Mortimer J., *The New Capitalists: A Proposal to Free Economic Growth from the Slavery of Savings*. New York: Random House, 1961.

Kelso, Louis O. and Hetter, Patricia, *Two-Factor Theory: The Economics of Reality*. New York: Random House, 1967.

Kelso, Louis O. and Kelso, Patricia Hetter, *Democracy and Economic Power: Extending the ESOP Revolution through Binary Economics*. Lanham, Maryland: University Press of America, 1991.

Kurland, Norman G., "Beyond ESOP: Steps Toward Tax Justice," *The Tax Executive*, April and July 1976.

Kurland, Norman G., "A New Look at Prices and Money: The Kelsonian Binary Model for Achieving Rapid Growth Without Inflation," *The Journal of Socio-Economics*, 30 (2001) 495-515.

Law, John, *Money and Trade Considered, With a Proposal for Supplying the Nation with Money*. Edinburgh: Andrew Anderson, 1705.

Miller, John H., ed., *Curing World Poverty: The New Role of Property*. St. Louis, Missouri: Social Justice Review, 1994.

Moulton, Harold G., ed., *Principles of Money and Banking: A Series of Selected Materials, with Explanatory Introductions*. Chicago, Illinois: The University of Chicago Press, 1916.

Moulton, Harold G., *The Financial Organization of Society*. Washington, DC: The Brookings Institution, 1930.

Moulton, Harold G., *America's Capacity to Produce*. Washington, DC: The Brookings Institution, 1934.

Moulton, Harold G., *America's Capacity to Consume*. Washington, DC: The Brookings Institution, 1934.

Moulton, Harold G., *The Formation of Capital*. Washington, DC: The Brookings Institution, 1935.

Moulton, Harold G., *Income and Economic Progress*. Washington, DC: The Brookings Institution, 1935.

Moulton, Harold G., *The Recovery Problem in the United States*. Washington, DC: The Brookings Institution, 1936.

Moulton, Harold G., *Financial Organization and the Economic System*. New York: McGraw-Hill Book Company, Inc., 1938.

Moulton, Harold G., *Capital Expansion, Employment, and Economic Stability*. Washington, DC: The Brookings Institution, 1940.

Moulton, Harold G., *The New Philosophy of Public Debt*. Washington, DC: The Brookings Institution, 1943.

Rommen, Heinrich A., *The Natural Law: A Study in Legal and Social History and Philosophy*. Indianapolis, Indiana: Liberty Fund, Inc., 1998.

Rommen, Heinrich A., *The State in Catholic Thought*. St. Louis, Missouri: B. Herder Book Company, 1947.

Say, Jean-Baptiste, *Letters to Mr. Malthus on Several Subjects of Political Economy*. London: Sherwood, Neely, and Jones, 1821.

Say, Jean-Baptiste, *A Treatise on Political Economy*. Philadelphia, Pennsylvania: Claxton, Remsen and Haffelfinger, 1880.

Smith, Adam, *The Wealth of Nations*. New York: Alfred A. Knopf, Inc., 1991.

Thornton, Henry, *An Enquiry into the Nature and Effects of the Paper Credit of Great Britain*. London: George Allen and Unwin, Ltd., 1939.

Thornton, William Thomas, *Over-Population and Its Remedy, Or, an Inquiry Into the Extent and Causes of the Distress Prevailing Among the Labouring Classes of the British Islands, and Into the Means of Remedying It*. London: Longman, Brown, Green, and Longmans, 1846.

Thornton, *With the Outlines of a Plan for Their Establishment in Ireland*. London: John Murray, 1848.

Thornton, William Thomas, *A Treatise on Labour: Its Wrongful Claims and Rightful Dues, Its Actual Present and Possible Future, Second Edition*. London: Macmillan and Company, 1870.

Thornton, William Thomas, *Old-Fashioned Ethics and Common-Sense Metaphysics, With Some of Their Applications*. London: Macmillan and Co., 1873.

Thornton, William Thomas, *A Plea for Peasant Proprietors; With the Outlines of a Plan for Their Establishment in Ireland, Second Edition.* London: Macmillan and Co., 1874.

Thornton, William Thomas, *Indian Public Works and Cognate Indian Topics.* London: Macmillan and Co., 1875.

Thornton, William Thomas, "Agriculture," *Encyclopedia Britannica,* 7th Edition (1875).

Tocqueville, Alexis de, *Democracy in America.* New York: Alfred A. Knopf, 1994.

Tocqueville, Alexis de, *Memoir on Pauperism.* Chicago, Illinois: Ivan R. Dee, Inc., Publisher, 1997.

Tucker, George, *The Theory of Money and Banks Investigated.* Boston, Massachusetts: Charles C. Little and James Brown, 1839.

Joining CESJ as a member is one way to support the Just Third Way and work for the passage of a Capital Homesteading Act. Information about joining CESJ can be found on the Center's website,

http://www.cesj.org

XV. Revisions from the 1848 Edition

**Rewritten for the 1874 edition from pages 8-16
in the 1848 edition:**

From a comparison of the number of persons engaged in agriculture, with the supposed extent of cultivated land, it appears that one such person is employed on every twenty-four acres of such land in England and Wales. Twenty-four acres (even though, according to the proportion usual in England, only two-fifths of that quantity be under tillage, and the remainder pasture) are probably more than can be cultivated in the most efficient manner by a single person, whether he be a hired servant, or a small farmer;[1] but of the two, the latter, provided he be a leaseholder on reasonable terms, and not a rack-rented tenant-at-will, is pretty certain to obtain the largest amount of produce. He may perhaps set about his work less systematically; he may not command the same means of economizing labor, but, nevertheless, from some cause or other, his labor is pretty sure to be more abundantly rewarded; his land generally bears by far the heaviest crops. In the year 1837, the average yield of wheat in the large farms of England was only twenty-one bushels, and the highest average for any one country was no more than twenty-six bushels.[2] The highest average

---

[1] *Encyclopedia Britannica*, Art. Cottage System.

[2] See Table in Macculloch's *Statistics of British Empire*, vol i. p. 482. In Mr. Muccolloch's latest work on *Succession to Property*, p. 117, the average produce of wheat in England and Wales is said to be "certainly not under thirty bushels" per acre; but no authority is given for this statement, whereas that for 1837 was founded upon separate returns for every country. It is evidently impossible that such extraordinary progress can really have been made in so short a time, and there can be little doubt that the average of a few greatly improved districts is represented as that of the whole kingdom. Great improvement has certainly been made of late years, but not so much as to invalidate the comparisons drawn in the text; for agriculture, while advancing in England, has not been stationary in other countries. In Guernsey, in 1835, four quarters per acres were considered a

since claimed for the whole of England is thirty bushels, and, according to a statement resting on the same authority, the produce of the seed is "seldom less than twelve-fold, but if drilled, fourteen-fold, and if dibbled, sixteen, or even twenty-fold."[3] In Jersey, where the average size of farms is only sixteen acres, the average produce of wheat per acre was stated by Inglis,[4] in 1834, to be thirty-six bushels; but it is proved by official tables to have been forty bushels in the five years ending with 1833.[5] In Guernsey, where farms are still smaller, four quarters per acre, according to Inglis, "is considered a good, but still a very common crop." In Flanders, where the most numerous class of farms consists of those between five and ten acres, the average yield of what is at least thirty bushels.[6] Mr. Macculloch, indeed, without quoting his authority, sets it down at no more than twenty bushels and a half per acre; but this, though only a trifle below the average ascribed by the same writer to the whole of England, and higher than that of one-half of the whole number of English counties, is evidently incorrectly stated, and must be considerably below the truth, as Mr. Macculloch likewise says, that the seed sown produces more than twenty-fold.[7] It should be observed that the soil, both of Flanders and of the Channel Islands, is, for the most part, of a light sandy character, ill adapted for the growth of

---

good crop of wheat; but at the last meeting of the Guernsey Agricultural Society, the largest yield of white wheat was reported to have been not less than nine imperial quarters per acre, and that of red wheat seven quarters and a half. These crops would be thought so prodigious in England that I at first suspected the account to be exaggerated. Its accuracy is, however, attested by a gentleman who is not likely to be mistaken, Mr. Le Beir, the able secretary of the Guernsey Agricultural Society. His letter on the subject will be found in the Appendix [I].

[3] Speech of Mr. E. Chadwick, at a meeting of the Farmers' Club in the early part of 1847.

[4] Inglis's *Channel Islands*, vol i., p. 186.

[5] *Guernsey and Jersey Magazine*, vol. iii. p. 106.

[6] *Flemish Husbandry*, pp. 8 and 76. From a remark at p. 92, the average in the Pays de Waes would seem to be between four and five quarters.

[7] *Geog. Dict.*, vol. i. pp. 331-2.

wheat. Of barley, a more suitable crop, the quantity in some parts of Belgium is sometimes as much as eighty bushels per acre, and the average is forty-five; while in England it is only thirty-three bushels.[8] Of potatoes, the average produce in England is certainly not more than 300 bushels, or 22,200 lbs. per acre, and is probably not nearly so much. In Belgium it is ten tons, or 22,400 lbs.[9] and in Jersey 35,000 lbs.[10] Clover, another most important article of farm produce, is nowhere found in "such perfect luxuriance" as in Flanders, where it exhibits "a vigor and weight of produce truly surprising," more especially when it is considered "that such prodigious crops are raised from six pounds of seed per acre."[11] These proofs may be thought sufficient to establish the superior productiveness of small farms; but if others be required, they may be found in England itself, among the smallest of small farmers, the allotment-holders of a quarter of an acre, who seldom fail to obtain a profit of at least five pounds sterling even from that morsel of ground. It appears then that the small occupier, in spite of his disabilities, real or imaginary, would be able to get a good deal more from his land than it would yield if it formed a portion of a large farm. After paying, therefore, rent at the same rate as the large farmer, and after taking for his own use the same sum as would be applied to the maintenance of the cultivator of an equal portion of a large farm, he would have remaining, not only as great, but a much greater relative surplus wherewith to continue his cultivation. Acre for acre he would be able to spend in improvements, not only as much, but a good deal more than his rival. The whole of his profits would not indeed enable him to do some few things which are occasionally done by managers of large properties. Assuredly he could not, "to improve the breed of his sheep, give a thousand guineas for the hire of a single ram, for a single season," nor "send across the kingdom to distant provinces for new imple-

---

[8] *Flemish Husbandry*, pp. 8 and 32. Table in *Stat. of Brit. Empire, ut supra.*

[9] Macculloch's *Geog. Dict.*, vol. i. p. 332.

[10] *Guernsey and Jersey Mag.*, vol. iii. p. 106.

[11] Macculloch, *ut supra*, p. 331.

ments, and for men to use them," nor "employ and pay men for residing in provinces where practices were found which he might wish to introduce." But with all deference to Arthur Young, who says that such efforts are common in England, they neither are nor need be made, except very rarely, and by very few even of large farmers, and all the ordinary expenses of cultivation the small farmer is equally able to bear. With as much ease as the tenant of two or three square miles he can afford, if need be, "to cover his whole farm with marl at the rate of 100 or 150 tons per acre," — "to drain all his land at the expense of two or three pounds per acres," — "to pay a heavy price for the manure of towns, and convey it thirty miles by land carriage," or "to float his meadows at the expense of five pounds per acre." What reason is there for doubting his ability to do this? The original capital, whether of a great or of a small farmer, must, in fairness, be assumed to bear an equal proportion to the extent of the farm; its only certain source of increase is the profits of farming, and the small farmer's profits have been shown to be the greatest. In proportion to the size of his farm, therefore, he must have not merely as much, but a good deal more money to spend on cultivation.

In effect, his expenditure is often proportionably the greater of the two. The richest English farmers are less prodigal of manure than those of Belgium, who, by the continual intermixture of animal and vegetable refuse, have converted a sterile sand into a dark rich loam of unsurpassed fertility. In the Channel Islands, also, manure is employed with almost equal liberality, ten cart-loads of seaweed worth fifty shillings, besides stable dung, being the allowance for an acre.[12] Drainage is an operation which, in many situations, cannot be effectually executed, unless it be undertaken on an extensive scale; but that the necessity of combining for the purpose does not prevent small occupiers from properly performing this important part of their business is shown by the example of the Netherlands, the country, above all others, in which drainage is most indispensable, and in which also it is best provided for. Combination

---

[12] Duncan's *History of Guernsey*, p. 294.

equally enables small farmers to construct expensive works for irrigation. Perhaps the most ingenious contrivances of the kind which anywhere exist, are to be found, not among the scientific and wealthy agriculturalists of Europe, but among the Bedouins of some Arabian oases, which owe their fertility to the labor and skill exerted by the inhabitants in order to obtain supplies of water. The greater part of the country being destitute of running streams on the surface, springs are sought in high places beneath it, and in order to reach them, the ground must often be opened to a depth of forty feet. "A channel from the fountain head is then, with a very slight descent, bored in the direction to which it is to be conveyed, with apertures at regular distances, to afford light and air, to those who are occasionally sent to keep it clean. In this manner water is frequently conducted from a distance of six or eight miles, and an unlimited supply is obtained. The channels are usually about four feet broad and two feet deep, and contain a clear rapid stream."[13] If the small farmer use only the "simplest machines," it is probably because experience has taught him, as we shall hereafter see, that the simplest tools are by far the most efficient. If he keep no horses, it is commonly because he selfdom has occasion for them, and that it is cheaper for him to hire them when necessary; and with respect to his alleged inability to avail himself of the services of others of the "lower animals," it is sufficient to remark that the livestock of a Belgian farmer of no more than six acres, commonly consists of two cows, a calf or two, one or two pigs, a goat or two, and some poultry."[14] Such a farmer in Belgium would use the spade only for trenching the ground; but among equally small occupiers in the Channel Islands, whether from attachment to old customs, or from some other cause, not only is the plow in general use, but a plow called "la grande querrue," so large and lumbering, that not

---

[13] Wellsted's *Travels*, vol. i. p. 93.

[14] Mr. Nicholls' *Report on Holland and Belgium*. "It would startle an English farmer of four hundred acres of arable land, if he were told that he should constantly feed one hundred head of cattle; yet this would not be too great a proportion if the Flemish system were strictly followed." — *Flemish Husbandry*, p. 94.

less than eight or ten horses or oxen are often employed to draw it. Very few of the peasants are rich enough to possess one of these ponderous engines, or the number of cattle required for it; but the poorest has no difficulty in borrowing both the one and other from his neighbors, who, moreover, cheerfully assist each other in busy seasons. The good feeling subsisting between the people of the Channel Islands, allows this exchange of services to be effected by barter; but even if money were employed in the transaction, it is obvious that every one, with the hire of his own services, would be able to purchase an equal quantity of work from others, and that thus the division of labor could be practiced even on small farms, although not nearly to the extent to which it is carried on in large ones. So much must be admitted in favor of the latter; but of all the claims hitherto enumerated, set up on their behalf, this is the only one which can be even partially conceded. There is certainly not the least foundation for the assertion that a suitable rotation of crops is impracticable in small farms. Every owner of a few perches of garden ground has room enough to prevent his bends of cabbage, peas, beans, and lettuces, from repeatedly occupying the same sites, and until some reason to the contrary be shown, the tenant of five or six acres must be supposed capable of taking a similar precaution with respect to his crops of grain and roots.

Rewritten for the 1874 edition from pages 26-27 in the 1848 edition:

Still, it cannot be denied that small farmers do not, in general, avail themselves to the utmost of the means at their command. Living always on the same spot, with little taste or time for reading, they know little of what goes on beyond the bounds of their immediate neighborhood; and, like all persons in similar circumstances, they are exceedingly averse to change, unduly attached to old habits and proportionately disdainful of foreign practices. The most skillful and successful of all small farmers, the Flemings, are, perhaps, as obnoxious as any to this reproach. None adhere more pertinaciously to hereditary usages, or are more unwilling to adopt modern inventions, or to listen to the counsels of modern science. No fields can be more carefully tilled than theirs; nowhere is the ground more frequently turned up, more thoroughly drained or kept freer from weeds. But the implements of husbandry are, in general, rude and clumsy; the horses are oppressed by massy wooden collars, and broadcast sowing, in spite of the manifold objections to it, is still very commonly preferred to drilling. But is this prejudice in favor of antiquated absurdities a reason for the unqualified condemnation of small farmers? Does it not rather furnish the strongest possible proof that there must be some extraordinary excellence in a system which, in spite of such glaring defects, is more than a match for all the efforts of capital and science combined? The small farmer may be ignorant, may work with bad tools, and may not distribute his labor in the most economical manner; but with all his stupidity and awkwardness he nevertheless contrives to make his land yield more than a large occupier, with all his skill, could obtain from it. This has been already shown to be the case, and it is, indeed, so well known to all who have taken the trouble to enquire into the matter, that if the question at issue between large and small farms were to be determined by their respective amounts of gross produce, a verdict would infallibly be given in favor of the latter.

Rewritten for the 1874 edition from pages 29-38 in the 1848 edition:

This might, perhaps, at once be taken for granted, if the average size of small farms were not below twenty-four acres — the extent of land which, as we have seen, affords complete occupation to one cultivator on the large farms of Great Britain. For, as the small farmer would obtain a much larger gross produce than the other cultivator, he might retain for his own use as much or more than would have been consumed by the latter, and yet have a greater quantity left for sale. But in countries in which small farms abound, their average size is frequently, perhaps generally, less than twenty-four acres; in France, it appears to be eighteen acres; in Jersey, sixteen; and in Guernsey, where land is more minutely divided than perhaps in any other part of Europe, is little more than eleven acres. Of course, the number of cultivators on land so divided must be greater than on an equal extent occupied by large farmers; in Guernsey, for example, the agricultural population is three times as dense as in England. But it is by no means so obvious as some writers imagine that, "where a great proportion of the inhabitants is directly supported by the produce of the soil, there must be less of it to support others."[15] Undoubtedly, if the gross produce be the same in both cases, more will remain when the subsistence of only one, instead of that of three cultivators, has been deducted. But it the combined exertions of the three can augment the gross produce by a quantity sufficient for the consumption of two, the surplus remaining beyond their consumption will be precisely the same as if only one had been employed. Now, the consumption of the family of a cultivator in England may be estimated at about one-fifth of the produce of the portion of land cultivated by him — that being the numerical proportion borne by the agricultural class to the rest of the community. If, therefore, three cultivators can obtain from a piece of land crops exceeding by two-fifths those which a single person could raise, they will have precisely the same neat produce remaining after their own wants are satisfied, and will be able to send precisely the same quantity to market. Now, taking Mr. Macculloch as our authority as to the productiveness of English agriculture, (for Mr. Chadwick's higher estimate is certainly applicable only to a few of the most improved counties, and probably only to a few of the best managed farms,) we have twenty-one bushels of wheat as the average produce per acre. But in Guernsey the average wheat crop has never been stated at less than thirty-two bushels per acre; that is to say, considerably more than two-fifths above the English average. Thus, three persons may be employed in Guernsey on land, which in England would afford occupation only to one; and yet, after feeding themselves with the fruits of their labor, will have not only as much, but a good deal more food remaining for other people, than would have been reserved by the English cultivator. In corroboration of this conclusion, it may be mentioned that a Flemish farmer of six acres of moderate land,

---

[15] *Encyclopedia Britannica.* Art. Cottage System.

obtains from two acres and a half, as much grain, potatoes, butter, pork, and milk, as are required for the consumption of himself, his wife, and three children, and sells the produce of the remaining three acres and a half.[16]

One thing, which by itself might seem to prove that markets are better supplied by small than by large farms, is the fact that land, when divided among many occupiers, commonly pays a much higher rent than when united into one extensive holding. Thirty shillings an acre would be thought in England a very fair rent for middling land; but in the Channel Islands, it is only very inferior land that would not let for at least £4, and Switzerland the average rent seems to be £6 per acre. Rent being that portion of the produce of land which remains after the expenses of cultivation are deducted, it is evident that small farms, as they pay the highest rent, must also yield the largest surplus produce. So much, at least, is incontestable; but the portion of produce remaining over and above what is reserved for the cultivators, is not all that is sent to market, for part of the share of the cultivators is also sold, in order to furnish them with the means of procuring the various articles they require in addition to food; and it is certainly possible, though there is not the least reason for supposing it, that the cultivators of a large farm may sell a larger proportion of their shares than those of a small farm, and may compensate, by that means, for the deficiency of the portion which they appropriate for the payment of rent. We shall hereafter find, that there are no grounds whatever for this hypothesis, and that it is not only not true, but directly opposite to the truth; still, although actually erroneous, it might by possibility be correct, and it must therefore be admitted, that payment of the highest rate of rent does not afford absolute proof, but merely very strong presumption, that small farms send likewise the most abundant supplies to market.

The same inference might be drawn from the fact that some of the countries in which land is most minutely divided, are also among those which maintain the largest manufacturing and commercial population. Belgium, for

---

[16] *Flemish Husbandry*, p. 74.

instance, is second in this respect to Great Britain alone; and Switzerland, and the Rhenish provinces of Prussia, may also be cited as examples. It may indeed be objected, that non-agricultural classes may not be entirely dependent for their subsistence on home produce, but may derive part of their supplies of food from abroad, and it may generally be impossible to discover what portion is imported. This objection, however, does not apply to the Channel Islands. We are there able to ascertain pretty accurately the quantities of food imported and exported, and after making the needful allowance on that account, we shall find that two small territories occupied exclusively by small farmers, and affording employment to two or three times the number of cultivators that would be thought requisite on large farms, do nevertheless furnish a sufficiency of food, not only for those cultivators and their families, but for a larger non-agricultural population in addition than is maintained by an equal extent of land, even in Great Britain, the model country of the eulogists of large farms.

The extent of cultivated land in Great Britain is estimated at nearly thirty-four millions of acres. The population in 1841 was 18,720,394 persons, of whom twenty-two percent belonged to the agricultural class. The class so denominated, however, included not only the persons actually engaged in agriculture, but likewise their families, the number of the former being only 1,480,880, or about one-twelfth of the population; so that the number who, in the largest sense of the word, might be termed non-agricultural, was not less than 17,239,514. But these were not entirely dependent for subsistence on the produce of the British soil. The quantity of grain annually brought to market in the United Kingdom is estimated at thirty millions of quarters, of which, previously to the repeal of the Corn Laws, about two millions, or one-fifteenth, came from abroad. This statement, it will be observed, applies to the whole of the United Kingdom. Of the grain brought to market in Great Britain alone, between two and three millions of quarters, equal probably to one-tenth of the entire quantity, were annually brought from Ireland, so that supposing an equal proportion of other provisions to have been of transmarine production, one-sixth of the non-agricultural population may be considered to have been fed on imported provision. The number of persons, exclusive of the cultivators, who subsisted on home produce, was between fourteen and fifteen millions, or one person to about every two acres and a half of cultivated land.

The proportion between the agricultural and other classes in the Channel Islands is not stated by the late Census Commissioners, but all the other particulars required for a comparison with Great Britain are procurable. Jersey contains 26,600 acres of cultivated land; her population in 1841 was 47,544; the number of persons engaged in agriculture 2,392, or one-nineteenth of the whole; and the non-agricultural population (using that term in the same extended sense as before) 45,152. In the year 1835 foreign provisions were imported to the value of about £80,000; but whereas corresponding imports into Great Britain are purchased almost entirely with manufactured goods, in the Channel Islands they are, to a large extent, bartered for other agricultural produce. The exports of provisions from Jersey in 1835 were worth nearly £60,000, so that the value of the net imports was little more than £20,000, which, even at the very low rate of £10 a head, would suffice for the maintenance of only two thousand persons. Deduct this number from the non-agricultural population referred to above, and there will remain 43,152 persons over and above the cultivators to be fed with the produce of 26,600 acres. This is at the rate of four persons to every two acres and a half.[17]

17

Imports	£	Exports	£
Wheat, 22,914 qrs. at 40s	45,828	Wheat, 4,694 qrs. at 40s	9,388
Barley, 2,369 " 25s	2,961	Potatoes, 211,559 bs. at 1s	10,577
Oats, 2,634 " 20s	2,634	Cows, 1,135, at £10	11,350
Oxen, 2,784, at £6	16,704	Butter, 25,000 lbs. at 1s	1,250
Sheep, 6,602, at £1	6,602	Apples, 224,611 bs. at 6d	5,615
Lambs, 1,243, at 10s	621	Cider, 413,815 galls. at 1s	20,690
Poultry, 28,821, at 2s	2,882		
Eggs, 96,950 doz. at 6d	2,423		
	£80,655		£58,870

Guernsey and Jersey Magazine, vol. iii., pp. 106-9

The results exhibited by Guernsey are still more striking. The cultivated portion of that island contains 10,240 acres; the total population in 1841 was 26,649; the number of cultivators 1,494, or rather less than one-eighteenth of the whole; and the non-agricultural residue 25,155. In the year 1834 foreign provisions were imported to the value of £81,400, but provisions were exported to the value of £27,500, so that the value of the net imports was £53,900. This sum might suffice for the maintenance of between five and six thousand persons, leaving nearly 20,000, besides cultivators, to be fed with the produce of 10,240 acres. This is at the rate of very nearly five persons for every two acres and a half.[18]

Pages 39-40 of the 1848 edition, omitted from the 1874 edition:

By what means they accomplish this end is comparatively unimportant. A tree is judged by its fruits, and the conflicting claims of agricultural theories should be de-

---

18

Imports	£	Exports	£
Wheat and flour, 21,955 qrs. at 40s	43,910	Wheat, flour, and biscuits, 4,660 qrs. at 40s	9,338
Barley, 6,295 qrs. at 25s	7,868	Barley, 859 qrs. at 25s	1,073
Peas and beans, 1,295 qrs. at 30s	1,942	Peas and beans, 524 qrs. at 30s	786
Oats, 2,645 qrs. at 20s	2,645	Oats, 229 qrs. at 20s	229
Cattle, 1,332, at £6	7,992	Cattle (Guernsey) 506, at £10	5,060
Calves, 240, at 30s	360	Do. (foreign) 8, at £6	48
Sheep, 6,358, at 20s	6,358	Calves, 68, at £3	204
Poultry, 47,147, at 2s	73	Pigs, 399, at 30s	598
Eggs, 13,972 doz. at 6d	4,714	Eggs, 12,390 doz. at 6d	309
Potatoes, 1,788 bs. at 1s	349	Potatoes (and equivalent of potato spirits,) 100,000 bs. at 1s	5,000
Butter, 101,980 lbs. at 1s	90	Apples, 1,824 bs. at 6d	45
	5,099	Cider, 29,410 galls. at 1s	1,470
		Pears, 12,175 bs. at 5s	3,043
		Butter, 5,380, at 1s	269
	£81,400		£27,472

Martin's *British Colonies*, vol. v. pp. 481-2. I have taken those years both for Jersey and Guernsey, for which I had the fullest information. The quantities of butter are misstated by Martin. In the table above, they are given upon the authority of a paper obtained from the Guernsey Custom-house.

termined by observation of their practical results. Improved machines and processes are not valued for some intrinsic virtue of their own — for the mere pleasure found is making use of ingenious contrivances, but solely for their effects. The final object for which they are used in farming is to increase the net produce left unconsumed by the cultivator; but if this object can be attained equally well without their aid, surely nothing remains to be desired. The small farmer, though destitute of some of the appliances of the large capitalist, nevertheless manages to get more from the land, and after reserving sufficient for his own consumption, has a larger residue for sale. He might, perhaps, do better still by imitating some of the methods of the large capitalists; but, even as it is, he does better than the other, and his plan must, on the whole, be preferable. To admit that he has the largest produce to dispose of, and yet to quarrel with him because he has not acquired it *secundum artem*, or to sneer at small farms, because, forsooth, they might more properly be styled gardens, is a singular preference of the means to the end. Dr. Purgou might with equal reason have blamed *le malade imaginaire* for persisting in living, when, for his neglect of the rules of medicine, he ought, by rights, to have died.

About the Author

William Thomas Thornton was an English economist. He was born at Burnham, Buckinghamshire, on February 14, 1813. In 1836 he became a clerk in the London office of the Honourable East India Company, "John Company." In 1858, after the British Crown assumed direct rule of India following the Great Mutiny, he became secretary for public works in the India office, a post that he held until his death. In 1873 Thornton was created a C.B., a "Companion of the Most Honourable Order of the Bath," a title and order conferred on British and Commonwealth citizens in recognition of conspicuous service to the Crown.

His first major work was *Over-Population and its Remedy* (1846), a counter to Thomas Malthus's 1798 *Essay on Population*, in which Thornton proposed a plan by means of which propertyless Irish peasants could "homestead" waste (unused) land in Ireland by having the government purchase undeveloped land at a low price and allocate it to people who would develop the land and repay the government out of future profits.

In 1848 Thornton published *A Plea for Peasant Proprietors*, in which his proposal was developed in greater detail and urgency in light of the Great Famine. This was followed by *On Labour* (1869) in which he engaged in a friendly dispute with John Stuart Mill over the latter's adherence to the "wage fund doctrine"; and *Old-Fashioned Ethics and Commonsense Metaphysics,* a volume of essays opposing utilitarianism, published in 1873. The next year, in response to the reoccurrence of famine and an upsurge in discontent in Ireland over the ineffectiveness of the various land reform acts, Thornton published a revision of *A Plea for Peasant Proprietors.* In 1875 Thornton published *Indian Public Works and Cognate Indian Topics.* That same year he contributed the article on "Agriculture" to the 7th edition of the Encyclopedia Britannica. He is credited with some volumes of verse, among them *Life's Mystery* (1873).

William Thornton died in 1880.

About the Editor

Michael D. Greaney is a Certified Public Accountant and Director of Research for the Center for Economic and Social Justice. He holds a BBA from the University of Notre Dame, and a MBA from the University of Evansville, Evansville, Indiana. He has been a Senior Field Accountant for the American Red Cross, Medical Center Auditor for Georgetown University Medical Center, and auditor with the Federal Election Commission, and is Director of ESOP Administration Services for Equity Expansion International, Inc., an ESOP investment banking and consulting firm that specializes in helping workers and others without savings to become owners of capital as well as labor.

Mr. Greaney has written numerous articles for such journals as *Social Justice Review*, *Military History*, *Military Heritage*, *Learning Through History*, and Krause Publications' *World Coin News*, for which he received the 2002 Numismatic Literary Guild award for best article or series of articles for his series on Medieval Irish coinage. In 1997 he wrote a weekly column on economic and social justice for *Ultimas Noticias*, the largest daily newspaper in Uruguay.

Books published to date include *Curing World Poverty* (1994) and *Capital Homesteading for Every Citizen* (2004) as contributing author, and *In Defense of Human Dignity* (2008), *Supporting Life* (2010), and *The Restoration of Property* (2011) as sole author. He has edited and written forewords for the novels of Nicholas Wiseman, Blessed John Henry Newman, and Robert Hugh Benson, for which he compiled a reader's guide, *So Much Generosity* (2011), and is working on the novels of Patrick Augustine "Canon" Sheehan. His daily blog, "The Just Third Way," is read in an average of fifty countries.

Mr. Greaney spoke at the 2001 "Witness" conference in Toronto, Canada, and delivered the keynote addresses at the Centenary of the Central Bureau of the Catholic Central Union of America in St. Louis, Missouri, USA, in 2008. He has been interviewed on *The Challenge* and *The Skip Mahaffey Show*, and spoken before various civic groups. In 1994 he received the CESJ "Soldier of Justice" award, and the CESJ "Scholar's Award" in 2007. He is a member of the Irish "SIG" of Mensa, and the Col. John Fitzgerald Division of the Ancient Order of Hibernians of America in Arlington, Virginia.

Index